LIBERALISM AT ITS LIMITS

ILLUMINATIONS
Cultural Formations of the Americas

John Beverley and Sara Castro-Klarén, Editors

LIBERALISM AT ITS LIMITS

CRIME AND TERROR IN

THE LATIN AMERICAN

CULTURAL TEXT

ILEANA RODRÍGUEZ

UNIVERSITY OF PITTSBURGH PRESS

Published by the University of Pittsburgh Press, Pittsburgh, Pa., 15260

Copyright © 2009, University of Pittsburgh Press

Manufactured in the United States of America

Printed on acid-free paper

10 9 8 7 6 5 4 3 2 1

Library of Congress Cataloging-in-Publication Data

Rodríguez, Ileana.

 Liberalism at its limits : crime and terror in the Latin American cultural text / Ileana Rodríguez.

  p. cm. — (Illuminations—cultural formations of the Americas)

 Includes and index.

 ISBN-13: 978-0-8229-4368-6 (cloth : alk. paper)

 ISBN-10: 0-8229-4368-9 (cloth : alk. paper)

 ISBN-13: 978-0-8229-6019-5 (pbk. : alk. paper)

 ISBN-10: 0-8229-6019-2 (pbk. : alk. paper)

 1. Liberalism—Latin America. 2. Violence—Latin America. 3. Civil society—Latin America. I. Title.

 JC574.2.L29R63 2009

 320.51098—dc22   2008052969

Proponents of the application of a model of deliberative democracy to actual political processes in imperfect democracies with injustices suggest that the more that public life and political decision-making motivate political actors to justify their claims and actions and be accountable to their fellow citizens, the more the arbitrariness of greed, naked power, or the cynical pursuit of self-interest can be exposed and limited. When public debate gets beyond soundbites and manipulated opinion polls, issues often are seen as more complex and less polarized, and thus more open to minority voices.

IRIS MARION YOUNG, *Inclusion and Democracy*

contents

acknowledgments

SPEAKERS of foreign tongues need help in conveying their ideas clearly in English. In this text, the English-language experts who walked side by side me were John Crider and Kathryn B. Auffinger. John edited chapters 2 through 6; Kathryn the rest of the manuscript. They proved to be excellent and incisive readers of texts. My whole heartfelt thanks to them.

After many drafts, I submitted the manuscript to the press and, on my second revision of it (after complying with the readers' suggestions), Professor Sebastian Knowles offered to read the text over when he was already the associate dean of the college. I am sure no faculty member has ever been the recipient of such personal generosity from a college dean. I am forever indebted to him and promise to remember that one metaphor per sentence is enough.

There were three very well chosen readers for the manuscript. Their comments and suggestions were very valuable, and it is thanks to them that I have covered all my bibliographical bases. Peter Kracht and Devin Fromm, University of Pittsburgh Press editors, were very efficient in the handling of the text; Devin Fromm meticulously revised it, and his advice was always punctual and encouraging. The series editors, Sara Castro-Klarén and John Beverley, my fellow subalternists, were prompt in considering its publication. Ohio State University College of Humanities gave me several grants to improve the manuscript and to present the work-in-progress at various international conferences. To all of them I express my deep gratitude.

Books are collective enterprises, even if just a single name appears on the front cover. My gratefulness also extends to all of those who examined the questions treated in this text before I did, and to all the people who, in telling their life experience or in gathering the experience of others, made it possible for me to read, in disbelief, of the horrors at the heart of cultural texts.

LIBERALISM AT ITS LIMITS

introduction

Cross-Cultural Dialogues
in a Global World

ON THE MORNING of September 11, 2001, the twin towers of the World Trade Center collapsed under the impact of two airplanes piloted by members of Al Qaeda, an Islamic organization. In disbelief, the whole world watched the images of these two planes that struck the U.S. security system at its real and symbolic financial heart in rapid succession—images that were transmitted relentlessly by CNN throughout that entire day and for days and years to come. Astonishment, fear, and outrage colored the most immediate reactions at home. Two simple words—terror and terrorism—covered the entire semantic field in an attempt to explain this seminal act of the complex politics that is fundamentalism. The instantaneous awareness of the momentous outcomes of that event stopped me cold.

There are numerous historical and theoretical conditions of possibilities for such taxing acts. Terror and terrorism are the expressions of potent and absolute political closures, acts of political desperation: war by other means. However, although terror, terrorism, and war are extreme and desperate forms of violence, they enjoy radically different epistemological positions. Whereas war, after Clausewitz, as a legitimate and well-planned action of a state, is understood to be the continuation of politics by other means, terror and terrorism are comprehended as the irrational (albeit well-organized) and "evil" performances of people without states—or worse, by people belonging to rogue, marginal, incomplete, or failed states. The radical disparity between the two forms of understanding politics compels us to treat them differently. Using the ordinary political (or moral, if you will) categories of analysis does not deliver a proper or even useful understanding of these new forms of political warfare, due to the fact that terror and terrorism are forms of struggle that transcend all the major Western frames of political thought. New associations between countries we now call global strongly contribute to the scrambling of relationships between people, obstructing the formation of the world's common good. There is a correlation between the breakdown of major categories of analysis —such as civil society, the public sphere, and the state—and all kinds of organized, albeit delegitimized, forms of investments and labor that impinge upon the stability of states and tear apart their respective civil societies and public spheres: here I include all those profitable manners of making money grouped under the rubric of *maquilas* and/or "traffics"—in organs, drugs, and perverse sex.

FOR over two decades, cultural scholars and philosophers of law have argued for the necessity of understanding the nature and possibilities of cross-cultural dialogues. They have insisted on the multicultural and multiethnic nature of the global world and warned that the problems of cross-cultural communications lie at the basis of geopolitical struggles. After September 11, 2001, however, the urgency of cross-cultural communications has taken a dramatic turn and can no longer be dismissed as the abstract and theoretical work of academic in cultural studies. These academic concerns now occupy the minds of politicians, including pressing questions on the nature of democracy and whether or not nondemocratic societies can make the transition from their own vernacular forms of governance to democratic rule. Can liberal democracy be the answer for a troubled world, or is it already a philosophy at its limits?

Within the cultural context for some of today's public policy debates, it is time to challenge the assumption that liberalism can constitute the ground for cross-cultural communication. In Guatemala, Colombia, and Mexico, forms of extreme and multifaceted violence and mass murder wreak havoc and threaten governability. In these societies, state-sanctioned mass murder and campaigns of terror and genocide reveal the extent to which liberal concepts have become inoperative and no longer capable of explaining new forms of violence or accounting for a wide variety of cultural conflicts. Bruised and battered survivors, and even the lifeless bodies of the less fortunate, appear in the public space and are discussed as part of public culture only *after* an insidious clash of values and ideas has already taken place and laid the groundwork for such spectacular acts of terrorism. This clash forces various forms of cultural exchange into a single pattern.[1] When this occurs, there is a tug of war between vernacular forms of social behavior and liberalism as universality is contested by local ideas. There is an unwitting use of liberal concepts such as *civil society, public sphere, state,* and *labor.* At stake are the content, form, future, and viability of democratic regimes.

Women and ethnic groups are agents of both material and discursive disruptions; they are both social actors of and figures and tropes in discourse. In my earlier study of women in transition, as well as in my analysis of the fiction of Central American revolutions, I demonstrated how the dramatic entrance of women and ethnic groups into the social history of the nation-state marks all kinds of distortions in the rhetoric of the nation.[2] Here I argue that they disturb the prose of globalization to an equal extent.

Women and ethnic groups have sufficiently documented this fact in testimonial literature, as well as in the wealth of legal depositions filed in court records and in anthropological and sociological research. Through their testimonials, women and members of ethnic groups speak loudly about the disparity or disjunction between concepts and lived experience. In this regard, testimonials do not merely reflect a given sociopolitical moment but are responses to, engagements with, and contestations of enduring issues. By contributing to the public sphere and constituting counterpublic spheres, they participate in the reconstitution and reformulation of democracy and democratic practices. Testimonials are related to embodied legacies of resistance and categorically help to position women and ethnic groups as ideal cross-cultural mediators on a global scale. For this reason, textual studies and discourse analyses are fundamental elements in the analysis of political violence.

Liberal scholars of multiculturalism and multinationalism, as well as philosophers of law and jurisprudence, have raised a host of concerns about liberal democracies. Their disclaimers lead me to question the nature and possibilities of dialogues across cultures.

In civil society and public spheres, I examine the use that women and ethnic groups make of those two core and supposedly cogent concepts of liberalism, specifically in Guatemalan society such as it is viewed by Rigoberta Menchú in *Rigoberta: La nieta de los Mayas.* How is it possible for an indigenous woman to speak about civil society and the public sphere within a society characterized by the criminality of the state, a state that has massacred thousands of indigenous people in the last decades of the twentieth century? Feminist and ethnic theories and scholarship assist me in this discussion and help me answer these questions.

In regard to the state, I inquire about the forms, styles, and protocols of multinational states. Different groups view the contractual relation between citizens and governance through consensus or the lack thereof, and how free-market exchanges that are declared illegal shred the fabric of social life. The testimonials of Colombian men, women, and children gathered by Alonso Salazar and Alfredo Molano speak to the criminality that pervades Colombian society, perpetrated by the state, the guerrillas, the paramilitary groups, and the drug lords.

In the domain of labor, my main interest lies in the moment that labor encroaches, trespasses, and therefore reorganizes the politically constituted borders of supposedly sovereign states. The fantastic takes over and covers up all kinds of free-market deals and as the traditional forms of labor organization in trade unions wilt, the magical and the demonic are the terrains from which to discuss the relation between labor and profits. Testimonials, compiled by concerned journalists and nongovernmental organizations, of mothers whose daughters have been murdered in Ciudad Juárez, Mexico, illustrate how these things occur.

Treading these paths takes us through examples of illegitimacy, illegality, and criminality, the very obverse of a well-regulated state governed by consensus and created for the common good. Nevertheless, such factors are undeniably present and emerge as predictable results of reading liberal democracies through the gaze of difference, cultures, and nations. Liberalism itself is implicated in this contradiction: that is, cultural texts understand and, more often than not, misuse (when not simply projecting as a fantasy) the core principles of liberalism and its paradoxes. One useful by-product of my probe is a broad illustration of the stock from which debates on ungovernability and criminality draw their force.

My discussion on the main theoretical difficulties pertaining to cross-cultural dialogues on the political ideology and principles of liberalism, as they occur both nationally and internationally, draws on the most recent contributions to the debate on multiculturalism, multinationalism, and difference. As a counterpoint, I lay out the perspective of theorists of plural societies. In this process, three tensions at the heart of liberalism itself are overriding: that between freedom and collaboration; that between freedom and equality; and that between laissez-faire and the welfare state.

If nothing else, these tensions call into question the notion of liberalism as a universal value. To talk about them, then, means to revise the universality of liberalism and examine the premise that liberalism is merely a particular philosophy in disguise, one that has successfully hegemonized global signification and established the limits of the political. In fact, each society has its own perception of universals and its own ways of inscribing its specific traumas within the symbolic organization of the social, as Renata Salecl has claimed.[3] Thus, for liberalism to ever be universal, it must achieve the impossible: obtain global consensus on the meaning of civil society, the pubic sphere, and the state. To do so, it must engage with concrete communities and mediate the relations they establish among themselves socially. If liberal ideology can do this, it will become truly liberal politics.

1

Cultures, Nations, Differences

THE PARADOXICAL FANTASIES
OF LIBERALISM AS DEMOCRACY

Sou um mulato nato
No sentido lato
Mulato democrático do litoral.

    Caetano Veloso, "Sugar Cane Fields Forever"

AT THE CLOSE of the twentieth century, the demise of socialism and the victory of capitalism as a one-world system drove the world into a deep conservative recoil.[1] The long march toward a utopian world came to a full stop, and the drift to globalization held sway apparently uncontested. Severely shaken by its untenable identification with socialist politics, Marxism lapsed from the ideology of liberation to just another classical German philosophy, and the struggle for social justice came to be relocated at the heart of liberalism.[2] Socially concerned liberal scholars turned their gaze inward to seriously reconsider the tenets of such political ideology, and the struggle continued within the liberal front. The grating sounds this shift produced are still audible.

In its wake, legal, political, cultural, and philosophical debates on the nature of multinational, multicultural states and on difference have ensued. These debates are twofold: they represent, on one hand, the tail end of a search for liberation that mirrored the anticolonialist and anti-imperialist thrust pervading the political space throughout the entire last century, and, on the other, the intellectual offensive against the strategies that the "new religious right" is mounting against the great majority of the global population under the guise of democracy. The most recent developments in the Middle East—Afghanistan, Iraq, Palestine—and in several localities of the African and American continents are patent examples of this struggle. Grappling with these situations is part and parcel of my quest to determine the nature and possibilities of cross-cultural dialogues in a multiethnic and multicultural global environment where liberalism may seem to be at its limits. At the root of this quest is an attempt to come to terms with the contradictions of liberalism. For, if the axiom is true that liberalism was born as a contested political ideology—sometimes more conservative and prone to the preservation of property as good governance, sometimes more radical, advocating an end to different rules for the poor and the rich—then the aporias inherent in liberalism suggest up front that it is not likely to be successful in its stated goals.

The overall strategy of this plunge into the philosophies of liberalism is to investigate the truth content and universal character of natural and human rights, and thereby test the limits of a doctrine that is organized around a set of seemingly paradoxical relationships. In this vein, I explore the possibilities of bringing the incongruous fantasies of liberalism—such as democracy, justice, and the common good—to bear in the organization of the neoliberal, democratic, postmodern, and now global state.[3] The unstated, yet related, concerns of this internal probe are, first, an anxious search for the locus of social hope and, more pressingly, the question of the possibilities of world politics.[4] The high stakes of this probe involve reviving the radical possibilities of liberalism, before global differences come to be the only explanation for criminality, terror, and terrorism. These acts, together with their misinterpretations, threaten to curtail, or at least heavily encumber, struggles for civil and human rights worldwide.

Myriad well-researched scholarly works on identities, cultures, and nations already document the violence inflicted by colonialism upon people that are considered different. In the Latin American field, most of our "native" categories of analysis—acculturation, transculturation, heterogeneity, and hybridity—speak to that issue directly. However, to converse about human rights using this contemporary vocabulary of liberal struggles simply acknowledges the standard idioms of the current ideological debate and tackles the questions within the same terrain. Thus, speaking liberalism in this way signals that there are no contested ideologies, no counterhegemonic projects, and that we are on the threshold of a new postmodern modality of colonialism that is devastating and ferocious. It is a modality, following Masao Miyoshi, that begins with a total indifference for regions of the world outside the megastates of Europe and the United States, known as "Fortress Europe" and "Fortress United States."⁵

This indifference amounts to nothing less than an all-out offensive against people outside these two fortresses—although some, considering the multilateral effects of policies such as outsourcing, will argue that the offensive is also internal. The irony is that this offense is carried out under the banner of liberalism and a larger strategy that calls for the establishment of "democratic" regimes. Here, "democracy" only gives the impression of a cover for the ability to control natural resources throughout the world. The condition of this possibility is the eradication of all forms of multiculturalism worldwide. In this context, democracy and its corollary, modernization, simply come to suggest a total disregard for the multicultural nature of the world: that is, to put it bluntly, a disregard for the nature and character of individual, historical, and particular cultural formations, which is tantamount to selling them off at a discount price. If carried to its conclusion, this campaign quite simply promises to deliver instability into all forms of modern institutions, and, worse yet, to induce political chaos throughout the world, all in the name of liberalism.

It is my purpose, then, to demonstrate the aporetic and politically untenable position of a particular philosophy of freedom whose only condition of possibility is the eradication of difference through the politics of indiscriminate force. My point is to demonstrate that liberalism is specifically grounded in a particular form of historical development, and that this specificity does not seem transferable or translatable—no matter how attractive and desirable the liberal philosophy may be. Consequently, cultures with different historical developments do not easily reproduce it. What they do, instead, is to interpret it, or more precisely, to adapt the core principles of liberalisms to their own specific circumstances and act on them accordingly. The result is, at best, a skewed and bizarre performance, an illiberal form of liberalism that all but enhances the paradoxes of the creed. Proof of this is provided by the examples of Latin American scholarship I rehearse in this book.

LIBERALISM AS A POLITICAL IDEOLOGY AND AS COMMON SENSE

The difference between liberalism as politics, as philosophy, and as common sense is a pertinent point of departure for my discussion. The theoretical distinction between philosophy and common sense that I use has been thoroughly rehearsed by Antonio Gramsci, and I would refer the reader to his body of work.[6] The problem I embark upon is the fact that although liberalism provides the basic political atmosphere for our lives in the West (that is, for us, liberal philosophy has lapsed into common sense), most of us are far from understanding the intricate detours of liberal, democratic governance that is liberalism as politics. Furthermore, few of us can grasp the conundrum that colonialism, imperialism, native indigenous populations, migration, heterogeneity, and the more recent phenomenon of outsourcing bring to the heart of liberalism.[7] To glance at these vast and complex webs of meaning—to which the entire body of postcolonial, gender, and ethnic studies have dedicated their efforts—we ought to understand first some of the internal tensions within liberalism itself, and, second, the queries that multiculturalism, multiethnicity, and difference have raised toward it. My purpose is to bring the totally unfamiliar displacements, shifts, and adjustments world scholars perform into the theater of discussion in order to fit the intricacies of the particular socialities they examine—like those of Latin America—into the liberal philosophical and political code. These adjustments, displacements, and shifts constitute, if not our political unconscious or our deepest desires to belong, then simply an all-out case of bad faith.[8]

LIBERALISM is a totalizing philosophy. It is a distinct framework organized around a set of core concepts that constitute the ground for calculating, reading, and interpreting political, social, cultural, and economic life. Following Stuart Hall, philosophically, we can say that liberalism stands for "individualism in politics, civil and political rights, parliamentary government, moderate reform, limited state intervention and private enterprise economy."[9] Politically, it "entails sovereign individuals casting their votes, political parties representing the people and competing for the right to shape the will of the sate, and elected representatives deliberating on their behalf in legislative bodies in between elections. The state is neutral with regard to the competing conceptions of the good, government and elected officials are generally attentive to public opinion, relevant players abide by the rule of law, and external actors do not intervene in domestic politics."[10] Liberal democracy is "representative government, the rule of law, a regime of entrenched rights, the guarantees of certain freedoms."[11]

Although the imaginary horizon of liberal politics in practice is much less tidy, in common practice it has also come to stand for a form of practical reasoning and thought. This is an attitude that stands for being open-minded, rational, and freedom-loving, "a taken-for-granted discourse of everyday life that shapes the 'practical consciousness' of the masses."[12] In this sense, the stock from which liberal thinking draws its major tenets recedes from memory, and the historical struggles that inform its function appear as merely natural. This gives liberalism its resonance with an immemorial past, while simultaneously projecting it forward into a concept of eternal time. It is this all-encompassing logic that enables liberalism's transition from a philosophical ideology to common sense, and this shift is precisely what grants liberalism its sense of universality. Beyond this universal claim, all of its core concepts only make real sense when they are understood against the background of European history and the emerging social order of the bourgeoisie. Liberalism, which in those days was a socially progressive and democratic ideology, is therefore intimately related to the rise of the modern capitalist world, where it informs modernism by opposing feudalism. For instance, the idea of popular power first appears in contrast to the absolute power of the monarch, freethinking is a response to ideas of order that ascribe it to some source, and the notion of individual freedom emerges against the tight grip of religion.

As a broader discourse, liberalism is a seventeenth- and eighteenth-century philosophy born in England out of English struggles for the freedom of trade and correspondent forms of governance. It is reasonable, then, to surmise that as a political philosophy, liberalism serves English—and later western European and U.S.—history well. However, when it migrates to other contexts, such as the Latin American countries (not to mention Africa and Asia, and even Eastern Europe) liberalism, like all traveling theories, requires heavy adjustments and goes through a severe and at times bizarre process of analogues. For example, in Latin American scholarship, the interests of the *criollos,* as the emerging social group seeking their independence from Spain in the late eighteenth and early nineteenth centuries, are implicitly considered analogous to the interests of the Whigs in England—an absurd idea. And while this fallacy is nourished by the historical fact that the *criollos* used liberal ideas for their struggles, and in many instances were both ideologically and financially supported by English groups, the radical differences between the two social formations ought to be enough to bring us to a full stop. In actuality, the historical development of Latin American societies more closely follows Caribbean scholars' descriptions of the process of creolization, and multicultural theorists' examinations of multiethnic and multinational societies, in marked contrast to the liberalism that emerges from the western European tradition.

As a political philosophy, liberalism claims to be an open system. However, it is a very well worked out totality in which all kinds of procedures work to fasten tight the social contract. Liberals call this a civil (or civilized) way of being that ensures the common good, a system that depends upon a firm, tight matrix of attractive core concepts—civil society, public sphere, the state, and markets. But what these concepts, in fact, do is define the conditions of possibility of the structure. They map out what can be said and what is off limits. Individualism is the solid and unswerving bedrock upon which liberalism firmly rests and to which all the other concepts of liberalism refer; all liberal concepts flow from individualism, and nothing can be understood outside of it. In actuality, human and natural rights are coterminous with the rights of the individual. Together they constitute a synergy that holds together the edifice of liberalism and that underwrites its particular claim to universality. Hence, if this core concept is flawed or insufficient, as historians of colonialism have strongly demonstrated, the whole theoretical edifice is tremulous, ready to collapse under the weight of its own tacit assumptions and presuppositions.[13]

Given that the relationship between liberalism and the bourgeois western European worldview has been in the intellectual market for some time, one wonders about the urgency with which multicultural liberal theorists repeatedly return to it nowadays. Their body of work on liberalism posits several concerns that I will here group into two: the recognition of the unresolved tensions at the heart of the doctrine—tensions that are aggravated when the political philosophy is exported to different social sites; and the need to preserve the universal validity of the system and to honor the open character of its philosophy. With these interests in mind, liberal scholars of multiculturalism working to analyze the nature of multiethnic states have offered a series of amendments to make room for the inclusion of all sorts of people defined as "different." Whether or not these people classify as individuals has been the burden of postcolonial, subaltern, gender, and ethnic studies.

These shifts toward a more inclusive form of liberalism as a philosophy of rights informing governance signals a tacit recognition of the homogeneity upon which the internal coherence of the system rests (a theme we will return to later). Furthermore, it is a struggle that liberalism permits. Michael Walzer has argued this issue in his discussion of two forms of liberalism, what he calls "Liberalism 1" and "Liberalism 2." Liberalism 1 "is committed . . . to individual rights and . . . to a rigorous neutral state, that is, a state without cultural or religious projects or, indeed, any sort of collective goal beyond the personal freedom and the physical security, welfare, and safety of its citizens." Liberalism 2 "allows for a state committed to the survival and flourishing of a particular nation, culture, or religion, or of a (limited) set of nations, cultures, and religions —so long as the basic rights of citizens who have different commitments" or who do not have any such commitments at all "are protected."[14]

We need not review the entirety of world history to realize that the synergy of a natural individual and his or her human rights is a concept deeply and absolutely contradicted by the narratives of other social formations, such as those based on slavery, debt peonage, indenture, and many other forms of labor. These social formations are responsible for transforming human individuals into chattels and have determined the form and shape of political governance in many parts of the world. Furthermore, these systems not only cohabit with liberalism; they have actually been sponsored by it. Thus, world history brings us to one of the most severe and unresolved questions at the heart of liberalism: namely, the question of human rights.

In order to understand the aporias of the system, we must review all those abundant narratives that offer samples of liberalism at its limits. In this case, it is important to revisit and reappraise the documents that speak about population segments that lack all kinds of human rights, live under perennial states of exceptionalism, and circulate in texts only under generic names.[15] Such is the case of *indios, cholos, serranos, sambos, selváticos, jinchos, cabecitas negras,* and *huachos* in Latin America; blacks, Native Americans, Mexican Americans, and now Latinos/as in the United States; Jews, *pienoirs, moros,* and Turks in Europe. Generally, liberal thinkers tend to claim that these proliferating descriptions of difference occur only in illiberal societies. However, such categories are easily accommodated by a liberal, democratic, and universal philosophy; furthermore, liberal human rights are precisely the flip side of these lacks of rights, as liberal ideas not only foment these distinctions and differences but even benefit from them. In this case, the burden for liberalism is then to explain and account for the legal and philosophical status of these population segments and make a statement as to whether or not it is important, necessary, and plausible to dialogue with them. Judging by the number of studies, the answer is in the affirmative. Therefore, what is at stake is the validity of the system itself: its universal, and now global, feasibility. Today, more than ever, it is imperative to prove that human rights are not the prerogative of one ethnic group alone, nor of one nation; they must be the right and prerogative of all human beings, regardless of race, gender, religion, or national origin, lest liberalism become just another particularism disguised as the universal. In this way, the interrogation of liberalism by ethnic, gender, and multicultural studies and scholars constitutes a truly democratic gesture. In today's world, this is the only possibility of politics and governance.

It is well known that liberal governing practices across the globe (from Latin America to Asia, Africa, Eastern Europe, and even western Europe and the United States) are contrary to the philosophical principle that understands the individual to be a social agent unencumbered by the limitation of status, position, and so on, free from constraint, and endowed by his or her natural birth with inalienable human rights. Histories of maltreatment and abuse carried to the extreme of massive killings or pogroms in some of these societies force us to reflect on the nature of human rights.[16] In their political practices, these governments drastically trample upon the principles that sustain the notion of the individual in liberalism. For them, human rights are not grounded on nature and do not bear on all forms of social intercourse; they do not "belong to individuals as individuals in the state of nature and [are] therefore [not] prior to entry into society."[17] In these particular historical instances, liberalism loses all its universal philosophical seduction. It stands as a theoretical abstract and, at best, an idealist philosophy, one that is the source of much confusion when it attempts to explain forms of governance whose conditions of possibility are precisely contrary to what liberalism predicates in matters of universal human rights. In the nations under study in this text, in no way or manner could liberal principles be viewed as respectful of human rights, or as the expression of the common good upon which the foundation of political society—or the state—rests. This fundamental disparity accounts for my proposal that Latin American nations historically have developed in manners more akin to the models of multicultural, multiethnic, or so-called Creole societies/states, than those of liberalism, even when qualified as plural.

To offer an example of how this disparity spans the entire gamut of liberal literatures and illustrates my point, the distinction between natural and native suffices. Both natural and native are idioms that have circulated within the field of liberal philosophies for sometime. The critical difference between them is that whereas *natural* refers to the citizen-subject, *native* names the colonial subject. Thus, although the concept of native carries connotations of primitivism that the concept of natural lacks, primitivism, in the sense Freud granted this term (a presocial form of being) subtends both concepts. *Natural* and *native* are terms that could be conflated and work as synonyms, however much they seem to establish a radical opposition and deepen the distinctions between humans and their rights.[18]

From the beginning of modernization, the difference between European states and Amerindian societies produces a covenant that divides natural from native rights. People without well-established states are people without history.[19] In Hegelian terms, history is contingent upon the formation of the state and is hence the history of the state. Considered within a Hegelian epistemology, *native* refers to the rawest state of being, a quasianimal, primitive ontology, previous to civil society (civilization) and the social organization of labor to fit human needs. *Natural,* in contrast, already implies a transition into civil society, a step previous to political society, where labor in the abstract will deliver the organization of the state.[20] Natural society is the society of needs. Civil society is the society of organized labor. Political society is a society in which labor in the abstract is the organizing principle of the social. In civil society we already find in operation the foundational principle of liberal individualism, a condition that precedes the foundation of the state and the full realization of human nature. In the course of human interaction, the logical development from natural, to civil, to political societies suffers an *interruptio* that preempts the possibilities of state formations and produces the societies of natives. Scholars of colonialism attribute this *interruptio* to colonialism itself. Colonialism marks the divide that sunders humanity and explains the caesura between native and natural, who throughout history stand poised on the opposite sides of a partition later to become the distinction between civilized and uncivilized or primitive. Hence, the merging of native and natural is only the labor of political desire and of political opportunism visible in sentimental and romantic fiction. In the late eighteenth and early nineteenth centuries, the categories native and natural are willfully merged in these genres so that Latin American states become plausible.[21] Borrowing from postcolonial scholars, these narratives can be read as marketing techniques, making the "native" a good item for purchase when native stands for natural. Doris Sommer argues this eloquently in

"Sab c'est moi," where she maintains that *criollo* writer Gertrudis Gómez de Avellaneda speaks of herself when speaking for and about her slave, Sab. Through the work of such narrative, *native* (later to become mestizo, hybrid, Creole, migrant, *cholo,* or what have you) enjoys ample circulation and becomes a common dividing idiom, an empty signifier that continues to refer to those without names in the metropolitan public sphere to this date.

European and Latin American romantic and sentimental literatures go on to circulate the homology between the pure and innocent native as a natural man—perhaps, in the best of cases, as a catachresis of his "natural" European counterpart. The dramatic creation of the Latin American states thus occurs through the idealization of natives—Ladinos, acculturated Indians, mixed breeds, mestizos, mulattoes—frail and flawed fictional characters usually associated with the romantic literatures of the period of independence. Sab, Oronooko, Hamel, María, Enriquillo, Yariko, the "good woman" of Anotto Bay, Mary Prince—these are just a sample of those agents whose social pacts with the *criollos* would enable the latter to fashion a temporary common-front politics and thereby establish their own liberal states in which their natural human rights would prevail—"Sab c'est moi." Romantic literature and its native characters here constitute the medium for the illusory establishment of the analogies, as absurd as they may be, between Latin American *criollos* and English Whigs or the people of the French Commune.[22] Scholars of postcolonialism discuss these ideas regarding the native in sentimental and romantic fiction at some length.[23] But aside from this instrumental use of nativism as grounds for individualism, individualism is primary, in essence, because the idea itself is grounded in nature, on the notion of instincts and drives, on the primitive of totems and taboos, as Freud has amply demonstrated, and easily underwrites the sign of native as a natural man. This also occurs in the case of its flip side, the idea of a natural man as native. Native, however, is never granted the status enjoyed by natural. In fact, native could be interpreted as a category halfway between animal and human. It names an arrested development, a frozen state of being, that which was bred by the policies and politics of liberal colonialism, a stateless being.

The significance of natural (as primitive and primary) in individualism is that it facilitates and firmly grounds the notion of the state.[24] And here is where the idea of reason enters the scene: first, as the protocols of discussion (Hegel calls it transcendence), the logic that brings all concepts together to constitute a system; and, later, as that part of being that conflicts with instincts (the primitive) and establishes a perennial tension that the state will come to mediate. Freud formulated it as the distinction between Eros and Thanatos, civilization and its discontents. In this way, reason is doubly articulated: first as rules and protocols, and then as that which is unnatural, a transcendence of nature. Moreover, reason is also that which names the distinction between competition and collaboration or regulates competition for the sake of collaboration.

Here we see that in classical liberalism, nature and the state are poised as the opposite poles of natural being. Furthermore, the distinction between reason and instincts also subtends the divide between citizens and natives, states and societies, nations and empires. One argument that runs throughout the system is that the egotistic (or individual) pursuit of happiness or the good life, which is mediated by labor in its abstract form, provides the basis for the social contract, whose ontological foundations are all predicated on nature. It is only through free consent that individuals sufficiently abrogate their natural rights to create society and government. Consent is thereby the sole condition for legitimacy. This certainly seems like an attractive proposal. In contrast, colonialism is just the opposite of government by consent, and consequently the flip side of reason, state, and human rights.

As the domain of public duties and responsibilities, the state, in exchange, provides the conditions so that individuals are free to pursue their own affairs both in private and in public. Yet, the ascription of primitivism to individualism explains why the theories of Freud and Lacan are necessary addenda and supplements to liberalism and its critics. This additionally explains why Freud begins his examination of death, in *Totem and Taboo,* by studying prestate forms of societal organization: that is, the relationship between the native and the natural. For, if liberty means freedom from constraint for the individual to realize "'his natural, egoistic drives and instincts," then theories of the unconscious (like those of colonialism and postcolonialism) serve to explain the lingering presence of unreason even in societies based on consent.[25] Law and the unconscious, as Lacan clearly saw the link between them, are the basis for understanding the constitution of primitive individualism and modern citizens' identities, as well as their counterpart, as forms of oppression of individuals that are kept hovering at the margins of liberal human rights.

Understanding how the system works philosophically is of the essence in understanding how it works politically. It is useful, in turn, for the present work in showing that liberalism is, in fact, at its limits, as evidenced by a curtailment of human rights today that is every bit as severe as the lack of human rights that has prevailed under the systems of colonialism, both neo- and post-. Further evidence appears in the curve of liberalism that has moved from classical and communitarian to social-democratic forms, and from there back to a neoclassical stance, the form and content of what we call neoliberalism. May I suggest that this return is a sign of weakness, a form of empowering its disempowerment, a strategic necessity, but one that nevertheless comes to haunt the liberal state from within, as theorists of multiculturalism attest?

Here, vast arrays of old and new varieties of criminality defy the liberal state, as if all forms of the primitive, the instinctual, and the natural, as well as the native, have been let loose in the midst of the most organized forms of labor and states. A neonatural and neonative society from below threatens to dissolve the divide between natural, civil, and political, whereas from above, political society moves in parallel, complementary, and opposite directions. Both do so in full force. The medium for this discussion passes through the hurdles of the basic concepts of civil society, public sphere, state, and labor, as we will have the opportunity to examine in the chapters that follow. But first it is necessary to examine how the invisible hand of the human as native and as natural haunts the borders of a disorderly state.

If the philosophy of liberalism as a refined totalizing system is flawed in the arena of human rights and contingent on a contradictory notion of natural and native, then its political ideology, as it works through the medium of the state and governance, is much more complex. As different scholars have already addressed a variety of problems within liberalism as politics, I shall review those concerning the state, civil society, the public sphere, and labor, which are the concepts whose contradictory relations I examine in subsequent chapters. The three contradictions outlined by Stuart Hall, the queries raised by multiculturalism as represented by the work of Charles Taylor and Will Kymlicka, and the nature of Creole and mestizo societies each will assist me in traveling between two distinct forms of liberalism: one in central nations and the other in peripheral societies.

All of the crucial problems of liberalism seem to emanate from a need to make the natural individual and his freedom the keystone of the philosophies of rights, the founding agent of democracy, and the pivot around whose needs and desires market exchanges turn. Consequently, it is urgent that we work out the relation of the individual and the social—what liberals call communal or group interests—and that of freedom and equality in relation to the state. Only in this way will we come to understand the cogency of this totalizing system, or lack thereof, and examine what Benjamin Arditi has so appropriately called "politics on the edges of liberalism" or liberalism's underside: "a gray zone of phenomena where one is tempted to suspend the qualifier 'liberal' when describing politics, or at least where it is difficult to assert unambiguously that what happens within it is governed by a liberal code alone . . . a zone where experimentation with political innovation questions the liberal consensus. The 'edges' . . . refer to phenomena that either push the envelope of liberalism to seek to go against and beyond it."[26]

Part of these edges are constituted by the class character of liberalism, which is connected from the very beginning. Hall argues that liberalism is not tied to any particular class interest, although not one but two revolutions came about as a result of the Civil War of 1640 in England: one won civil, political, and economic rights for the new men of property, the Whigs (as the wars of independence won those rights for the *criollos* in Latin America at the beginning of the nineteenth century); the other revolution placed less emphasis on property and was designed to eliminate poverty and social injustice. The two strands exist simultaneously within liberalism, and liberalism emerges as an arena of struggle. Hall notes,

Liberalism actually emerged as a contested space already divided into its more conservative and its more radical tendencies—a tension which has been repeated again and again throughout its history. Depending on which tendency was the dominant one, liberalism could be articulated to the demands of different social strata. . . . Both conservative and radical tendencies were premised on the fundamentally liberal concepts of individual liberties and rights and a conception of society as an association of free and rational persons bound by contract and consent. The quarrel between those who saw good government as the extension and the preservation of their property and those who saw liberty as the end of "one rule for the rich and one for the poor" was a quarrel between different classes initially within liberalism.[27]

The debate on multiculturalisms, multinationalisms, and difference thrives on this idea and digs profoundly into the tensions within liberalism, insisting on the principle of universal human rights for those individuals classified under the rubric of special-interest groups or communities.

THREE PRIMORDIAL TENSIONS AT THE HEART OF LIBERALISM

Stuart Hall identifies three tensions within liberalism that bear witness to the severe stretch and strain to which the system is subjected in its efforts to iron out contradictory ideas or oppositions. The first tension is between freedom and collaboration, the second tension is between freedom and equality, and the third is between laissez-faire and a welfare state. After being slightly rephrased by different multicultural scholars, these tensions appear as: (1) those between individual and communal or group interests, (2) those between freedom and equality (this tension remains the same), and (3) those between a strong state and a noninterventionist state. These three tensions enable us to distinguish the different strands of liberalism—radical, conservative, and social democratic—and thus understand the difference between the communalist and the procedural approaches to liberalism.

Tension 1: Between the Individual and the Communal or Group Interests

The tension between individual and group needs follows from a distinction between freedom and collaboration. This distinction is fundamental to liberalism as it negotiates the radical difference between group interests and needs and societal interests and needs. The essential divide here is that whereas *societal* putatively refers to the whole society, groups are understood as special-interest associations of individuals that stand paradoxically separate from the whole. Within multiculturalism, group interests are understood as ethnic, gender, or difference interests, which appear disengaged from the interests of the society as a whole. They are interests that, while existing within the social, only belong to portions, segments, and parts of the society and might therefore impinge upon the rights of others. A problem emerges immediately in that group interests are not defined as common interests, but rather as partial and special interests. Thus, if we take *group* to mean society as a whole, then we are not operating within liberalism. But, the problem is more complicated still, as the existence of groups that are within, but not of, the society not only posits a tension between freedom and collaboration, but is also the essence of discrimination (understood as unequal civil rights, an example of the divide between naturals and natives), denoting an illiberal locus of liberal societies—a catachresis. The tension between freedom and collaboration underpins the discussion of multiculturalism and therefore constitutes the foundation for the debate between procedural and communitarian and between conservative and social democratic forms of liberalism.

Furthermore, the idea of the individual and the idea of the group—implicit in the first tension, between freedom and collaboration—are antithetical, which constitutes the overlaying tension that subtends the philosophy of liberalism as a political ideology. Charles Taylor has worked amply on this subject. In his work he examines this question by referring to the relationship between public and political spheres. In his article "Politics and the Public Sphere," Taylor takes on the concepts of private, public, and political spheres and attempts to demonstrate how the three remain separated in principle.[28] However, in so doing he underscores the tension produced by this separation.

The tensions between public and private thus arise from the contradictions of a theory predicated on the freedom of the individual, which now has to explain how and where individuals interact with each other and how they seek the common good. The main strategy to solve these seemingly opposing principles —the individual and the communal (which are never conceived as group interests)—has been to think of a happy medium, a medium endowed with a certain autonomy, a space for free public interaction. Civil society is such a happy medium. Taylor understands *civil society* to mean "the host of free associations, existing outside of any official sponsorship, and often dedicated to ends which we generally consider nonpolitical. . . . But civil society . . . exists where beyond these multiple associations, or through their combination, society can operate as a whole outside the ambit of the state. I mean by this ways in which society can be said to act, or to generate or sustain a certain condition, without the agency of government."[29] Thus, in contrast to the state, which is the sphere of the political, civil society is the field of play for the realization of individual self-interest. Civil society is thus defined as a privileged domain beyond the reach and regulation of the state. The three major zones of civil society are (1) the private, domestic world of the family, (2) the market as the arena of free and contractual economic activity, and (3) the domain of voluntary social and political association.

The two major components of civil society are the public sphere and the market, which together constitute the arena for individual expression of the public. The public sphere is "a common space in which the members of the society are deemed to meet through a variety of media: print, electronic, and also face-to-face encounters; to discuss matters of common interest; and thus to be able to form a common mind about these things."[30] The public sphere is that real, metaphoric, or virtual space of discussion where individuals can agree: that is, reach consensus on matters pertaining to their common good. Markets then follow as the "perfect instrument of such a system because, in market society, central economic decisions . . . result from the impersonal movement of prices reflecting the push and pull of forces of demand and supply which arise from a multitude of individual decisions and wills."[31] Thus, individual (human) rights, as well as political and civil, are matched by a vigorous economic liberalism in which competition (which to me is the expression of individual freedom in action) is the governing principle. This is a materialistic and utilitarian conception of the economic and the political grounded in the calculus of rationally pursued self-interest and advantage. And here we must stop and reflect on the multiple meanings of the public, for it is in the public sphere where the tensions between the individual and the communal are played out.

First of all, the public is simply that which is not private. If in the private sphere individuals reign supreme and are in full command of their rights and freedoms, in public they must abide by the rules and procedures of reason constituted into law. The public is thus an intermediary zone, a corridor connecting the private and the state, a space paradoxically construed as within, yet simultaneously outside, the political. In this space individuals are free to exchange all kinds of goods and ideas, provided they follow the rules, procedures, and protocols established for interactions between individuals and for public interaction: this is the meaning of reason as instrumental. The public is, in this sense, an arena of exchange (of goods, ideas, opinions), and the societal interactions of individuals in public are hence on the one hand market interactions and, on the other, political interactions. From this we can gather that the economic always underwrites the notion of the public. This gloss on the fundamental principles of liberalism leaves us here with three outstanding questions that will be taken on in the subsequent chapters of this text: (1) Is individualism construed differently in the private and the public spheres? (2) Are the rules and procedures of public discussion restricted to the public sphere, or do they extend to the private?[32] (3) Is reason merely instrumental?

The bridge between the individual and the collective is the public sphere. Liberal society, "one which is trying to realize in the highest possible degree certain goods or principles of right . . . [and] trying to maximize the goods of freedom and collective self-rule, in conformity with a rule of right founded on equality," thus holds on to the notion of the individual and his or her human rights because that is the keystone of a theory of markets—of the open exchange of goods and ideas.[33] This theory of markets, in turn, has to propose a theory of the societal in order to introduce politics (law and order) into exchange. This is what Hegel called the transition from civil into political society (the state) mediated by labor in the abstract. Here we come into another conundrum within liberal philosophy: namely, the relation between all the spheres of liberalism—markets, labor, public sphere, civil society, and the state.

The key issue for us now is that no matter how we look at any of the articulations of liberal democratic principles, we are always confronted with the problem of the individual and the collective, of the private and the public, of civil society, public sphere, states, and markets. In this section we are trying to unravel the paradoxical relationship between the individual and the communal, which is another way of stating the relationship between freedom and governance. So is governance—political society—really the end point of this discussion? Hegel seems to think so: the apex of his philosophy is the state. Considered from this point of view, it seems, in all fairness, that in the public sphere civil and natural rights are at odds with each other, because whereas civil rights invoke the social, natural rights favor the individual. And civil and individual rights are not the same, although they are usually thought of as one. The designation of natural comes first; it comes from birth and is essentially ahistorical and asocial (a truly neutral ground). The designation of civil, on the other hand, is essentially political, a fiduciary form, the product of communal living and voluntary surrendering, and related to the state. From here it seems only logical to conclude that in the political philosophy of liberalism, individual human rights are first made to be coterminous with civil rights, and subsequently with political rights—law and order. This is the bedrock upon which civilization, state rule, and political society stand.

To solve the tension between the individual and the communal, then, the mediation of the state is necessary. The argument goes as follows. Through a focused public discussion, free individuals become of one mind. Consensus is that mechanism by means of which everyone speaks with one voice. Hence, through consensus the tension between the individual and the community relaxes. In the public sphere, dialogical reason turns freedom into consensual (and hegemonic) governance. Thus, the tension between the individual and the communal is solved in governance. Political society is, as Hegel upheld, the resolution of all the tensions within liberalism.

Now the question is: governance by whom? And the answer is: governance by the same individuals who have come to an agreement in their public discussions on matters concerning their common good. And, here again is where semantic problems become political and ideological queries, as, for good or for ill, the notion of the public tends to become coterminous with the communal —all the individuals becoming one individual. Common interests give rise to laws that emanate from the orderly exchange of words, from procedural (reasonable) discussions over matters of interests to all. These discussions are, in principle, devoid of all spirit of partisanship and related to the issues at hand. Group and party interests are considered negatively and thought of as antithetical to the communal. The social contract has a compelling character, which is constitutionally stated in the rule of law. Managing the notion of the public, then, entails considering the individual as a member of a social community; although the public is the medium to express common concerns and forge agreement on issues of common interests, under no circumstances ought it be confused with the societal. Trouble arises when one has in mind altogether different referents while employing these terms.

For me, this is one way of going over the logic of the system, to experience the ways in which every core concept connotes the other concepts and to reveal how all of these terms together constitute a closed and self-referential system. This is also a way of deducing a logic that departs from the concept of entrenched individual rights and ends in the rule of law and judicial action—a way of understanding the public and the political, and of moving from abstract philosophical principle into concrete political action. No liberal theoretician would disagree with these statements except when confronted with what are referred to as group rights (or interests), which in the societal context of central nations are the human rights of ethnic communities, special-interest groups, and gender. I will elaborate on this point later, but for the moment, it stands to reason to conclude that the public sphere is the vehicle enabling communal or societal formation and which thus takes the individual off center within the frame of a liberal state. Could we then provisionally conclude that in public, the tension between the individual and the communal is resolved when the individual and the communal become one?

I know liberal theoreticians will accept this logical consequence momentarily: if and when people reach an agreement and are of one mind, the individual is realized collectively. The caveat resides in making an unbridgeable distinction between the societal communal and the group communal. We are therefore compelled to conclude that some people belong to the societal communal and others to the group communal. The next question is, does not the societal communal constitute a group? Liberal thinkers will be reluctant to admit this, for admitting it is tantamount to accepting that liberalism is truly a group philosophy, a particularism based on the time-honored homogeneity of its members and their communal or group interests. Therefore, to avoid this dilemma, they create a series of infinite mediations that never allow the individual to be superseded by a group or a community. Nonetheless, and in a contradictory fashion, they readily accept that there are groups: that is, that there are certain people that either identify themselves or are identified by others as a community, and that these communities are differentiated by race, by gender, or by sexual orientation, among other traits. The result is that these groups stand separate and apart from the political society, from the state. It is logical, then, to conclude that what liberalism fails to accommodate is not the relation between the individual and the collective, but rather equality-in-difference.

This brings us to another problem that liberal philosophers have to explain: the inside/outside of power that the categories of public sphere and the market enjoin. Civil society, we are told, is separate from the state. Civil society and the state are two different domains. One cannot be confused or taken in by the other. The unstated corollary is that civil society is the terrain that guarantees that human associations are pre-, extra-, or apolitical, because the public space in which they occur is defined as neutral. Neutrality, however, does not account for the fact that such social exchange presumes at least some pattern of public maintenance, rules, and procedures that are well established and agreed upon—in most cases, the rule of law. If public space is the space where people come together, we must ask: What are the preconditions for this space to exist? What are the conditions of possibility of drawing rooms, coffee houses, salons, trade unions, newspapers, novels, print capitalism, games, movie theaters, and even friendships and affect? How should one think about them without invoking the presence of private property and the law—matters of "common interest" that need consent and agreement?

It is clear that the public sphere is "the locus of discussion potentially engaging everyone . . . in which the society can come to a common mind about important matters." It is clear, too, that critical debate produces a common mind. However, it is not clear how civil society "is an association which is constituted by nothing outside of the common action we carry out in it"; how it is "a discourse of reason outside power, which nevertheless is normative for power." And it is still less clear how the extrapolitical status in which all the members of a political society "should be seen as also forming a society outside the state," when "it is true that in a functioning public sphere, action at any time is carried out within structures laid down earlier" in a "de facto arrangement of things" that "does not enjoy any privilege over the action carried out within it." My interest, then, is in how public debate can be disengaged from partisanship and devoid of social conflict, and therefore ultimately in the relationship between conflict and freedom. We can think about these ideas in abstract forms only if we think about them philosophically, not politically. The moment we state that the public sphere and the public opinion it generates play "a crucial role in [the public sphere's] self-justification as a free self-governing society, that is, a society in which (a) people form their opinions freely—both as individuals and in coming to a common mind, and (b) these common opinions matter: they in some way take effect on or control government," we are talking politics.[34]

The systemic problems always boil down to the same paradox: arguing for individual human rights while explaining society's formation, existence, and rule of law. Freedom, the most central of human rights, is then construed as always subordinated to consensus in order to achieve the common good. The individual is always subordinated to the social—or the private to the public, as liberalism likes to call it. In liberalism, this subordination of the individual-private to the collective-public is mediated or attenuated through the construction of the public sphere as a public space for discussion. Freedom exists in the public sphere, and this freedom is what allows for the rule of law. The public individual is not subordinated to government, power, or the state; on the contrary, the state, government, and power are subordinated to the individual, provided the individual speaks with one collective voice. Government is always, in theory, responsive and responsible to public opinion, which means "(1) to be the product of reflection, (2) to emerge from discussion, and (3) to reflect an actively produced consensus."[35] However, the increasing overlap and conflation of the major zones of civil society that characterizes corporate rule provide the ground for Foucault's and Deleuze's proposition of the withering of civil society. The new social movements also contend that the logic of corporate society is ever encroaching on the procedural, impartial nature of state regulations. This is another pressure that philosophers of liberalism have brought to bear on the system.

Tension 2: Between Freedom and Equality: Minority/Majority Rights

Tension number two refers to the relation between freedom and equality. The problem here is that although by law all individuals are equal subjects, equality is a value derived from freedom and natural rights. Individual freedom presides over all others, equality included. This is the general idea of Anatole France's famous ironic dictum that anyone is free to sleep under a bridge at night if he so wishes. In constitutional democracies, everybody is free and equal to pursue his or her own egotistic self-interest, while competing with others with equal chances. But not all obtain the same results; some succeed while others fail. Why? That is what multicultural philosophies want to explore. The theory of the survival of the fittest is not sufficient, because the discussion is no longer situated in the natural but in the political. Tension number 2 thus refers to the paradox of how a basically egalitarian posture generates unequal positions. Legally, the question is: must the law be mute before inequality but not before freedom? Indeed, the law leaves the difference between formally abstract and concretely substantive equality unspecified. The law offers formal and systematic public criteria: neutral procedures. It also maintains fairness, secures contracts, protects individual rights, because "the business of the laws . . . is not to provide for the truth of opinions but for the safety and security of the commonwealth and of every particular man's goods and persons."[36] The key word is *neutrality,* because it constitutes the substantial divide between minority and majority constituencies. In democratic societies, majority rules.

The distinction between equality and freedom moves indistinctly from the domain of political philosophy to that of political economy, as equality is discussed first in terms of whether or not the state should intervene in defining a good life as the common good. Here the divide is between the good life and the common good. The good life is a private prerogative and an individual right, while the common good is the consensual agreement reached by all of the individuals composing the society to create a state. The catch is that the state must not interfere with the former but rather must create procedures for the latter. This tension marks the locus of another important divide between communal- and procedure-oriented scholars of liberalism, or Walzer's two kinds of liberalism. Whereas communitarians believe states must intervene in the definition of a good life for all, proceduralists think procedures suffice. Communitarian liberals call for a social-democratic and welfare form of state, while proceduralists support a more neoliberal type of noninterventionist state, which operates according to laissez-faire, laissez-aller policies.

One of the most pressing tasks of the philosophies of liberalism is to explain why there are disadvantaged minority communities and why minority groups do not fare as well in the equal market of opportunities. This is the crux of tension number 2, between freedom and equality. In *Liberalism, Community and Culture,* Will Kymlicka addresses this and, as a good liberal theoretician, subsumes all human rights into the rights of the individual and subordinates "minority rights" to individual rights—a very reductionist stance.[37] His subtext in this move is the question of how to manage the recognition of injustice, the battering of a vast array of cultures, the lopsided (misadjusted and maladjusted) lifeways that are characteristic of cultures created by the confrontation between freedom and equality. In our case, I instead propose to confront this tension in terms of how to accept the role of cultural membership (or citizenship). In relation to this interrogation, it is also legitimate to wonder if people have an interest in ensuring the continuation of their own culture when other types of culture are available for purchase in the market, or if they are ready to exchange their own cultural idiosyncrasies for the sake of integrating into larger and more powerful societies where the state is ready to make a substantial social investment in homogenizing cultures. For, as Kymlicka acknowledges, there is no doubt that cultural minorities have a distinct legal and political status and that within the liberal theory of equal rights, they have the right to develop their distinct cultural lives, however much these cultural lives present themselves as a liability to the "universal" mode of being and the pursuit of "the good life."

As I explained in the previous section, in principle liberal theoreticians oppose special status for any collectivity or minority group (culture) on the grounds of a conflict of interest between individual and collective rights. Any proposal which limits individual rights for the sake of collective rights will never be supported by liberalism. There seems to be zero tolerance within the moral ontology of this system for the idea of collectivities, other than its own. The problem is that, from a minority standpoint, the defense of individual rights takes the form of a confrontation between majority and minority rights. Liberals' championing of individual rights is viewed as a pretext to defend the rights of majority groups. Minority groups, in whatever ways they are formulated—be it in terms of ethnicity, gender, or disability—have already accrued lengthy and important bibliographies that prove that the concept of the individual does not apply to everyone equally. The individual, far from being a universal concept, is a very particular perception contingent upon availability of and access to collective decisions. Minorities are always seen as a group. Therefore, group (cultural) membership, a new term liberal theoreticians have to contend with, must play a role in the public discussion of human rights. The successful strategy here lies in the definition of majority and minority, since, in a democracy, the majority rules.

One important point that carries over in this discussion is to understand that minority rights usually refer more to rights of nondiscrimination rather than to special treatment for different cultures. This clarification is necessary because the struggle for cultural rights creates the impression of a petition for special rights. In fact, the case for minority rights argues against the special rights of majority groups. Cultural rights expose the existence of a double standard of governance, one for majorities (defined as the common good) and the other for special-interest groups. At issue here is a need to secure equal opportunities for the members of these minority groups, as well as a more supple type of basic liberties to redress inequalities and to compensate for what historically has been taken away from them, thus leveling the field of play. What we need is a historicization of liberalism that will allow us to understand why so-called cultural minorities do not fare as well as so-called cultural majorities.

The continued existence of minority communities may require societal restrictions of choice, as well as differentials in opportunity, unless liberalism stands for unequal forms of citizenship and unequal access to a common field of opportunity. If such differentials of opportunity are not in place, then some minority cultures are endangered cultures. Liberalism has to stop viewing aboriginal rights as matters of discrimination or privilege and begin thinking of them as matters of equality. The rights of minority cultures cannot continue to be theorized as in competition with liberalism but as an essential component of liberal political practices.

This distinction exposes the real problem facing liberalism today: the question of past offenses, and liberalism's need, therefore, to seriously consider a theory of equities. Here, damage repair must play an essential role in redressing former inequalities, as otherwise liberalism can never completely fulfill its tenets to become a true doctrine of universal individual rights. Furthermore, this means seriously questioning the aporias of liberalism, which currently resolve themselves by means of addenda and theoretical caveats, in concepts such as peripheral development, or traditional or so-called premodern cultures. It is thus also necessary to question the need to restrict, regulate, and control freedoms that endanger the very existence of the minority community or communities.

Otherwise, to accept these aporias of liberalism is tantamount to accepting that liberalism requires the practice of some illiberal measures, making it an unviable concept. Kymlicka addresses this when he argues that "liberal values require both individual freedom of choice and a secure cultural context from which individuals can make their choices." For instance, Kymlicka states that liberal values require the liberalization of certain things, making acceptable the previously unacceptable, as with homosexuality and ethnic and gender rights.

That is to say, broadening the tolerance of choice is a way of defending minority rights and liberalism simultaneously, and thus everything does not depend on our ability as individuals to make our own way in the modern world of seemingly unlimited possibilities. On the contrary, much depends on the existence of a "structure of social understanding which points out the dangers and limits of the resources at our disposal."[38]

Defenders of liberalism must realize that the concepts of liberalism have been heretofore understood within the politics of cultural homogeneity. In this case, liberalism is simply the hegemonic cultural structure of overdeveloped societies. The pressing question for liberalism today is to consider the historical role of other social and cultural formations, many of them devalued by the dominant society, and the role they play within liberalism, as well as to recognize that liberalism has already done away with many of them. Here, notions of the heterogeneous and the nondialogical, such as they have been systematized by scholars from around the world (in Latin America, primary examples include the works of Antonio Cornejo Polar, Edward Kamau Brathwaite, Ralph Premdas, and others), gain relevance.[39] The issue is, then, how to liberalize liberalism with respect to minority cultures, which seems to be the agenda of multicultural and postcolonial scholars. This agenda is predicated upon the revision of the past and the confrontation of liberal fears of disintegration upon contact with the outside.

Here the value of literature emerges in full force. Literature has long documented the disparities of rights between peoples as they are glossed over by governments in the name of philosophical principles and abstractions. Oral and testimonial literatures, diaries, and letters, in particular, are literary forms readily available to those disenfranchised by the state. However, transferring such representations to other arenas of discourse can be difficult. If and when the representations of the civic rights of culture are taken out of literature and placed into the arena of law, they immediately trouble legislatures, as they hold the state responsible for the relegation of the civic and human rights of these people. When philosophers discuss these rights publicly, the question of minority or cultural rights also weakens the pillars upon which hegemony and its vehicle, high culture, perch.

Several points can serve as guidelines in discussing the tension between freedom and equality. One is the notion of the individual as a purposive, conscious agent, someone who is accountable and who serves as a carrier of values. Another is the idea of self-respect, which John Rawls defines as the feeling that one's plan of life is worth pursuing.[40] A third one is the idea of choice. What would be the consequences of changing or losing one's values, of applying Rawls's principle to minority rights, to consider the context of choice? The variables are so complex that we always return to the distinction between homogeneous and heterogeneous societies. In homogeneous societies, every application of choice is easier, even visible. For instance, choices occur within cultural structures. In fact, the only meaningful options are provided by cultural structures, to the extent that this calls into question the notion of choice itself; we are not able to discern, in some instances, if changes occur *because* of the choices made or *despite* the choices made. Along these same lines, we must also consider whether the individual agent is well equipped to understand the consequences of his or her own choices. Another item of importance is the problem of devalued cultures, or those that find it difficult to sustain self-respect. In these cases, their context of choice and their capacity to produce localities—to build the institutions, forms of organization, and social relations we associate with the liberal state—is severely impaired. Devalued cultures find themselves in a protracted war with dominant or valued cultures. Their members can make use of role models to avoid despondency, escapism, and cynicism.

Tension 3: Between a Strong State and a Noninterventionist State

Tension number 3 refers the relationship between strong and noninterventionist states. Paradoxically, liberalism is a multilayered system that begins with individual freedom and ends with state coercion, which is chosen voluntarily as a collective necessity and condition for an organized social life. Coercion is simply a procedure against those who break the consensus. However, there are two different ways of conceiving the organization of society through the state: communal liberalism argues that the strong competitiveness of human nature requires the establishment of a strong state; procedural liberalism believes the state should meddle as little as possible in the societal affairs. The more classical the conception of liberalism, the more limited the intervention of the state in the affairs of people. Neoliberalism is the postmodern expression of the most classical form of liberalism.

Tension number 3 is expressed in the two kinds of liberalism outlined by Walzer above, as well as by Hall in his premise of a contested liberalism: that is, one concerned with social justice on one hand, and with the protection of property and different rules for the rich and for the poor on the other. Basically, the tension is between the argument that "a good liberal (or social democratic) state enhances the possibilities for cooperative coping" and the argument for a classical liberal state that does not. Walzer's point of departure is John Dewey's communitarian criticism, which he shared with his contemporary pluralist critics, for whom "the state is not 'only an umpire to avert and remedy trespasses of one group upon another' but also 'renders the desirable association solider and more coherent. . . . It places a discount upon injurious groupings and renders their tenure of life precarious . . . [and] it gives the individual members of valued associations greater liberty and security; it relieves them of hampering conditions. It enables individual members to count with reasonable certainty upon what others will do.'" However, these ideas are "constrained by the constitutional establishment of individual rights, which are themselves . . . not so much recognitions of what individuals by nature are or have as expressions of hope about what they will be and do. Unless individuals act together in certain ways, state action of the sort that Dewey recommended cannot get started."[41]

Walzer moves on to discuss the nature the non-neutral state, which he understands in republican terms as the provider of "much of the substance of contemporary communitarian politics." However, his contention is that neither Dewey nor John Rawls would recognize such notions as the public or the social union as versions of republicanism, if only because "republicanism . . . is an integrated and unitary doctrine in which energy and commitment are focused primarily on the political realm. It is a doctrine adapted (in both its classical and neoclassical forms) to the needs of small, homogeneous communities, where civil society is radically undifferentiated."[42] This particular version of the state thus identifies liberalism with representative government, but not with universal democracy. And, with liberalism here caught between its competing ambitions, we see the confluence of the underlying tensions discussed above, as the philosophy struggles to cope with individuals and groups, freedom and equality, and the role of the state in mediating their respective roles.

PLURAL SOCIETIES AND CREOLE SOCIETIES

The use of the term *plural* by Dewey's critical group allows me to move into the different ways liberal pluralism is interpreted. In contrast to Western societies ("A" societies), in which multiculturalism constitutes an internal obstruction or an opposition to the presumed notion of homogeneity, in Creole societies ("B" societies), the term *plural* presumes a model type where heterogeneity is the norm and where race, class, and color play a major role in structuring group relations across the social spectrum.

These societal models, A and B, represent two extremes, and the current question today is how these two will adjust to one another: that is to say, whether postcolonial societies can move from model B to model A, despite the effects of colonization and colonialism, or if, as one of the effects of the politics of globalization, type A societies have already been or are rapidly becoming type B societies. Scholars of multiculturalism are invested in studying the possibilities within this evolution and in proposing models of individual, civil, and state interaction to illustrate the kind of modifications that liberalism can accommodate. The bone of contention here is the role of race, class, and color in the maintenance of social order and respect for human rights. Thus the question is essentially twofold: on the one hand, it is posed as an ethical question, hinging on the question of natural rights, while on the other it is a political question, regarding either the implementation of social justice or the maintenance of law and order.

The first distinction to make is between the concept of plural, Creole societies and that of American pluralism, as they are two very distinct ideological regimes. American pluralism presumes consensus, order, and cohesion between different social groups, with one scale of values at the apex accepted by the majority. I have already discussed above how the presupposition of one value system for all has created tensions between groups and communities, curtailed consensus, and sparked a discussion on homogeneity that renders liberalism a particularism. This means that the consensus within plural type A societies is solely an ideology, a fantasy. As such, homogeneity of race, class, and ethnicity becomes the sole condition for the practice of truly liberal democratic regimes or imagined liberalism. To think otherwise is to speak about "mixtures," "edges," and "internal peripheries," gray zones where mainstream and edges meet. These gray zones in turn "confront liberalism with its 'unthought,' defy the common sense belief that our politics is unquestionably liberal, or spearhead political interventions that move into less liberal or even post-liberal scenarios."[43]

The pluralism of Creole societies (type B societies), on the other hand— which I will follow as the model for Latin American societies—stresses such difference, conflict, and distrust: those edges that for Arditi are always a "foreign internal territory," that in Rancière's formulation do not count, or that in the theorization of Deleuze and Guattari break away or depart from the existing code, to avoid being overcoded (stereotyped) and thus "becoming minoritarian."[44] This type of social order is not based on consensus and does not share a central value system; it is sharply sundered by ethnicity. Order is maintained by the monopoly over political power held by one segment of the society, and generally by force, control, and coercion. There is no choice; there is no, or very little, crossing of the color line, either by marriage, education, or trade. This rule by force imposes domination, in sharp contrast to hegemony and its rule by consent. Such rule by force can be understood by looking at all the institutional subsystems of the society, such as kinship structures, family types, education, and occupation, and examining how these systems interact with each other. Sheer numbers and head counting could indicate the degree of consensus and domination and forecast tendencies toward destabilization and restructuring of societies. For instance, in Jamaica, "four-fifths of [the] society is 'black', nine-tenths of the rest is coloured, 'of mixed ancestry', and tiny minorities are white, Chinese, East Indian, Syrian, Jewish and Portuguese."[45] Similar proportions in the race, ethnic, and class composition of Latin American societies could serve as the ground for the discussion of Latin American versions of the politics of pluralism.

In considering such a "plural (Creole) society," Stuart Hall brings up three criticisms. The first is the fact that in Caribbean and Latin American societies, "the patterns of race/colour stratification, cultural stratification and class-occupational stratification overlap" and are "massively over-determined"—that is, there is little or no upward mobility if you belong to an oppressed race group. The second is that "the 'plural society' model blurs the distinction between parallel or horizontal, and vertical or hierarchical segmentation"—color lines are arbitrarily drawn. The third is "that the overall cohesion of the society is achieved via the domination of one segment, by coercion in the political institutional order"—that is, politics does not work via common consent.[46]

Hall is right to point out that the plural society model stresses plurality in cultural values at the cost of overlooking the structures of legitimation and of displacing the historicity of the structure upon which Western liberalisms rests. Hall's task, then, as well as our own, is to rehistoricize this structure and to remember that such social structures are laid down in slave or *encomienda* societies. It is within the plantation/*encomienda* systems that race, color, and class (or caste) status was established as the legitimate structure. It is already a truism that "the whole idiomatic framework of 'normative degradations' is cast by the syntax of slave [and *encomienda*] society."[47] All previous cultural and ideological structures of African and American indigenous societies were broken, and they persisted only through accommodations—the so-called acculturations, transculturations, *mestizajes,* and hybridities—that Latin American thinkers theorize. Therefore, all postcolonial cultural institutions result from this domination or "normative degradation," and thus the theoretical idioms above merely signal the adaptation of a differentiated but single socioeconomic world system, not plural segments of equal cultures. These so-called pluralities were, in fact, only articulated differently, with their political and ideological function being to highlight the hierarchies and to deepen the divide. In spite of all of this, could we accept Hall's idea that "the most profound alternative cultural process to cultural domination…is creolization," or in the Latin American case, *mestizaje?*[48] That is something to ponder, and a discussion of this possibility is currently under way in the Andean bibliographies, where Indianness, rather than whiteness, receives most of the emphasis of the mixture invoked in *mestizaje,* hybridity, and acculturation.[49] That is the context and content of the term *heterogeneous,* after Antonio Cornejo Polar.[50]

In postcolonial, Creole, plural societies, legally enforced ethnic and racial barriers are currently undergoing a process of erosion. This, in turn, allows a transition between caste and class, enabling a new "colored" or mestizo population to gain some political prominence. This is an indication of social mobility across the border of difference, although the new acculturated or assimilated individuals rarely surpass the lower rungs of occupations and professions, thus testifying to the subterranean stability of social stratification and the considerable economic, political, and cultural power that white minorities wield. However, the profound meaning of these new mestizos and "colored" is that they succeed to the degree that they ape the language, dress, educational manners, and values of whites—hence the term *acculturation.* In this way, a sort of consensus arises, but one that here comes to honor the perennial overlapping of race, color, and class and testifies to the unshakable barriers and the inflexibility of the structure. Even when whites lose their political grip on these societies, they hold a great degree of economic power; they represent the absent paradigm and ideal value system, and they are bearers of profoundly internalized social symbolisms which are the source of the system's own legitimation. Any white person stands in for the system and validates the hierarchical structure. These multiply articulated mixtures make such systems among the most complex on earth. Thus, as Ralph Premdas claims, "Transferred to the Third World . . . this [liberal democratic] framework that has been so successful in Britain is the cause of a nightmare of unending ongoing difficulties. Not the least of these problems has stemmed from the multiethnic unintegrated cultural structure of the Third World environment."[51] This structural tendency suffers from local variations, yet, as a tendency, it remains steady.

LIBERALISM, *DERECHOS DE GENTES,* AND POSTCOLONIAL SCHOLARSHIP

In the discussion of multiculturalism, which is the rubric under which Western democratic societies debate the human rights of non-Western peoples, or equality-in-difference, we can distinguish at least four different problems pointed out by scholars of colonialism, which will be rehearsed in the analysis of concrete cultural situations that ensues. These problems are: (1) the restricted frame of reference, (2) the fallacy of the argument, (3) the definition of identity and culture, and (4) the historical legacy of colonialism.

Let us begin with the first problem, the restricted frame of reference. As we have seen, liberal democratic scholars from the West tend to depart from the Hegelian premise that liberal Western democracies, and the states they organize, are the ultimate goal of human political development. The extensive discussion on the premises of liberalism outlined above is the strong and irrefutable point of departure. Instead, the apex of political development becomes the rule of law, representative government, a regime of entrenched rights, and the guarantees of certain freedoms. These principles constitute the fundamental frame of discussion, and the frame is nonnegotiable. This frame already restricts the discussion to an epistemological space that is severely and radically contested by the presence of national groups (indigenous peoples) that were involuntarily incorporated, and by migrant groups that voluntarily come to the ambit of Western nations. These groups give the nation its multicultural character.

However, making the distinction between peoples and characterizing them as indigenous groups and peoples of foreign descent (minority people) severely cuts into the universal character of liberalism, revealing it as a particularistic doctrine predicated on a homogenous and historically organic group. The telltale sign is the concept of difference. The universal predication of liberalism comes to a full halt when dealing with people considered different—different from what? In this regard, multiculturalism names a contention and calls, at the very least, for a discussion, if not a modification, adjustment, reconsideration, or clarification, of the principles of liberalism. On this account, multiculturalism and postcolonialism share the situational privilege of inhabiting a multiframed universe, the famous in-betweens or third space so much advocated by Homi Bhabha. This condition brings us inside a field that is permanently destabilized and defamiliarized. It is a case of what Russian formalists called *ostrenanie*—estrangement—and what Arditi identified as the "underside": a symptom, meaning "the return of the repressed," a metaphor intended to signify "the notion of internal periphery, one that is designed to capture the peculiar status of an outside that belongs, but not properly so," because "the distinction between inside and outside is a matter of dispute and cannot be thought outside a polemic."[52] Were we to call that difference "color," the politics of color blindness or color specificity would constitute instances of defamiliarization or "undersidedness," and symptoms that would come to bear on the main operative principles of liberalism, such as the state, law and order, civil society, public sphere, labor, markets, freedoms and rights. The same holds true for any other variable—gender, sexual preference, or culture.

This takes us directly to problem (2), the fallacy of the argument of the two positions within liberalism, with one defending the universal rights of man (human beings) and the other advocating the recognition of the particularities of groups—ethnic, migrant, national, gender, physically challenged— that is, the admission of the nonuniversality of human rights. The fallacy resides in glossing over the fact that the modern world is the product of colonialism. With colonialism, the illusion or fantasy of homogeneity comes to a sudden and final close. Therefore, there must be recognition of the double legacy of the modern in liberalism and colonialism: that is, the politics of equality and the politics of difference. Adjudicating difference to all but one group is merely bad faith. Thereby, in the same manner that Hegel's vision of the political universe is a given in the discussion, so is the fact that whiteness, maleness, and bourgeois heterosexual rule is the measure of the individual and his rights. We are talking about particularisms, are we not? It is the policy of color blindness toward whites that subtends the use of politically charged vocabulary such as "particular ethnic groups" and "ethnic minorities," and it is the policy of gender blindness that privileges men over women, as heterosexual blindness creates queerness. In other words, all of the groups subsumed under the rubric of difference or underprivilege receive this same treatment as essentially unequal.

Actually, we must cut to the chase and avoid the philosophical dilemmas in which the polemic about rights and equality is couched, and introduce into our purview what Charles Taylor in all candor considers the cruelest and most upsetting attack. His claim is that "the supposedly neutral set of difference-blind principles of the politics of equal dignity [rights and freedoms] is in fact a reflection of hegemonic culture. . . . The charge leveled by the most radical forms of the politics of difference is that 'blind' liberalisms are themselves the reflection of particular cultures. And the worrying thought is that this bias might not just be a contingent weakness of all hitherto proposed theories, that the very idea of such a liberalism may be a kind of pragmatic contradiction, a particularism masquerading as the universal." We will do equally well to recognize that "the politics of difference grows organically out of the politics of universal dignity" and that it is the development of the modern and or postcolonial notions of identity that gives rise to the politics of difference.[53]

Problem (3) involves the definition of identity and culture. Here we find a real snag. This is due to the fact that culture is defined in many different ways. It is one thing is to speak about high culture: that is, production that is literary, cultured, written, haloed and hallowed, as modernism, the Frankfurt school, and Dinesh de Sousa defined it.[54] It is another to consider the concepts of culture that ensued from the so-called culture wars. In these debates of the late twentieth century, high culture was superceded by a more comprehensive, anthropological idea of culture. This was a debate carried forward into the multistranded versions of culturalisms espoused by cultural, subaltern, and postcolonial studies.

Last but not least, I turn to problem (4), the problem of history and the underside of modernity, which is the history of colonialism. Postcolonial historians and critics like Enrique Dussel and Walter Mignolo are meticulously examining the multiple articulations of Western, democratic, and liberal ways of thinking and being.[55] Little by little, they are filling the empty spaces of the modern/colonial debate and working on its genealogies. In the coming pages, I follow their lead.

Western Texts, Indigenous Histories, Feminist Readings

THE STRUGGLE FOR CIVIL RIGHTS
WITHIN THE CONTEXT OF LIBERALISM

> Domination is so successful precisely because it sets the terrain upon which struggle occurs at the same time that it preempts opposition not only by already inhabiting the vectors where we would resist . . . but also by having already written the script that we have to argue within and against.
>
> Wahneema Lubiano, "Like Being Mugged by a Metaphor"

> For some, I am still the Indian woman, the offensive woman, the subversive, the woman born in a humble bed, the woman without knowledge. I continue to be the maid, the servant, as some mestizos from the capital say.
>
> Rigoberta Menchú, *Rigoberta: La nieta de los Mayas*

WHEN I READ Menchú's text *Rigoberta: La nieta de los Mayas,* I am puzzled by two things: one is her use of categories such as public sphere and civil society; the other is the mixing of these philosophical, liberal, and juridical categories with terms like *millenarian cultures* and *creencias.*[1] How can an indigenous woman speak about public sphere and civil society when, I presume, these two terms have been effectively outside her realm of lived experience? And how can she mix categories of analysis as if they belonged to the same domain and made sense within it? To answer these questions, and to assess the strengths and weaknesses of her enunciatory strategies, I take a grand detour and visit the bibliographies of multicultural, feminist, and legal philosophers. They help me to support my hypothesis, which is that Menchú (a woman schooled in insurgency and metaphorically graduated from the informal foreign service of the guerrillas with an internship at the United Nations) uses the liberal vocabulary strategically, either to expose the aporias of liberal philosophy or to push at its borders and make it deliver a more comprehensive type of democracy. Further, I believe she uses the concepts of millenarian cultures and *creencias* as the hard ground to argue that human rights (*derechos de gentes*) extend to the rights of indigenous people like herself.

One principle that organizes the multicultural debate refers to translations, appropriations, interpretations (and misinterpretations), and I explore this through Norma Alarcón's essay "Conjugating Subjects in the Age of Multiculturalism," in which she discusses "the difficulties of articulating . . . sites across languages, cultures, races, genders, and social positions" that "convey the convergence of discourses of identity-in-difference as linked to the 'essence-experience' binary."[2] Another principle refers to the discursive and tropological terrain in which any discussion occurs, and for this, I read Wahneema Lubiano's "Like Being Mugged by a Metaphor," which helps ground my discussion within the field of domination, understanding that "domination has everything to do with how we think about the internal complexities of [subaltern] groups and their relationships to larger dominating groups. . . . Domination is so successful precisely because it sets the terrain upon which struggle occurs at the same time that it preempts opposition not only by already inhabiting the vectors where we would resist . . . but also by having already written the script that we have to argue within and against."[3] Whereas Alarcón calls our attention to the problems of translation, Lubiano stresses the tensions that already exist within the logic and rules of argumentation.

To argue the simultaneity of certain ways of thinking oppositionally, or the convergence of "discourses of identity-in-difference," Alarcón cites three examples that are pertinent to discussing terms like *public spheres* and *civil society* within a context of cultural citizenship and *derechos de gentes*. The first is Kafka's parable, which situates women between a series of opposing forces: the hermeneutical and the political; history and theory; discussion and litigation; and, for Hanna Arendt, the forces of past and future.[4] In Kafka's parable, one force presses from behind, while the second blocks the road ahead. This parable serves as a metaphor for the danger of paralysis inherent in discourses of identity-in-difference. The second example is Sartre's translation of *négritude* into class and Fanon's rejection of this translation. For Fanon, the translation of one term into another is an extrapolation that erases the specificities he precisely wants to preserve. For him, *négritude* is the product of his own history, of the categories the body carries with it, of the "psychobiological syncretism" which constitutes Fanon as a black subject, and as a black intellectual.[5] As Alarcón points out, Gloria Anzaldúa's concept of *mestizaje* follows Fanon's *négritude* line of argument. The third example is Jean-Luc Nancy's metaphorization of the concept of *mestizaje* and his use of *mestizaje* as a metaphor for otherness. Everything that alters him, makes of him a mestizo.[6] For Alarcón, all these hermeneutical strategies subtract the biological, racialist content of the term, which is a marker of its historical meaning.

Alarcón makes use of these three examples to discuss the drive toward "differential self-insertion through which 'a double gesture, a double science, a double writing [like Menchú's] practice an *overturning* of the classical opposition *and* a general displacement of the system.'" These examples are also useful in her debates on the particularistic/concrete and the abstract/universal, and to illustrate how "the very inflected force of the selected theoretical frameworks from a universalizing center expels the narratives and the textualization of difference and resistance."[7] Paddling against the current, Alarcón proposes to validate Fanon's and Anzaldúa's proposition of *négritude* and *mestizaje* as "psychobiological syncretisms" that are historically produced and carried forward. Her point is to explain how the translation of terms constitutes new prohibitions and appropriations, and signals Western intellectuals' fear of sharing or losing ground. The effect, according to Alarcón, is to keep unexplored "the possibilities that the combination of gender with race may transform our mode of speaking about the constructedness of the subject."[8]

Like Alarcón, Lubiano is also concerned with "differential self-insertion," and she begins to speak on this subject by explaining the tensions that already exist in the logic and rules of representation and argumentation. Her point of departure is a proposition: political subjects "as subjects who imagine their position in the world and act, but who are also subject to state power" can be mugged by metaphors. By this she means that language is a field that serves to attack and that the analytical power of language is a weapon that kills. But this figure of speech also indicates the overpowering presence of the state in the cultural and multicultural narratives "with which we imagine the world." As an example of these narratives that kill Lubiano brings forth the representation of race that is used to "proletarianize the whole racial group 'Black' or 'African American' so that it functions socially and politically as a class." Her goal is to counter this state narrative and to advance the position of the intellectual as black. In this way, she establishes the fact that she is speaking from the position and perspective of a black intellectual.[9]

Black intellectuals must intervene at the site of education because they can exert pressure on the tensions that tie larger structural global concerns and policies. She urges them not to "give up the ground because of what they [Western intellectuals] can do in the name of the ground on which [black intellectuals] have chosen to fight," and she quotes David Lloyd's statement that "culture is the ground for both accommodation to and contestation of state desires." To consider how language constructs the political subject is useful for our discussion on human rights and cultural citizenship, because, as Lubiano suggests, "what we think of ourselves in relation to the world, what we image ourselves to be in relation to the world, is also, under most circumstances, at least partially a state project."[10] This is another way of saying that domination sets the terrain of analysis and inhabits the vectors we use to think. What counts as authentic opposition, then, has to contend with the power of the state to publicly define who the subject is. It is to counteract this power in public that Menchú emerges as an indigenous intellectual with the distinct grain of her thought directed toward "secrets," the secrets of millenarian cultures she held tight in her breast.

Some years ago, interrogating the complicity of the intellectual and the state and fleshing out the role of the intellectual in the reproduction of the international division of labor, Gayatri Spivak wrestled with similar questions. Her argument is worth revisiting here, because it dovetails with Alarcón's and Lubiano's and gestures toward the discussion of human rights in the constitution of *gentes* as indigenous peoples, which is part of Menchú's agenda. Spivak spoke about the Western intellectual as a dominant subject (S) who is nonetheless a "concealed Subject" and who, speaking about the universal and the abstract, claims to have "no geo-political determination"[11] From this assumed no-place, the dominant subject intends to constitute a radical critique of Western epistemology. For Spivak, this gesture reveals the intellectual's own uncritical attitude toward his own positionality. She claims that no true criticism of ideology could emerge unless the dominant subject (S) acknowledges the power implicit in his own institutionality. If not, the dominant subject (S) can never truly unveil the concreteness of the oppressed subject (S), nor decenter the dominant subject (S) and construct a theory of pluralized "subject-effects." For, although his intellectual maneuvers may provide the illusion of undermining the sovereignty of his own position as dominant subject (S), they simultaneously mask those other subjects (s) as subjects of knowledge. Behind the dominant subject's (S) own position of centrality and privilege are hidden the problems entailed in representation: namely, the distinction between speaking *for* and *about*. The dominant subject (S) is narrativized by law, political economy, and ideology, and his production reinscribes politics into culture. To underscore the difficulties of the production of a radical critic of hegemonic discourse, Spivak makes the distinction between a descriptive and a transformative class consciousness, and then deprivatizes class consciousness, resettling it in the domain of the community—the national, the public arena, the collectivity, and the party.

Therefore, there are two ways of teasing out the problem of translation. One is to look at it as interpretation or appropriation—the interpretation of the interpretation. The other is to consider the ways discursive rules set the terrain, inhabit the vectors of analysis, and write the script of opposition, as we have seen in our discussion of Lubiano. Menchú's indigenous text articulates these two problems and addresses the question of identity-in-difference (ethnic and national) pointed out by Alarcón. The concepts argued by multiculturalism from the theoretical terrain of ethnic and postcolonial studies can be carried to the discussion of public affairs and the philosophy of law, and those from discussions in the North American academy can be applied to the domain of Latin American studies. But first, let us examine how translations work in Menchú's indigenous text.

INDIGENOUS HISTORIES
IN INDIGENOUS TEXTS

In *Rigoberta: La nieta de los Mayas,* Rigoberta Menchú writes about her personal experiences in organizing forms of civil struggle for the Maya people after the period of insurgency that disrupted Guatemalan society from the 1970s to the 1990s. The book chronicles the obstacles she encountered in her political practice and returns to the theme of millenarian cultures, *creencias,* and secrets, which she spoke about in her testimonial book, *Me llamo Rigoberta Menchú y así me nació la conciencia,* written in collaboration with Elizabeth Burgos-Debray.[12] What struck me immediately the first time I read *Rigoberta: La nieta de los Mayas* were the multiple instances of simultaneous translations of cultural materials. Some of these translations occur between the indigenous and the Ladino[13] worlds, others between Spanish and Quiché, and others between Quiché and other languages—like Latin. Still others transpire between men and women; between *tu* and *vos;* between high, popular, indigenous, and mass-culture registers; and between oral and written experiences. Very often in the text we find the formula "X means Y." This formula is highlighted in the series of footnotes scattered throughout the text.

In general, whenever Menchú uses a Maya word, there is a footnote explaining what that word means. For instance, when she says, "Hemos hecho de esta casa una pequeña aldea, una copia de Laj Chimel [We turned this house into a little hamlet, a copy of Laj Chimel]," the footnote explains, "The name of the place is Chimel. Laj is the diminutive prefix; in Quiché: 'little Chimel.'" When one of her relatives uses the pronoun *usted,* as in "Quiero hablar con usted tía [I would like to speak to you, aunt]," there is a note explaining that in Guatemalan Spanish it is very frequent to pass from *tu* to *vos* even within the same phrase. In the same manner, words like *pepitoria, chilacayote, ayote,* and *achiote* are explained with a description that follows their translation either into the precise biological term or into Latin, thus supplying a scientific nomenclature—*cucurbitacea, cucurbita ficifolia, calabaza,* and *bixa orellana* respectively for those mentioned above. The same occurs with terms like *guipiles, cortes, perrajes*—annotated as "telas para hacer vestidos indígenas [fabric used to make indigenous dresses]" for the first term and "del Quiché peraaj: *rebozo* (Marroquín)" for the last. Whenever Menchú offers a detailed explanation of a cultural event, there follows a detailed explanation of the same event, as when she explains what the word *pul-ik* means.[14]

As a reader, I wonder what the function of these footnotes might be. My first guess was that translations were intended to help non-Quiché speakers understand Quiché terms; however, this seemingly helpful device often repeats the same information that Menchú has already provided in her text, and in some other cases, such as with the names of fruits and vegetables, these names are clearly understood by Spanish speakers. The notes are, then, gratuitous interventions in that they add nothing to Menchú's thorough explanations, however much they might construe themselves as clarification, addenda, or legitimation. The question is: do the footnotes authorize or simply ratify Menchú? I contend that the footnotes in Menchú's text constitute a *criollo* cultural supplement to the indigenous cultural text. In fact, the footnotes mark what cultural studies regard as the hybrid, the multicultural, or the transculturated.[15] These explicit translations, shuttling back and forth between cultural systems of meaning, are the constructive principle of modern indigenous histories like Menchú's, but they are also implicitly present in colonial-era texts like the *Popol Vuh, Chilam Balam,* and the Huarochirí manuscript.[16]

It is no secret that, as a Quiché-speaking person, Menchú herself has always required the intervention of translators, be it Ladino writers or their equivalents (Gianni Miná and Dante Liano, or Elisabeth Burgos-Debray) to discuss her ideas within the public sphere. Hence, both of Menchú's texts are hybrid and plural (the two concepts are not coterminous), and the indigenous identities, consciousness, and worldviews they present are mediated by a Western techné. Here the problems implicit in translations pointed out by Alarcón reveal their full multifarious complexity, and the polemic about the testimonial genre and authorship can be reread under Alarcón's conflictive light.[17]

Many of the terms Menchú uses have well-established genealogies. The terms we want to work with here include *civil society* and *public sphere*, as well as others like *diversity, marginalization, millenarian cultures, creencias, minorities* —terms used to discuss civil rights, cultural citizenship, and *derechos de gentes.* Given that any text is already situated in various hermeneutical spaces, hybridity will be understood here as the braiding together of various cultural discourses (hence its multiculturalism) and logical procedures, of mixing procedural and critical reason with the logic of millenarian cultures and prophecies in order to produce a utopian vision, an imagined community that for Menchú is modern but not Western. In the same manner that the footnotes ground the text in Guatemalan Ladino and indigenous cultures and concretize their tensions— explaining language formation, geographical characteristics of Guatemalan topographies, ways of addressing people, uses of *tu* and *vos,* herbs and spices used in food preparation, weaving techniques and colors, and even Latin names of plants and animals—the words in the text pertaining to public affairs and the *res publica* reference discussions on liberalism, feminisms, and multicul- turalisms (specifically within Latino/a and black studies). For these reasons, an intervention on Menchú's text is a hermeneutical exercise carried out simul- taneously within various domains, including the cognitive parameters and epis- temes of dominant groups (Spivak's subject S) that Lubiano warned about in the epigraph to this chapter.

The real theoretical burden for us is twofold. One consists in not inter- rupting the various voices articulating Menchú's text but rather hearing them all without falling into the prohibitions that Alarcón pinpoints in Sartre's in- terpretive gestures on Fanon's work, or of Nancy's on *mestizaje.* The other con- sists in recognizing that what makes a text indigenous is not cultural purity, but rather the intensity of its hybridity. Here the claim is that a dominant text is not hybrid. The real challenge is not to squeeze Menchú's voice in between the two opposing forces of the past and the future, but to let her persuade us of her case. The difficulty of her case rests in that it is being articulated around dubitable, nonmodern grounds: the two discredited antimodern epistemes of millenarian cultures and *creencias*. My hope is that an epistemological reading can be both a political practice and an act of solidarity with Menchú's *creencias* and "psychobiological syncretism." The main dilemma is that the reader is situated between Western epistemologies and millenarian cultures' *creencias*. Therefore, to hear her voice correctly we must first understand what she means by civil society and public sphere, as well as by millenarian cultures—a concept underscoring *derechos de gentes* that we translate as cultural citizenship, a utopia for the oppressed and marginalized, a prophesy, according to Richard Rorty (more on this further on). This gesture will enable us to understand why Menchú believes the indigenous situation in Guatemala requires a political solution, a transformation of political culture, rather than bureaucratic paternalism and charity. It is Menchú's conviction that indigenous people can contribute "a pacific and plural understanding, making of it the sacred patrimony of a nation, of a continent"—of the world.[18]

Apparently, for Menchú, all these ideas can be understood without mediation or interpretation if we simply place them as part of the discussion of the civil rights of people within liberalism. However, and this is the claim of multiculturalists, *derechos de gentes,* when applied to indigenous and "minority" subjects (Spivak's subject [s]), bring into cognition the limits of liberalism. For never have these *gentes* partaken in the meaning of "people," the individual postulated by liberalism; hence, theoretical warnings—such as Benjamin Arditi's on turning difference into another essentialism—remain at a level of tidily and academically enjoying theoretical gestures.[19] It is easy today to forget that indigenous people were originally coded as animals, not as *gente de razón*. In the first centuries of colonialism they were narrativized through the language of nature ("natives") and not through the language of law, political economy, or culture, as Spivak claims the dominant subject (S) is. The emerging concepts of cultural citizenship proposed by anthropologists, as well as the legacies of millenarian cultures rescued by Menchú from the domain of archaeology, are ways of adjusting these logical and historical deficiencies and inconsistencies as they now come to bear in a multicultural, gendered, and embattled discussion of civil society and the public sphere.[20] Hence, Arditi's remark that advocates of difference critical of liberal democratic politics feel quite comfortable advancing their agenda within that setting.

Lubiano and Spivak have already shown us some of the parameters demarcating the current debate, and Alarcón discusses the relations between European intellectuals (Sartre, Foucault, Nancy) and intellectuals from other worlds—Fanon, Anzaldúa. Menchú invokes this border when she says she does not belong to those who get As, or to those who run after a piece of paper. She belongs to those whose memory "never qualified as being important."[21] So in her texts, words like "civil society," "continental movement," "practices of diversity," "desire for the future," "utopia of the oppressed," "political problems," and "recognition and respect"—which run through the sciences of interpretation—hold a different meaning. Our task is, then, to examine how the indigenous subject (s), Menchú, negotiates Alarcón's identity-in-difference (ethnic, gendered, and national) and multiculturalism (ethnic, cultural, and political). Further, we are interested in the way she handles *derechos de gentes,* and how her new articulations circulate in the public sphere.

These queries take us directly to the languages of prestige within which these concepts are discussed and to examine how the political identities of plural and multicultural societies (the two terms are not synonymous) mark the limits of democratic and liberal societies—their aporias.[22] I work with three notions of public sphere utilized by Menchú, Jürgen Habermas, and Nancy Fraser, with a purpose like Alarcón's, namely, to "convey the convergence of discourses of identity-in-difference" and to pinpoint the "difficulties of articulating sites of identity across languages, cultures, races, genders, and social positions."[23]

WESTERN, FEMINIST, AND INDIGENOUS NOTIONS OF THE PUBLIC SPHERE

Although discussion on the public sphere has enjoyed much attention by scholars recently—among the preeminent are Michael Warner, Laurent Berlant, Iris Marion Young—in this section I limit myself, for the sake of contrast, to examining three representative notions of the public: Rigoberta Menchú's, Jürgen

Habermas's, and Nancy Fraser's.[24] Habermas's classical notions of public sphere and civil society are modified by the feminist and ethnic reconceptualization of the same undertaken by Fraser and Menchú; and one of the central themes in Menchú's understanding of the public sphere is the discussion of the hybrid.[25] When words like "public sphere" and "civil society" appear in her text, they bring in an extraneous and transcendent element, another episteme that has to be absorbed, modified, and translated. In Menchú's text we have to contend not only with the overlapping of indigenous, *criollo*, and mestizo epistemes but also with those that come directly from the center of Western cultures.

By civil society Menchú understands a complex of civic organizations that represent the socially marginal groups who do not enjoy full rights of juridical citizenship but who do have well-established cultural citizenships. Examples of these organizations include the CUC (Committee of Peasant Unity), the URNG (National Guatemalan Revolutionary Unit), the RUOG (United Representation of Guatemalan Opposition), CONAVIGUA (the National Coordinator of Widows); the academic, popular and trade-union movements such as the National Coordinator; and even organizations such as the Institute for the Blind and Deaf.[26] These civic organizations are separated from the army and the government, and their task is to bring into the theater of public discussion all matters of primary importance to their constituencies. In this manner, these organs of civil society make a momentous contribution to the notion of democracy, in that they represent formerly unrepresented groups and publicize their plight and goals. This is, in fact, the contribution that the different popular sectors make to the nation, and, in so doing, their social performance fundamentally alters orthodox and bourgeois notions of civil society (like those of Hegel) and follow more closely the democratic model envisioned by Antonio Gramsci. In this sense, they solidify ground on which democracy rests.

It is worth noting that indigenous texts never speak in the name of universals and transcendence. Menchú's text is primordially local. Her point of reference is the small social community of Chimel, a speck on the Guatemalan highland map, from which she moves to the national scene before being propelled to vaster political contexts—international, continental, and global. When she goes international, her notion of civic organizations comes to include

GRULA (the Latin American Group), the continental movement Five Hundred Years of Indigenous, Black, and Popular Resistance, as well as other similar organizations in other continents, thereby referring to an alternate vision of globality. In any case, she does not mention these other organizations in order to universalize her struggle, but rather to trace the convergences of interests, the parallelism between networks at various levels, and the identities of the dominated, ethnic poor that could constitute common global fronts. In fact, Menchú tells us that one of the greatest lessons she learned while organizing the Quinto Centenario celebration concerns the diversity of experiences of indigenous people: "We are a diverse people and we have survived for five hundred years. We have survived amongst the rubble, and outlived massacres in different parts of the continent. We have diverse experiences, diverse identities; we also have multiple and diverse dreams. However, vital foundations exist in our cultures that unite us because they are millennial cultures. We have discovered that the indigenous peoples have always contributed immense riches in the form of their courage, their culture, their thought, their presence, their labor force, and their patience."[27]

In contrast to Menchú's indigenous definition of public sphere and civil society, which stems from descriptions of the concrete local social practices of the aforementioned organizations, Jürgen Habermas's definition of the public sphere is figured as the universal conceptual umbrella and frame within which notions of civil society, civil rights, democracies, and citizenships are discussed. It is in the public sphere that civil society holds discussions, and this public discourse is equated with "procedural rationality and its ability to give credence to our views in the three areas of objective knowledge, moral practical insight, and aesthetic judgment." The notion of the public sphere is predicated on "the quality of discourse and the quantity of participation," and both are thought of as constitutive elements of a democratic polity.[28] Thus, the public sphere is thought of as a neutral space where equality is practiced through discourse. It is assumed that, among peers, the best argument wins and serves to build consensus. Discussion among peers underlies the concept of democracy.

However, in spite of all of its democratic intentions, Habermas's notion of the public sphere contains contradictory predications. For one, at its inception, the concept is premised on private property (bourgeois), masculinity (man), and reason (be it called procedural or critical). The concept is, in addition, rooted in seventeenth- and eighteenth-century bourgeois life in only three European countries: namely England, France, and Germany, and hence it refers to an extremely localized historical experience. Historically conceived, for Habermas the term public sphere names the moment and place of bourgeois struggles against royalty and its "sovereign authority" as a form of centralized governance based on blood and prestige. Furthermore, reason is nothing more than the protocol of discussion (the script, Lubiano's restrictive frame, "the terrain upon which struggle occurs") underlying the rules and parameters of speaking. And, last but not least, the notion of public sphere brackets out other nonbourgeois sectors of the population. Class, gender, ethnic, and in general, group interests that are not those of the bourgeoisie are excluded, and this exclusion constitutes the conflicting terrain of liberalism on which multiculturalism blooms.

A third and revised definition of civil society is put forth by the feminist corpus. Summarizing Habermas, Nancy Fraser argues that the bourgeois public sphere acts as a counterweight to absolutist states and is the arena in which emergent congeries of voluntary associations, clubs, salons, and coffeehouses will provide the training ground to test the power and muscle of the new bourgeois *gentilhomme* who, in it, will constitute himself as a member of a new universal class with a new mode of governance. Adjusting Habermasian notions, she finds in this moment the genesis of bourgeois class formation, where an elite on the rise (Spivak's subject [S]) defines itself as different from both older aristocratic elites, whom they are about to displace, and the popular sectors they aspire to govern. In sum,

> The official bourgeois public sphere is the institutional vehicle for a major historical transformation in the nature of political domination. This is the shift from a repressive mode of domination to a hegemonic one, from rule based primarily on acquiescence to superior force to rule based primarily on consent supplemented with some measure of repression. The important point is that this new mode . . . secures the ability of one stratum of society to rule the rest. The official public sphere . . . was, and indeed is, the prime institutional site for the construction of the consent that defines the new, hegemonic mode of domination.[29]

What Fraser's feminist mediation on Habermas enables us to comprehend is that the public sphere is the foundational moment of a form of governance called democratic, if we restrict the meaning of democracy to the opposition between feudal and bourgeois. In this struggle, feudal rationality is displaced by a bourgeois logic. Bourgeois logic is the rationale of private property, individualism, laissez-faire market dynamics: a rationale that, with the development of capitalism, will increasingly become the form of bourgeois disciplining (Foucault) and control (Deleuze), what I call here the limits of liberalism or liberalism at its limits—Arditi's "underside" or "internal periphery," if you will. It is against this form of bourgeois logic that subaltern rationality defines itself. To make the shift between bourgeois thinking and the rationality of "subaltern counterpublics," Fraser rescues the concept of the public sphere from these historical moorings and reworks it in order to make it serve contemporary historical societies. For her, the public sphere

> designates a theater in modern societies in which political participation is enacted through the medium of talk. It is the space in which citizens deliberate about their common affairs, and hence an institutionalized arena of discursive interaction. This arena is conceptually distinct from the state; it is a site for the production and circulation of discourses that can in principle be critical of the state. The public sphere in Habermas's sense is also conceptually distinct from the official economy; it is not an arena of market relations but rather one of discursive relations, a theater for debating and deliberating rather than for buying and selling. Thus this concept of the public sphere permits us to keep in view the distinctions among state apparatuses, economic markets, and democratic associations, distinctions that are essential to democratic theory.[30]

For Fraser, there is a clear delimitation between the notions of civil society and the public sphere, and between publics and counterpublics. The reason for bringing all these concepts into dialogue with each other is first to mark their borders, tensions, and distinctions, and, second, to make clear the moment where the indigenous text departs from them. Here is where Arditi's discussion of Gianni Vattimo's idea of "oscillation" and Michel Maffesoli's "dynamic rooting," as well as his own proposal of the "underside of democracy" as the reverse of concepts and politics, provide a perfect ground to talk about Menchú's intervention. My argument is that Menchú's point of departure is bourgeois rights and that she discusses and deploys these rights strategically. She uses bourgeois concepts primarily as a springboard to speak about indigenous rights as basic human rights (or *derechos de gentes*), knowing full well that the pursuit of indigenous rights brings bourgeois modern reason to a moral halt. To illustrate how this theoretical closure occurs in real life, she repeatedly mentions her experiences at the United Nations, at airports, or when crossing national borders, where her mere physical presence disturbs Western bourgeois rights and discloses the contradictions of liberal discourse.

> I cross borders like any other citizen of the world, plump, dark-skinned as always. They are never going to take away this poor woman's face of mine. My Mayan face, my indigenous face, they can never take away either. As far as protocols go, I am a Nobel Peace Prize winner . . . [b]ut when I cross a border, the customs authorities don't have any patience with me. On several occasions they have been very rude to me, very racist. . . . The customs authorities still don't have any sort of social education program, and I always end up having to give them a lesson in social consciousness. After they have inspected me and taken my *guipiles* from me, when I am putting my things back into my suitcase, I take out my documentation and I say to them, "Look, see, I am a humble Nobel Peace Prize winner, and the humble president of a foundation that works for education for peace, civic education, and to raise the awareness of humanity toward the deep values of millennial cultures." The people are surprised.

And later she notes, "An indigenous person is recognized by her face and her thoughts. An indigenous person is recognized by the marks she leaves, by the humility of her soul. The clothes she wears do not matter—the indigenous face cannot be erased. People see only my face and immediately think that I am an immigrant or an illegal alien. In all of my years crossing different borders . . . , I had to take out a dozen elegant credentials in order to explain my indigenous face."[31]

Her narrative underscores her awareness of the shadow subalterns cast on dominance when they walk and talk within the boundaries of bourgeois public space. If her appearance causes so much hesitation, what could we expect will be provoked by Menchú's interventions on millenarian cultures, the site of her secrets, and her dread of being ridiculed?

THE PUBLIC/PRIVATE AND
THE COUNTERPUBLIC/COMMUNAL

Aside from the fact that the white male body seldom disturbs, concerns, or is the object of reflection for the Western masculine episteme, one of the major conceptual problems in bringing these three forms of public discourse—indigenous, bourgeois, and feminist—into dialogue with each other is each one's distinctive point of departure. In the Western bourgeois text, the point of departure is the public/private divide. The public is simply a meeting of individual minds, each of whom always speaks for himself and never for or about others. There is no presence here of that which Spivak calls transformative class consciousness, one which is not individual but remains within a feeling of community described in terms of the national, the collective, the party, or the ethnic group—or Menchú's millenarian culture. In this manner, public or the public never constitutes a community, a "we"—a difference between Guaraní's exclusive 'us,' *oré*, that does not include the listener, 'you,' and the "inclusive modality of the 'we' '*ñandé*,'" that includes both speaker and listener, 'me/we' + 'you,' a feature known as clusivity that illustrates not only different concepts of the collective us/we in indigenous texts but also how "in some contexts, the code-switching of bilingualism might do similar work of keeping the counterpublic horizon salient—just as the linguistic fragmentation of many postcolonial settings creates resistance to the idea of a sutured space of circulation."[32]

For Habermas, the concept of private and individual is the reason why discussion and persuasion prevail. It is only through talking, as it is through the protocols and procedures of discussion (critical reason and reasoning) that individuals (a male member of the bourgeois group, one who owns goods and persons) come to agree on something: that is, reach consensus. What this particular individual truly aims at is bringing his private economic interests and the public political into concurrence. This is another way of stating the relationship between the private and the public. Hence, the separation between the private, the economic, the political, and the public spheres that ground the bourgeois episteme is not quite clear-cut. I will come back to these distinctions later. As a form of social organization and articulation of human life, the public discursive field is clearly summed up "as the public of private individuals who join in debate of issues bearing on state authority."[33]

In Menchú's text—and in the feminist text too—there exists a conceptual unity. Public is, for her, a more Foucauldian notion: not a neutral space, but a space that is politically saturated, a space where the community does not come to engage in conversation to reach consensus but rather to engage in litigation to obtain rights. This is, I believe, a very important disjunction between the dominant Western and the subaltern indigenous (and feminist) text, a disjunction that accounts for misunderstandings and mistranslations.[34] In the feminist text, the line dividing the spheres of the public and the private is very porous. Fraser's public sphere, which is more compatible with Menchú's because it debunks the notion of bourgeois and makes it a place where the "subaltern counterpublics" operate, is still a safe zone in egalitarian societies. However, in stratified societies, it is a zone fraught with danger, where not only words but also bullets are often exchanged.

A second disjunction between Western and subaltern texts refers to the subject of enunciation and discussion protocols—a rough border divide. In the case of Habermas, as we said, the subject is a white male property owner. Consequently, public discourse is masculine, the property of men, and rational, critical discourse is the privilege and prerogative of the bourgeois man who has been initiated into its procedures. Thus, although they are very mediated and ideologically coded, discourse and procedural rationality are facets of the economic. The public sphere is economically saturated, and, consequently, consensus is achieved through reasoning among peers of equal economic means. Their aspiration is state management and control. These ideas serve as a point of departure for Lubiano's theoretical proposition of public discussion as preordained and for her claiming a place for intellectuals as black.

None of the Habermasian qualifications apply to Menchú's text. In her text, the subject is indigenous and dispossessed (a subject [s]), and her protocols of discussion are those governing direct depositions and legal claims concerning violations of indigenous peoples' civil rights. Reason is testimonial reason, which consists specifically in presenting one's own life and one's own body as both proof and witness. The body, Menchú's "Indian face" in this case, is itself the place where, as Renato Rosaldo has it, categories of analysis are extolled.[35] The body is the ground that supports the thesis of a "psychobiological syncretism," the carrier of those visible markers that Chela Sandoval calls the "non-yet" and even the "not-at-all."[36] The indigenous body is a text, a conspicuous written surface upon which discourse is constructed and directed: "They approached me to do interviews but not because they recognized me, but rather because of my Indian face. I didn't tell them my name because it didn't matter. I got the impression that the organizers [of the Rio de Janeiro World Conference on the environment in 1992] did not distinguish between the indigenous people and creatures of nature."[37]

It is clear that Menchú's physical presence, especially when crossing national borders and walking the hallways of public buildings, disturbs bourgeois discourse by taking it to its edges, when not turning it upside down. She only needs to appear in the public space wearing her indigenous clothing and people turn their gaze and look askance. What can be expected from the intervention of the subaltern in the public sphere is never consensus; at best it is a favorable legal ruling. Thus, in one model—Habermas's—reason is a protocol of discussion among economic peers, and in the other—Menchú's—it is litigation between unequal actors: a white, wealthy, and masculine state versus the feminine or indigenous community. Now, the question is, can these two types of reason, embodying two different conceptions of public and civic spaces, be made coterminous? Can Habermasian reason embrace the interests of indigenous reason—or of subaltern counterpublics for that matter? Can it bring about the equality-in-difference that indigenous and feminist reason advocate? The simplest answer to these questions is no, for this is not the case of a system representing equivalences between plural segments of equal cultures. Male bourgeois rights and feminine and indigenous rights are located at the opposite poles of predication and are construed each as the negation of the other. We can imagine this to be the true meaning of exceptionalism—liberal and American. To gauge the heterogeneous nature of the two epistemes—feminist and indigenous texts are dialogical—it suffices to give, as an example, the stylistic construction of the indigenous discourse that weaves together millenarian *creencias* and communal civic rights:

> One of the peculiarities that distinguishes indigenous peoples . . . is the elaboration of a thought system with respect to the earth. [An] ancient civilization constructs its thought in relation to the universe: the earth, the sea, the sky, the cosmos. It needs a community in order to exist and the community guarantees the continuity of transmission of its thinking throughout different generations. Mother Earth is not just a symbolic expression. She is the source. She is the root. She is the origin of our culture and our existence. The possibility of equilibrated coexistence on the earth has been undermined. According to our ancestors' testimonies, the ancient civilizations and the first nations possessed these values. In all aspects of life, this equilibrium should exist, and one of the most important sources of equilibrium is community.[38]

Indigenous discourse is not predicated on the private and individual but on the public/communal. Like the feminist text, the indigenous inverts the relation between public and private. Menchú speaks in the name of a collective "us" even if this collective "us" is deemed utopian, fictitious, or "premodern"—as Morales and Stoll would have it.[39] Thus, her public interventions are, from the point of view of bourgeois rationality, totally inconsequential and meaningless. Her way of organizing public discussion exceeds the limits and boundaries of procedural, bourgeois communicative rationality and constitutes the domain of subaltern knowledge and reasoning—or nonsense. What Menchú says is not to be heard. The ground of her argument is constituted through and by a utopian conception of a past sociality, the big and flashing episteme of millenarian cultures she wants to remember. This historical past, her precious memory, is a place of secrets. Secrets secrete being, and being, in the indigenous mind, is never private but rather public/communal. Nonetheless, precisely due to the manner in which she organizes knowledge, Menchú's reasoning becomes fantasy to outsiders, a site where bourgeois modern reason becomes inoperative. The idea that public discussion ensues among peers is moot in Menchú's world, where public exchange is a never-settled historical confrontation among ethnic groups over a terrain of pronounced differences. Discussion with the goal of consensus is litigation—Spivak's place where history is narrativized as logic. Consequently, Menchú calls for adjustments in Western critical and procedural reasoning and for a redefinition of the public sphere as either an instrument of domination or a site for the prophetic. We'll return to the prophetic further on.

In order to bring our discussion of indigenous and feminist rights to play in the arena of bourgeois democracy, we should consider the four adjustments to Habermas's model proposed by Fraser. First, she maintains that the public sphere must be an open and accessible stage for all. The public is no longer the meeting of communicative rationalists but a space open to all kinds of sectorial interests. In this way, by removing the property qualifications, the theater is open to pluralism, where pluralism is here understood as the possibility of discussing all kinds of issues relevant to communities based on gender, race, and the equality of cultures. Second, we must not bracket social differences, but rather highlight them so that these differences can be explicitly thematized and thus become the basis of the discussion. Third, a wide variety of protocols of style, decorum, and communicative procedures must be accepted—what Rosaldo calls "cultural citizenship"—the heterogeneous, hybrid, and multicultural, which basically is the meaning we want to give to "the neutrality" upon which the sphere rests, bereft of any specificity accommodative to all.[40] Finally, social inequalities must be addressed, for "societal inequality infects formally inclusive existing public spheres and taints discursive interaction within them."[41] My thought, after reading these four points, is that both feminist and indigenous texts call for a drastic rewriting of the epistemic system undergirding the economic and the political. Is that really possible or merely a utopian ideal? Can the public accommodate multiple subaltern counterpublics, or will it remain sequestered by only one interest group? Are multicultural groups to have their mutual relations regulated solely by the prophetic? Can indigenous struggles for representation bring about democracy in their own nations?

With these four adjustments introduced by Fraser we can better understand what Menchú calls civil rights and bring her ideas about *derechos de
gentes* into dialogue with Antonio Gramsci's notion of popular blocs. Through
the ongoing struggle around *derechos de gentes,* indigenous people are constituted as *la gente,* the community. Herein the indigenous sectors struggle to
obtain what can be properly called modern bourgeois rights. However, we are
not here invested in deconstructing the obvious or introducing the aporetic to
argue the impossible:—namely, that the popular cannot claim bourgeois rights
—because if it did it would cease being popular. Rather, we are interested in
following the thread of subaltern logic that begins precisely where bourgeois
logic ends. Instead, we claim that if human rights are universal, they are not
bourgeois; and if they are bourgeois, they are not universal. This is what Ranajit
Guha calls turning the world upside down, what Arditi calls the underside of
liberalism, and what Dussel calls the underside of modernity.[42]

It could be argued that this abstract way of thinking the public sphere is
utopian. Yet is it possible that the utopian can serve to enfranchise formerly
disenfranchised or bracketed sectors, the "subaltern counterpublics"? It is only
in the imaginary, in imaginary liberalism—what Menchú calls *sueños* (dreams),
"the only place in which we really exist"[43]—that the subaltern can have rights,
and it is only there, in her fantasy, that she can think of the possibilities of
equality in freedom. It is in this sense that the indigenous, like the feminist,
text is prophetic. For Fraser's feminist text, like Menchú's, is also a deposition,
litigation, a testimonial, and, therefore, it textually establishes the basis for
forms of political and cultural solidarity. What is useful for us is that Fraser deprivatizes: that is, she takes all the bourgeois qualifications out the public
sphere and opens it up to all kinds of interests. The public sphere thus conceived is a way of holding the state accountable to civil society via the public—
as Gramsci would have it—but it is also a way of constituting a different
domain for civil society. The public is a way of discussing sectorial (group and
communal) interests and of exchanging information among the civic organizations of the subaltern counterpublics. It is a way of guaranteeing free speech,
press, and the right of assembly to subaltern groups, and eventually of securing
rights and representation for subaltern counterpublics through parliamentary

institutions—quite an undertaking, I would think. Here is an example of the difficulties of bringing about this dream:

> In Guatemala, no one has taken an interest in whether the people vote or not. The traditional political parties are not interested in the citizenry's vote. . . . They don't even lie about it—they aren't interested in talking about the rights and values of the indigenous peoples. . . . The day that these relations change, surely we will make a change in Guatemala. . . . How can the basis for an international relationship between our peoples be created? During the Campaign (the National Campaign for Civil Participation), the linguistic experience was extraordinary. We would arrive to a town without speaking the language spoken there, without knowing its community structure. We would allow the town's professionals, its local leaders, to make our message their own. If they do not appropriate the message, we will surely carry out a formal project, but this would not be anything other than the same routine that many others have carried out. The experience reaffirmed the need for a deep respect for the local identity and the fact that one should not try to impose ideologies or partisan beliefs, only the logic of reasoning. The people were happy and were moved because they shared the message with us, the need for everyone to construct a democratic country by working together. The elections and the votes that were cast were seen by our people as Ladino customs; they say, "they are *kaxlan!*" ["Generally, *kaxlan* is understood to mean Ladino. *Kaxlan winaq* is a *kaxlan* person, while *kaxlan tziij* is the Spanish language."] Convincing them that these are the rules of the game nowadays was not difficult either. Our people decide.
>
> Some people might say, "Where is the indigenous presence?" I would respond by saying that the concept of citizen, as I understand it, is an integral one, a concept that is broader than that which is understood by most people. We directed the campaign toward women, and it would not have made sense to say: "as this is for the indigenous women, such a thing does not belong in the campaign." The Campaign for Civil Participation that was run by our Rigoberta Menchú Tum Foundation surprised many people because of its demand for autonomy. . . . I could not promise . . . that respect for indigenous peoples, necessary social reforms, and a fairer economic model would be guaranteed, or that the welfare of human beings would be considered the main objective. Who could be the candidate who would guarantee respect for women; an end to human rights violations; who would not only put an end to the armed conflict, but comply with the implementation of peace accords; who would encourage true peace process and honor commitments so that we would never again have war; who would respect the historical memory of Guatemala? Who was going to be that candidate?[44]

Here the problem is clearly one of discussing issues within the frames of liberal democracy, but Menchú's ideas of civil society evidently invoke this frame.

As stated above, the theoretical gesture of deprivatizing the notion of the public sphere and civil society, and of subordinating the state to civil society, coincides with Antonio Gramsci's notions of the public and the state. Gramsci's idea is basically that of making the public sphere and civil society a way of constituting the state. What he truly advocates is governance by the social, or the collapse of civil and political societies.[45] Like Menchú, Gramsci is interested in transforming civil organizations into governing bodies, a model for withering the present notion of the state. In this case, all the organizations Menchú speaks about will, according to a Gramscian model, come to replace the role of the state and stand for civil society, the more diverse and heterogeneous, the more plural and democratic. So if at the beginning of the formulation of the concept of the public sphere public and civic are distinct and even separate from the state, later on the civic becomes a counterproposal, another model for organizing society. In this model, the state will wither away, and the civic organizations will be in charge of the *res publica*. This was probably the idea informing the constitution of the central committees of the Communist parties in socialist societies, was it not?

One of the most important issues for Menchú is cultural citizenship. Menchú will come to disclose her secrets in the open when she speaks about the way indigenous people organize the world of meaning. In this, she establishes a South-North dialogue with Renato Rosaldo's notion of cultural citizenship and Fraser's revision of the public sphere. The three of them take up their discussion at the moment when nonbourgeois strata, subaltern counterpublics, and competing interest groups gain access to the public sphere with an agenda that questions all kinds of former arrangements. In the works of Fraser, Menchú, and Rosaldo the institutions change and the use of the public space differs—compare, for example, coffeehouses and salons with pubs and trade-union halls; and these with NGOs, cultural centers, mass rallies, and sit-ins as meeting spaces.[46]

After taking into account feminists' and multiculturalists' theoretical adjustments, we can see that the subaltern counterpublics have appropriated the right to public critical debate and have kept the notions of public sphere and civil society, the foundational principles of liberal democracies, alive, yet mediated. It could be argued that these adjustments are tantamount to a subaltern assault on the bourgeois notions of the civic and public spheres—at least conceptually. The move has an added bonus of bringing the subaltern counterpublics to the postmodern debate on the modern.[47] For the concepts of civic and public in Habermas not only define the bourgeois order but also, and most importantly, define modernity as just bourgeois. Pushing the subaltern into the theater of the modern is a way to displace or render moot concepts like pre- or a-modern, which in the past served to bracket indigenous and feminist subjectivities and to keep them parenthetically enclosed and separated from the real discourse of civil society and the public sphere. Once the subaltern becomes a player in the scene of the modern, modernity itself exposes its aporias, and alternative views of modernity come into the scope of theoretical reason.[48]

Open access to the theater of discussion means that subordinated groups construct alternative public spheres or "parallel discursive arenas where members . . . invent and circulate counterdiscourses to formulate oppositional interpretations of their identities, interests, and needs."[49] It is important to emphasize that the size of the constituency should not invalidate the claim of the group, and that all subaltern counterpublics "are situated in a single 'structured setting' that advantages some and disadvantages others. . . . [I]n stratified societies the discursive relations among differentially empowered publics are as likely to take the form of contestation as that of deliberation." Here Fraser establishes a useful distinction between what she calls stratified societies and egalitarian societies. Egalitarian societies "are societies without classes and without gender or racial divisions of labor." Although they need not be culturally homogeneous, in fact, they tend to accept the realities of multiculturalism and its effects. These societies permit a greater degree of free expression and association.[50]

The feminist- and indigenous-revised public spheres, then, are theaters for public discussion but also sites for the performance of social identities—in other words, cultural citizenship. Participation, then, means the enactment of many forms of heterogeneous expression. If the arena is to remain neutral, the content of the discussion is not. The problem faced by a heterogeneous public sphere is how to preserve diversity in consensus, how to establish the criteria for what is retained and what is negotiated, and more basically, how to determine what the participants will share in terms of values, norms, procedures, habits, and protocols to achieve a worthwhile deliberation aimed at reaching consensus. After all, "the activity of revolutionizing today means primarily but not exclusively to challenge the existing liberal-democratic consensus" or to practice Rancière's politics as the interruption of the given.[51] As discussed in chapter 1, issues of pluralism, multiculturalism, *creolité,* heterogeneity, and hybridity are pertinent here.[52] The common objective held by all the civil organizations discussed in Menchú's texts is the struggle for civil rights. What is still a matter of contention is the nature of indigenous *creencias* and their political usefulness.[53]

BEFORE I move on to discuss the nature of indigenous *creencias,* and Menchú's spin on it, a comment is in order concerning ethnicity as body performances and the fear of ridicule attached to speaking about *creencias* as a singular trait of what Michael Warner attributes to counterpublics. In his work on publics and counterpublics Warner takes issue with Fraser's proposal of subaltern counterpublics on the basis that her notion sounds too much "like the classically Habermasian description of rational-critical publics, with the word 'oppositional' inserted."[54] Counterpublics, for him, demand an altogether different set of requirements that he illustrates not with feminist or ethnic discourse (the contents and idioms of which have become multicontextual) but with queer ones. Although I find his criticism of Fraser unfair—feminism is a significant step for queer studies—I appreciate Warner's effort in countering a notion of state intervention in his workings of publics, as well as in his highlighting of performativity and the politics of the body that also subtend Menchú's text.

Warner proposes that publics are no different from the discourse that addresses them. Publics "exist *by virtue of being addressed.* . . . [T]he idea of a public . . . is text-based—even though publics are increasingly organized around visual or audio texts," and available "addresses are 'essentially imaginary' which is not to say unreal, or a matter of private fantasy."[55] Publicness is a space of interaction and the world of "strangers." Therefore, public discourse is a field of tensions, and being public, a risky endeavor.

In contrast to dominant publics, which take their pragmatics and lifeworlds for granted, counterpublics are structured by different dispositions or protocols, make different assumptions about what can be said or not (*creencias*), and maintain a level of awareness about their subordinate status (millenarian cultures). They speak against a dominant public, and their conflicts move beyond ideas and policies into other speech genres and modes of address (the indigenous face as body politics). Their idioms are not different or alternative but ones regarded with hostility and met with skepticism, if not contempt. Although they also address indefinite strangers, stigma is an assumed background of their practice, and their publics are socially marked by it. Stigma is then transposed to the conflict between modes of publicness. As a space free from normative protocols and marked by risk, a counterpublic discourse might circulate in special, protected venues where people will recognize themselves in its address. Counterpublics also project the space of discursive circulation among strangers; they are mediated by public forms and incorporate the personal/impersonal address. In so doing, they fashion their own selves around the conditions of public circulation and sociability, however much their address might be laden with intimate affect. But counterpublics aim at supplying different ways of imagining stranger sociability and reflexivity, a wager that the poesies (the bringing forth or coming out) of scene-making will be transformative and not merely replicative. Participation is active individually and at the level of a corporate entity created by the space of circulation—oscillating between *oré* and *ñandé*. And most importantly, "counterpublics tend to be those in which this ideology of reading does not have the same privilege. It might be that embodied sociability is too important to them; they might not be organized by the hierarchy of faculties that elevates rational-critical reflection as the self-image of humanity; they might depend more heavily on performance spaces than on print; it might be that they cannot so easily suppress from consciousness their own creative-expressive function."[56] The lesson here is that counterpublics can learn much from each other and that all of them, even when constituting part of a multicontextual discourse, raise the same question: how to imagine their agency.

Indigenous *Creencias,* Millenarian Cultures, and Counterpublic Persuasion

> Counterpublics are counter to the extent that they try to supply different ways of imagining stranger sociability and its reflexivity; as publics, they remain oriented to stranger circulation in a way that is not just strategic but constitutive of membership and its affects.
>
> Michael Warner, *Publics and Counterpublics,* 123

FEMINIST AND MULTICULTURAL texts inscribe the discussion of feminist and indigenous rights into an old and already occupied hermeneutical place. They write over the already-written script of public sphere and civil society, and by so doing feminism, at least, steps into the terrain of the prophetic. Richard Rorty's reading of Catherine MacKinnon's work illustrates this shift in the feminist text, which holds true for the indigenous text as well. MacKinnon states that "unless women [read also indigenous groups] fit into the logical space prepared for them by current linguistic and other practices, the law doesn't know how to deal with them." When Rorty understands that she means that "assumptions become visible as assumptions only if we can make the contradictories of

68

those assumptions sound plausible," then feminism (or ethnic studies) occupy the ground of persuasion, dissenting—interrupting the given, as Rancière advises.[1] Feminism, like ethnic studies, labors against the language of hegemony, treating consent as dominance.

Rorty takes this statement as a pretext for arguing in favor of expanding the logical space. He makes two observations in his reading of MacKinnon that are useful in our context. One observation is that feminist debate is acceptable because it is considered immanent and assumes that liberalism is flexible. The other concerns a consideration of feminism as a locus of the prophetic. This is clear when a woman claims that being a woman "is not yet a way of being human."[2] The question is: are both these observations valid for the ethnically indigenous? Are both feminism and ethnicity immanent and prophetic? Can both be read as discussions about justice within the boundaries of bourgeois law? Feminist, ethnic/indigenous, and multiculturalist rights could be turned into questions of numbers, but they are much more than that. Women, like multicultural constituencies, are also sets of unrealized possibilities—what Chela Sandoval calls the "not-yet"—that in their realization can burst the limits of bourgeois epistemology.

The awareness of this very possibility of noncontainment is the reason why Rorty suggests MacKinnon's words can be read as prophecy. The use of the term is telling, because it connotes the forecasting of something not yet seen, perceived, or realized. It is an indication of something in need of revision, or at least revisitation, making space for new descriptions, modifications, remodeling. As a pragmatist, Rorty believes in argumentation, discussion, and the expression of beliefs—some of which persuade, some of which do not. So he jettisons "the comforting belief that competing groups [i.e., feminist, multiculturalists] will always be able to reason together on the basis of the plausible and neutral premises." As a pragmatist, Rorty understands that not all discussions about the civil rights of counterpublics are plausible, but one wonders which are not. He concedes that, at least in the case of feminism (but not ethnicity or multiculturalism), there is an available cultural space where discussion takes place and prophecy becomes a site of comfort where "all non-violent political movements can fall back on when argument fails." According to Rorty, "argument for the rights of the oppressed will fail just insofar as the only language in which to state relevant premises is one in which the relevant emancipatory premises sound crazy"—which is the case of Menchú's secrets. Perhaps here the feminist and indigenous texts diverge.[3]

The force of prophecy is that it can create a language, a logic, a tradition, an identity. Momentarily, this identity, tradition, logic, and language are utopian in that they exist only in the imagination. However, this status as an idea already sets up practices different from the ones currently existing. Utopia and prophecy are the exercises of a radical critique of reason. Thus, Rorty maintains that "one will praise movements of liberation not for the accuracy of their diagnosis but for the imagination and courage of their proposals. Utopians . . . [a]bandon the contrast between superficial appearance and deep reality [the metaphysics of essence but not the hermeneutics of difference] in favor of the contrast between a painful present and a possible less painful, dimly seen future."[4]

Appealing to sense and sensibility (plausibility and neutrality) is the sign that betrays Rorty's pragmatism as a philosopher and prophet of the private sphere that can be open to prophets and poets pertaining to the subaltern counterpublics, because, for him, sensibility is another form of reasoning. Sensibility shares a border with ethics and morality. It is a more fluid realm of convictions and, likewise, a tool of persuasion, imagination, poetry, and courgage. Epic are the sensibilities making sense.

MILLENARIAN CULTURES
AND MENCHÚ'S SECRETS

Speaking about Rigoberta Menchú's first book, *Me llamo Rigoberta Menchú,* Scott Michaelson and David Johnson make a point about secrets that I want to reconsider.

> Anthropology comes after the secret understood as the private knowledge of culture, that which the other holds in reserve, that which in its reservations preserves the other and sustains the other's culture. . . . [This] marks the limit of culture. And al-

though Menchú takes the liberty of recording, on her own, a discussion of those rituals, it is nonetheless not clear that she doesn't share Burgos-Debray's understanding of one's relation to culture, for *Me llamo Rigoberta Menchú* concludes after nearly three hundred pages of revelation, with Menchú claiming that although she has given 'una imagen de [mi pueblo] . . . sin embargo, todavía sigo ocultando mi identidad como indígena.' . . . The self occults the secret in order to reserve to herself her identity, in order not to give it away. If the secret is a content, a datum . . . then *Me llamo Rigoberta Menchú* blows smoke in the anthropologist's face, telling her secrets in order not to give herself away.[5]

What is interesting about this quote is the aporetic nature of the construction of the Michaelson's and Johnson's argument. Although it is recognized that cultures do hold information in reserve to preserve themselves, in her interview with Elisabeth Burgos-Debray, Menchú speaks about three hundred pages of this information—rituals, as Michaelson and Johnson call them. Thus, in Menchú's text, cultural secrets held in reserve are revealed and therefore are no longer secrets. Right? However, even though Menchú speaks enough to fill three hundred pages, we are told she tells her secrets "in order not to give [her identity] away." This statement is so cryptic as to make us ask: how can she do that? Putting the quote in context, what becomes clear is that for these two authors, Menchú's secrets in *Me llamo Rigoberta Menchú* are not datum but a pretext to discuss the anthropological drive to disclose the nature of indigenous cultures, to open up the private to the public, to unveil that which is kept locked in order to preserve and guard an identity. But, then, we may ask, is identity private? The central idea of their argument, then, is more a questioning of anthropology and its disciplining of cultures than a discussion of Menchú's secrets. Johnson and Michaelson attribute such secrets to the inventions of anthropologists who habitually exoticize indigenous peoples and direct the discussion toward disciplines, knowledge, and power. Nonetheless, for me, the key idea in this quote is not the confusing statement that Menchú speaks without telling, or the daring albeit unexplained idea that Menchú and Burgos-Debray might share the same vision of "one's relation to culture," but that after Menchú has already spoken her secrets, she insists on speaking about them again. So let us listen to Menchú once more.

> When I worked on the book *Me llamo Rigoberta Menchú,* I said I kept some secrets and saved some parts that are very secret to our culture and I am sticking to that decision today. Many people have changed our history. Many people have pushed us into their schemes. They have put us within books and analysis. They study us and study us. They have studied us for centuries. And what is worse is that many people have taken our knowledge. I believe that this is infuriating when they convert us into subjects of experimentation. I have not wanted to tell the secrets because some like to ridicule our words. However, I would like to tell one of those secrets. When my mother was very young . . . .[6]

In fact, in her second book Menchú insists on keeping her secrets but explicitly agrees to tell one of them. Aside from the curiosity she strategically arouses in her reader, I wonder whether Menchú's notion of secret is the same as ours. Certainly, for Menchú secrets are not localized within the private and the individual but are rather encapsulated in a vision of the world she calls "millenarian cultures," a concept that in her book runs counter to the concept of minority cultures in Western liberal discourse, and one that serves her struggle for the *derechos de gentes.* In order to understand these secrets not as anthropology does, according to Michaelson and Johnson, not as rituals or datum, as they have it, but more in the sense that cultural criticism has given to them, I will read Menchú's secrets through the work of Norma Alarcón mentioned above.[7]

I have already pointed out how Alarcón brings together narratives of difference produced in distinct historical localities and weaves them together to show the diverse manners of articulating cultural politics of difference— *mestizaje* in Anzaldúa and Nancy, *négritude* in Fanon and Sartre. She does so to demonstrate how convergences in discourses of difference and identity are related to the binary of "essence and experience" invented by Western patriarchal discourse. One of Alarcón's points of departure is her thesis that differential insertions are, at the very least, double, because in them there is a convergence of various identities, writings, and positions. In point of fact, identity gestures of difference are always multiple. This means the subject is always on the border of meaning and always in between a welter of predications (Vatino's oscillation [multiplicity and contamination] as freedom, Maffesoli's dynamic rooting, nomadism, and intermittent intervention),[8] some of which are related to the historical present, some to the historical past, others to the cultural parameters of peripheral modernities, and yet others to the parameters worked on by central modernities. In the case of Menchú, it is clear that she stands poised in between a millenarian and a modern culture: the former presses her from behind, empowering her; the latter blocks the road ahead and places her in an embattled situation in which she has to struggle for *derechos de gentes* for her own people.

There is no question that some of her secrets accessed from her millenarian culture will be ridiculed—Warner's idea of the stigma attached to counterpublics. Or, if not ridiculed, at least they will be retranslated and reincorporated back into the discourse of modernity. All the stories and beliefs related to the owners of nature (called the *rajaaw juyub'*), all the readings of animal behavior as premonitions of things to come, conveyed to her by her grandfather and her mother, will easily be subsumed within the archaic, the animistic, or absorbed by the theories of magical realism in which peripheral modernities have been encoded.[9] It is in this sense that Alarcón speaks about Sartre on *négritude* as class, and about Nancy on *mestizaje* as otherness. The absorption of difference by sameness that occurs in this (mis)translation is what she objects to.

Alarcón's instances illustrate how Western thinkers appropriate all categories of thought by subsuming or absorbing them into their own system. I think this is exactly the gesture Michaelson and Johnson indicate in the case of anthropology. Reading, interpreting, and translating are the methods used by anthropology to appropriate what is produced by non-Western thinkers. The result, Alarcón writes, is that the different meanings generated by difference are not taken seriously. Through metaphorical substitutions, difference is glossed over and thinking is disqualified. This, she writes, is nothing less than the reflection of the desire for domination, the anxiety that Western intellectuals experience when coming across a form of thought they do not recognize as proper, one they do not own as their property. This is the same logic Spivak pinpoints when talking about the relationship between subject (S)—Western intellectual, author, and producer—and subject (s)—subalternized intellectual, subject of and subjected by knowledge. I situate Menchú's dilemma about her secrets here and take the essence of her secrets to be the indigenous epistemes she does not want to disclose for fear of ridicule. Indigenous knowledge is the content of millenarian cultures and her particular way of looking at the world.

To suggest that Menchú speaks but does not tell is likewise to establish the prohibition of difference—something Doris Sommer has understood very well; it is to interrupt a dialogue between what is different and what is the same— something Alarcón addresses properly.[10] To translate indigenous concepts is to dilute difference, to discount other meanings, and to subjugate other forms of interpretation. This is a good reason to take into account Sommer's approach to Menchú, which is essentially one of respect. She warns that Menchú's secrets are cultural and that cultural secrets matter. She counsels readers of testimonial literature not to confuse genres (specifically, testimonials and autobiographies) and to accept that not all their interests will be satisfied. Sommer advocates keeping the distance between reader and writer and understanding that particularist narratives baffle certain types of hegemonic master readings.

In Menchú's case, to go back to the indigenous past, to lean on it, may be interpreted as a return to forms of essentialism, the metaphysics of presence and of being. For, after all, isn't *millenarian culture* a term promulgated by Mesoamerican archaeologists? Does it not belong to Classic Mayan aesthetics? Was it not a term used to bypass the social and fix meaning in the splendor of buildings?[11] All this is true. However, simply understood as a legacy of archaeology, the concept is cold. It does not incorporate the sense of ridicule that Menchú feels about her secrets, the shame it brings her to speak about them publicly, or how the public reaction she expects goes directly to her guts.[12] Thus, it is only when she appropriates the term that *millenarian culture* becomes a powerful sign-carrier of her difference. The historical context of her secrets, added to the way she lives them, challenges the archaeological concept of millenarian culture.

My take on Menchú is that she shifts the term *millenarian cultures* from signifying the remnants of Mesoamerican buildings, "ruins," to signifying a system of interpretation of the world.[13] Millenarian culture is, for her, an epistemology, a conceptual divide that takes her back to the moment in which the historical development of that episteme was unseated from dominance and slipped into the subjugated.[14] The appropriation of the concept is her way of validating the past forms of that society, whose historical development was curtailed and whose dominance lives only as a memory passed on orally from the elders to their offspring. In this respect, millenarian culture refers to a past way of thinking that has survived in a latent state for centuries. In addition, there is the possibility of retrieving and putting it at the service of the world. Millenarian culture is thus a locus of value, a source of self-respect, a macrosignifier in the genealogy of oppression, whose ultimate worth is to link past and present and to be a vehicle for carrying the struggle of indigenous peoples for their civil rights. Millenarian culture is a term that expresses the best argument Menchú can muster against oppression. The struggle for civil rights is the act whereby a besieged historical subject reconstitutes itself (re-members itself) through the medium of a cultural past looked at as millenarian. Millenarianism is thus the clear water that washes out the stigma imputed to polluted and devalued cultures. Millenarianism, as with *mestizaje* in Anzaldúa and *négritude* in Fanon, rehistoricizes the subject and validates her experience.

Menchú is certain that the moment she discloses the ways her people organize their system of meaning, ridicule will descend upon her words. She knows, through experience, that her science is mocked, disqualified, reinterpreted, and ignored, or pushed back into myth, ritual, fiction, delusion. Menchú's epistemology is reiteratively thrown back to the state of nature, to the precivic and prepolitical, and hence, the premodern.[15] But, paradoxically, this very act of dismissal is the source of her energy. In Menchú, millenarian cultures and civil rights are two sides of the same predication that defines and constitutes her as an indigenous subject, a member of a community, the granddaughter of a culture. Millenarian cultures and *creencias* are expressions that point to the survival of old structures of meaning and feeling that, although no longer current, useful, or valid for modernity, are still endowed with the power and force that communities attribute to them. On this score, her way of formulating the question can be read more properly through the work of those who understand the meaning of being caught between webs of opposing forces—Alarcón, Lubiano, Spivak, Sommer.

Chief among these *derechos* is her right to speak her mind and be heard in the public sphere. Her presence in the public sphere, as I stated above, burdens that space simply because she is a multiply articulated subject: a carrier of millenarian cultures (which cannot be erased because she is a "psychobio-logical syncretism") and a modern indigenous woman, a Nobel Prize winner. Her race and ethnicity trouble the public space because her relation to the public is very particular: "To be indigenous is to automatically be a suspicious individual. We carry this in the depths of our souls every time we are con-fronted with an authority figure. I have felt as if it were a great sin, a great diffi-culty, as if one needed to prepare oneself to face tough situations, only because of being Indian."[16] She is always looked down upon as the Indian: "my Indian face, my face of a woman, the Mayan lineage—these things will not be taken from me."[17] The vestiges of a past, especially the survival of structures that are still real (Chimel is a flashing sign in Menchú's narrative), coexist with the structures of the present in her.

Once the internal and intimate is publicized, the individual is better ex-pressed in the communal and collective—be it indigenous or feminine. In the same manner, once we reverse the dominant direction of marking—when women mark men, when color marks white, when homosexuality marks heterosexuality—difference and diversity come to inhabit and trouble all the real and symbolic spaces. Millenarian cultures bring their weight to bear upon contemporary ones. Their historical and socio-symbolic spaces inflect the field of dominance. Ridiculing nature, the natural, the animal (a person's own *nahual,* a sort of personal totem), that is, Rigoberta's secrets—is to cover up the struc-tures of contention, negation, and translation that signify a theoretical fear, the process of erasure by absorption and the reformatting of a tradition to traverse it through and through. It is clear that Menchú's secrets have a place. They stand poised between the modern and the millenarian.

Under the banner of millenarian cultures, Menchú is the signifying agent producing a meaning that is opposite or contrary to the ones that negate her. She navigates the waters of oppositions, paddling in a counter direction. Every-thing that she produces is mixed, realigned, bizarre, and baroque—a text con-stituted by a discordant and dissonant subject, made up of explosive fragments. Affirming the "politics of the not-yet," "differential consciousness," and "tac-tical subjectivity" of Chela Sandoval, or the "strategic essentialism" of Gayatri Spivak, Menchú's texts ask not to get tangled in the net of procedures of bourgeois reason, whose deconstruction only leads to oscillation between two un-tenable opposing positions. Further, they seek to resist falling within the net tended by facile and exoticizing versions of multiculturalism, which are under-stood as a quick metaphorical fix, an inclusion through a reification of differ-ence, and a refusal to hear the implications that difference brings to knowledge production.[18] Menchú's aim is to stage the cultural politics of difference and to promote the reassessment of the material grounds upon which social and political histories are written. She is also invested in underscoring what the dominant culture fails to grasp: namely, the substantive claims generated by Cornel West's "new cultural politics of difference," Renato Rosaldo's "cultural citizenship," and Richard Rorty's prophesies and pragmatic utopias.[19]

CULTURAL CITIZENSHIP

Cultural citizenship is an area of comfort where the multicultural subject feels at ease. It is an area where she makes sense and where her agency is invested with courage and power. Within the domain of cultural forms of citizenship, the disabilities of certain identities become stabilized. Within these forms, those who have been labeled mad and marginal find a place of actualization, even if this place has been designated by power as meaningless, a place of ridicule, the abject. But what is cultural citizenship? Addressing the circumstances of Latino/as in the United States, William V. Flores and Rina Benmayor define it as a range of social practices that, taken together, claim and establish a distinct social space. This Latino/a social space is evolving and developing new forms of relation, many of them contributing to an emergent Latino/a consciousness and sociopolitical development.[20] For Renato Rosaldo, "cultural citizenship oper-ates in an uneven field of structural inequalities where the dominant claims of universal citizenship assume a propertied white male subject and usually blind themselves to their exclusions and marginalizations of people who differ in gen-der, race, sexuality, and age. Cultural citizenship attends, not only to dominant exclusions and marginalizations, but also to subordinate aspirations for defi-nitions of enfranchisement."[21]

To my mind, Michael Warner's counterpublics is another way of speaking about cultural citizenship. For instance, when he says that "within a gay or queer counterpublic . . . no one is in the closet; the presumptive heterosexuality that constitutes the closet for individuals in ordinary speech is suspended," I understand this gesture within the politics proposed by cultural citizenship. However, he adds, "The expansive nature of public address will seek to keep moving that frontier for a queer [ethnic] public to seek more and more places to circulate where people will recognize themselves in its address. . . . The subordinate status of a counterpublic does not simply reflect identities formed elsewhere; participation in such a public is one of the ways by which its members' identities are formed and transformed."[22]

With this in mind, we can return to Menchú's secrets and reread them through Rosaldo's cultural citizenship and Warner's counterpublics. For Menchú, the concept of cultural citizenship involves secrets and what she calls indigenous *creencias*. She tells us that she maintained her *creencias* in secret because she feared that she would be ridiculed for them—you enter the public at your own risk. Now, she wants to talk about them in order to establish a distinction between indigenous *creencias* and the Christian religion.

> I want to differentiate between the idea of religion as doctrine and the meaning of a people's beliefs. Our faith is to have something that can strengthen us, something in which to confide our hardships, something that will allow us to face life modestly in the face of pain, in the face of Nature, in the face of past generations and past epochs. To be strong enough not to feel discouragement, to believe in a life beyond ours; all of that is faith, it is to seek protection in a religious practice that cannot be categorized into one single concept. It means to have conviction in the greatness of life. The gift of prayer is a humble revelation of respect for the hereafter. . . . My mother used to pray to Nature. She would go out to burn the *pom* . . . to pay homage to the *raajaw juyub'*, the Master of the Universe. . . . Throughout her whole life, love for life, for the Sun, for the Moon, for the Earth, was present in all aspects.[23]

In this quote, the crux of the matter resides in the meaning Menchú attributes to the word *doctrine* in relation to *creencias*. *Creencias* appear, in this quote, as a kind of faith, something "to hold on to . . . [something] to trust. *Creencias* make you strong, make you 'have conviction.'"[24] *Creencias* stabilize certain identities' disabilities. *Creencias* group together all the forces and signs of resistance whereby the indigenous subject constitutes her being and agency, the intimate that will come to publicize the indigenous. *Creencias* constitute a type of cultural citizenship in that they attend "not only to dominant exclusions and marginalizations [pushing people into the closet], but also to subordinate aspirations for definitions of enfranchisement," as Rosaldo's quote above indicates. Furthermore, *creencias* refer to her maternal side and to her mother's legacy, and establish a social practice that is in synch with millenarian cultures. But (and here is the logical twist) *creencias* are also part of being deeply religious. She states:

> I am profoundly religious. I believe in Nature, in life, and in the different peoples. I am profoundly religious because I also believe in the faith of the people and their communion; I believe in the experience of life and the faith of the first Christians. . . . I believe that, as human beings, we should fight for creation. I understand creation to be every one of the particularities of life that move throughout the universe. I believe that it is necessary to believe. I am always quick to point out that each person's faith, the faith of the peoples, is something sacred and private, something that cannot be bought and sold.[25]

Here religion becomes *creencias* and *creencias,* religion. If that is the case, where does the disparity lie? In doctrine. Doctrine, in her vocabulary, points to many forms of disrespect. Doctrine is a colonial legacy and its sequel: the replacement of one set of laws by another—the indigenous by the Spanish. This is what Rosaldo calls an uneven field of structural inequalities. Through the use of the law, the colonial administration excludes certain forms of religious expressions from the domain of the sacred and deposits them in the sphere of *creencias.* Menchú's intervention calls attention to this asymmetry that subordinates and demeans indigenous spirituality, and promotes the restitution of *creencias* to the realm of the sacred. As an everyday practice, religion is faith, a force that helps the subject cope with life and to forge a communion with nature, whereas doctrine is a set of beliefs imposed by force, an umbrella for contemporary forms of repression, a cover-up for other types of political or economic interests. To elaborate the distinction between these two forms of religious practices is Menchú's way of highlighting forms of indigenous spirituality that she associates with millenarian cultures—the communication with the Earth, the Sun, the Moon—that becomes a strategy to ask for the official recognition and public respect for other forms of mystical beliefs. She advocates the reinstitutionalization "of Mayan, Incan, [and] Aztec" religions.[26] Indigenous ways of being religious thus differ greatly from the use of religion as doctrine, and, more importantly, from predicating which *creencias* are true and which are false.

To sum up, Menchú sees no conflict between *creencias* and religion. Both are forms of spirituality. Menchú is made of both—her mother's *creencias* from millenarian cultures; her father's Christian religion from the *españoles*—and together they constitute her dual consciousness. However, the divide is her pretext to speak about manipulation and to redefine religion as "a way to face life with modesty." Therefore, the problem here is not truly religion but the instrumentalization of religion as doctrine by politics. As it circulates in local public life in Guatemala, religion is a tool to serve the caciques, and results in corruption, defilement, plunder, and hunger: that is, religion at the service of crooked politicians. Having established this distinction, the struggle is between the *creencias* of the people and religion as doctrine, the two terms of the discussion that indigenous reason wants to make public. And it is *creencias* that become the real force propelling her struggle for *derechos de gentes.*

In Menchú, *creencias* become politicized and publicized; they shift from being secrets to becoming the basis for indigenous dialogue in the public sphere, the ground upon which her cultural and civic citizenship is predicated. Even as these *creencias* are sources of personal strength for her, she knows their place in the public sphere. She knows their public circulation invokes the ridiculous charge of being pre- or even antimodern, the means by which the indigenous are dismissed, disrespected, and neutralized. Therefore, part of her struggle is to give prestige to these *creencias,* to endow them with "full respect and a kind of institutionalization."[27] Her aim, then, is to expunge *creencias* from the ridiculous, to remove them from the place where they were hidden by history, and to relocate them institutionally to underscore their deserved prestige.

Creencias, as the locus and sanctuary of her secrets, are what interests Menchú. She explains that her strength, conviction, and trust—her cultural citizenship—come from her *creencias,* and her *creencias* in turn come from her mother. The sign *mother* embraces a dual representation, signifying a biological entity but also a cultural entity. Mother means a carrier of millenarian cultures, the supporter of cultural citizenship. To convey the meaning of what her mother represents, she tells us that she is a midwife, a natural doctor, and a seer.

> When it had been sunny for a week, Mama cured us in so little time that she left us as good as new. She was a *curandera,* a healer, and a midwife. She taught us about the *xew' xew* [a medicinal plant] and how to use it to cure aches and pains and to ward off "the evil eye," how to use *saq ixoq* [a medicinal plant whose name means "white woman"] for severe stomach pains; the tender stems of the *chilacayote* leaf to cure the wounds on our feet from the mud. We were never without *k'a q' eyes* [a medicinal plant] to cure the flu, a common cold, and fevers or *saq ixoq* to cure stomachaches caused by the cold or from having gone without food for too long.[28]

Menchú's biological mother draws her own sense of self from her knowledge of nature. Nature is her open book. Her wisdom consists in knowing how to read nature's signs. For instance, she can accurately read the strength of the winds, the sound of animals, their presence in unexpected places, the movement of time, darkness, and light: "Before Patrocino [Menchú's brother, who was burnt alive by the military] left the house, my mother tells how first she heard the call of the *xooch',* the bat, and followed by the call of the *tukur,* the owl. . . . When she heard the call of the bird, she said to Patrocino, 'Do not come with me. Stay here at home, son!'"[29] *Creencia* is thus a mentality, a spirituality, education, and conduct, a very localized tradition. And this very localized tradition comes from Chimel. Chimel, or Laj Chimel, is Menchú's place of birth and the first place she visits when she returns from exile in 1994.

> Chimel is the name of a magical place, deeply enchanted. It is a land rich in many varieties of trees, animals, birds, flowers, reeds, and mosses. It is a cloud forest, one of the few that remain on earth, those that are called "the planet's lungs." . . . All of Chimel is a mountain that cannot be broken. Chimel is a beautiful place. It has many rivers—that is where the quetzal lives. Because the quetzal is a bird that likes freedom, perhaps it flew to another place to defend itself. The people say that the quetzal has recently returned.[30]

And at the end of the book she states:

Chimel lives in my dreams. There are wonderful nights in my life when I dream about Chimel. I feel as if I had returned there after taking a long trip. I look at my mother, I talk to her, I look at the house. . . . I see the rabbits. . . . I see the peach tree grove. I see the short path that leads toward the river. I see the long path that heads out of the town toward Uspatan. I see the slope that heads toward Chimel, I see the whole village, and I see a house near the edge of the village. I remember the scent of the earth after the rain: a beautiful scent that comes out of the ground. I feel nostalgic. These dreams are those that I carry with me. The dreams that make me want to travel in the mountains . . . entrenched in my dreams, I continue living, because dreams are the only place where we really exist.[31]

Chimel is the *locus amoenus* of an episteme that speaks through smells and sounds. This is a move toward the poetics of knowledge. Menchú's entrance into Rorty's realm of the prophetic is posited as a radical and imaginative critique of reason, a courageous proposal that opens up a contrast between a painful present and a possible, less painful future.

The epistemological break represented by discussing *creencias* as secrets and *creencias* as knowledge is of enormous consequence. *Creencias* are not only given a status akin to religion; they are placed on a par with modern conceptions of science. *Creencias,* as a system, tax the conception of science itself by distinguishing the good from the bad in science. Bad is what serves as a weapon to control. Good is a way of approaching the natural world reminiscent of the ancient, millenarian ways—with respect. The effect is the affirmation of two kinds of knowledge for dealing with nature: one scientific, the other indigenous. Both vie with each other for consensus. Menchú's proposal is ethical. She calls for the reconciliation between modern science and the great majority of the world's population. She is against rampaging over "life, morality, ethics, dignity," and she instead condones millenarian cultures' capacity "to value the people, to value the collectivity, to value the community as a mechanism of social survival, as a way of living, existing, and developing within society." She condemns what scientific knowledge has brought to the indigenous world—technicians, students, and personnel interested in development, persons "who believe they understand the most intimate feelings of the people, imposing their own imagination over the facts," persons who work behind a desk for "years in a zone, educating the indigene, studying the indigene, teaching the people. . . . They finish their term . . . and go, leaving the people hopeless, the same or worse than when they came."[32] Though indigenous *creencias* and scientific knowledge are equally weighed by Menchú, her aim is to make her discourse seep through the cracks of a hopefully porous public sphere.[33]

Menchú's challenge, which we share, is how to bring her language to the negotiating table. Menchú's voice does not circulate in circumstances of equality. Her discourse belongs to the majority, yet it has been muted and reconceived as a minority utterance by the dominant culture. How, then, to valorize and amplify Menchú's voice? Shall we go back to the theories that speak about conceptual categories that are marked in the body, to the "psychobiological syncretism," to the circulation of markers to make them buzz? Should we globalize the margins, circulate the dissident traditions, and begin articulating dissenting knowledges? Walter Mignolo's work has long advocated this agenda as the politics of knowledge and knowledge production.[34] The present work is my attempt to articulate dissident discussions within the frames of Western epistemologies, in an attempt to contribute to Menchú's effort "to create new rules so that the construction of multinational, pluricultural, and multilingual nations can be guaranteed," or, to tap Hamid Dabashi's language, Menchú's task in " recasting . . . the world map in which the primacy is to local geographies, to the poly-locality of our historical exigencies, the poly-vocality of our voices, and the poly-focality of our visions."[35] My belief is that *derechos de gentes* begin with the possibilities of a different future where people will use their pain to great avail to defy the power, value, and hegemony of those who oppress them.

INDIGENOUS PEOPLE, MINORITIES, AND VULNERABLE SECTORS

In chapter 7 of *Rigoberta: La nieta de los Mayas,* Menchú vigorously endorses the difference between the categories of indigenous, minority, and vulnerable sectors and states her refusal to consider indigenous themes solely within the frame of ethnic minorities. Her reluctance brings us back to recent multicultural debates in the United States and Canada, which also aim at establishing specificities between the groups in question. Tracing the radical distinction between indigenous groups and ethnic minorities, she declares:

> There exists an unending discussion regarding the differences between indigenous peoples, ethnic minorities, and vulnerable sectors. . . . I think that there is a profound difference between these concepts. When we talk of ethic minorities, we are talking about a very broad concept. To begin with, there is the religious and cultural diversity that can exist in Asian countries, in African countries, and also in the countries of Eastern Europe. Actually, these are populations that have different origins and characteristics than the indigenous peoples. Naturally, it is necessary to listen to these peoples and get to know them in order to respond to their demands. However, many governments believe that to polemicize or to distort the discussion about indigenous issues by mixing it with ethnic-minority issues is a way to push back legislative advances concerning the rights of indigenous peoples. . . . In this way, they avoid progress in the recognition and respect for the rights of indigenous peoples and for minority rights as well.

She later continues, "I refuse to discuss indigenous rights within the framework of ethnic minorities. There is a great difference between a minority and an originary or millenarian people that has an ancient culture, a cosmic vision of the world, a philosophy of life, that is rooted in history. . . . Minorities are a product of the serious problems that humanity is experiencing. We Mayans are part of the great ancient civilizations of the planet."[36] Menchú defines indigenous people as "originary or millenarian," the carriers of ancient cultures. Originary and millenarian are terms born out of the colonial experience and are, therefore, rich, recondite categories, the by-products of jarring confrontations. These terms drive a wedge between histories, narratives, and cultures, and they separate before and after all those whose territories were invaded. Originary and millenarian peoples are the carriers and producers of grand and major narratives, peoples with large historical epistemological bequests.

In contrast, minority people are a product of the strategic fragmentation of societies under capitalism, a system vested in creating rifts, cracks, "the weapon of diversity," rather than collaborating toward social harmony and national unity.[37] Vulnerable sectors are mostly constituted through illness and total social destitution—street children, blind, deaf, disabled, the HIV-positive, those in the United States we call physically and mentally challenged, but who, for Menchú, also include those casualties of war such as widows and orphans—*los deshechables* (disposable people). The idea of grouping them all together under the same rubric derives from the political logic of international organizations like the United Nations, where Menchú did some of her training.

For Menchú, the idea is not to flatten but rather to enhance the differences between these groups, although she recognizes the mobility and multiple articulation of identities. For instance, indigenous peoples can be, and at times have been, transformed into minority peoples—i.e., reduced in status. It is imperative, then, to think about differences and similarities-within-differences. What makes indigenous peoples, ethnic minorities, and vulnerable sectors the same are systems of predication, the issuance of labels that anathematize difference and produce identities defined by lacks—of respect, of civil status, and of *derechos de gentes*. The philosophies of liberalism tend simultaneously to invalidate all notions of particular rights and to enhance minority status. This double move is what multicultural debates try to disentangle. Their aim is to discuss the particular and specific within the general abstract and how the particular is inscribed into, excluded from, or radically modifies the nature of the social contract—legally, politically, or otherwise. Multicultural thinkers take notice of how liberalism places indigenous peoples, minority groups, and vulnerable sectors under its own sway, and how it also has the power of using the might of the law to implement liberal views. For this reason, it is imperative to make this unheeded condition the topic of a radical rethinking, one that will map the contours of a new legal world order.

Menchú underscores the differences between the aforesaid sectors because she believes that viewing them as equivalent exacts too high a toll on each group's rights. Yet, it is clear from her definition that she embraces the understanding of the United Nations Working Group on Minorities—that there is a struggle in common between these sectors, in that they have been historically and politically defined as destitute. Along the lines discussed by Alarcón, Menchú's approach lies less in arguing the distinctions as in asserting simultaneously their commonalities-in-difference and their differences-in-commonality as a strategy to strengthen the rights of each group, and as a way of acknowledging and recuperating for each their specific cultural status. For Menchú, as for those discussing cultural citizenship in the United States, cultural and juridical status are commensurable.

Considered in this light, the adjective *millenarian* is simply a strategic essentialism, if you will (after Spivak), a way of reclaiming the right of indigenous peoples to remain on their present lands (not an inconsequential gesture) and ultimately to own them.[38] But millenarian means something else as well. It means to grant *creencias* the status of prophecy, which Rorty has granted to feminism, and to recognize *creencias* as a moving political force. It means to validate epistemic ways of thinking that benefit subaltern groups and to bring forth juridical and the cultural systems to discuss the contents and contexts of *derechos de gentes.* A new democratic legality would entail the recognition of alternative epistemological systems. That is, in essence, the putative nature of liberal traditions, of which John Rawls speaks eloquently: "The diversity of comprehensive religious, philosophical, and moral doctrines found in modern democratic societies is not a mere historical condition that may soon pass away; it is a permanent feature of the public culture of democracy. Under the political and social conditions that the basic rights and liberties of free institutions secure, a diversity of conflicting and irreconcilable comprehensive doctrines will emerge, if such diversity does not already exist. Moreover, it will persist and increase. The fact about free institutions is the fact of pluralism." Rawls makes the coexistence of this pluralism the foundation "for a conception of justice to serve as the public basis of justification for a constitutional regime," but for this regime to "be enduring and secure, this pluralism "must be one that widely different and even irreconcilable comprehensive doctrines can endorse," which "suggests the need for" what Rawls calls "a political conception of justice."[39]

I see here nothing but the overlapping interest of liberal jurisprudence and multicultural agendas. There are convergent strategies between Western philosophers of law and Menchú, Alarcón, and Lubiano.

We can now return to Menchú's secrets. Whatever impelled Menchú to keep her *creencias* secret in her first book—fear or shame—has been transcended in her second. At the crux of this shift are questions of respect and disrespect. Lack of respect, given the status of epistemological conflict, is, then, a good point of departure to discuss the *derechos de gentes* of indigenous and minority peoples and vulnerable sectors. But so is respect, for respect is at the basis of Menchú's willingness to speak about her secrets. A notion of respect that dovetails with Menchú is provided by a Chicana activist from San José, California. She puts the notion of *respeto* very simply: "About respeto my father gave me this advice: the first, first thing about respeto is to listen to the other person. Second, don't tell them that they don't feel something just because you don't. . . . Third, if you see something and they see something different, accept what they tell you. Fourth, ask a lot of questions to make sure you respect and understand. Fifth, you can be angry, but show respeto. Do not raise your voice, break things, or belittle the other person. Sixth, don't lie. All these consejos were taught by my father."[40]

Lacks, labels, and negativity are the ingredients synthesizing disrespect, but also the potential factors for consensus among groups that perennially have borne the brunt of rationality as violence concerning practices of discrimination. And if epistemological violence constituted the grain of past historical legacies, the recognition of that violence could now galvanize the formation of common fronts and become the ground for a political contestation in the present. This would be the logical and historical response to a violence that has inflicted emotional harm on people, disregarded or sidestepped their rights, and shown disrespect for their humanity.

Once Menchú establishes the differences that obtain between the groups mentioned above, she rhetorically asserts that "ethnic and cultural diversity is the nature of Guatemala."[41] This recognition situates her at a generative crossroads. Thinking about the national outside the *criollo/*mestizo paradigm and within the transnational logic of multiculturalist philosophers brings two consequences. One is that the collapsing of indigenous and originary peoples with ethnic minorities infuses a sense of shame about her *creencias* in Menchú, who learns to guard them as secrets as a mechanism of protection. The other is to reconsider the status of Guatemala as a nation and think about it not as a nation but as a minority. A nation that is given a minority status is considered as subordinated nation—a subaltern, failed state. In this manner, a discussion on multiculturalism and *derechos de gentes* dovetails with discussions of international politics.

From all this we can surmise that one common plight of the dispossessed is to be a by-product of universalizing concepts and traveling theories. A case in point is the subsumption of Menchú's defense of the rights of *pueblos originarios* under the same logic as migrant populations. The result is the establishment of a common bond between *pueblos originarios* and minority peoples. Thus, paradoxically, the overlapping of interests between indigenous peoples, minority peoples, and vulnerable sectors establishes the ground for common-front politics from below. And millenarian cultures become a dissident tradition, a strategy to secure cultural status and citizenship and to claim the terms of a discussion on human rights that is juridically transnational in nature. From this articulated stance, Menchú moves to the pragmatics of alliances with minority groups and vulnerable sectors.

IN the long story of confrontation between peoples, acculturation (or assimilation) has functioned as a dominant framing device. "Millenarian culture" appears throughout Menchú's prose as a term that stands poised in opposition to the proposal of acculturation. It is meant to counter the presumption that minority status is related to cultural deprivation, pertaining to cultures whose habits and protocols of conduct are considered ballast, a premodern, preindustrial, prescientific condition that holds people back. In opposition to John Rawls's ideas of overlapping consensus, the UN Department of Economic and Social Affairs states that for economic progress to take place, "ancient philosophies have to be scrapped; old social institutions have to disintegrate; bonds of caste, creed and race have to burst; and large numbers of persons who cannot keep up with progress have to have their expectations of a comfortable life frustrated. Very few communities are willing to pay the full price of economic progress."[42] A corollary presumption is that, in order to be part of the nation, minority peoples must accept deculturalization, forsake their own cultural values, shed those old forms, and, in the meantime (that is, during the process of becoming one with the dominant culture) acquiesce to a lesser ontological status. Accepting this idea amounts to a de facto recognition that *minority* stands as a metaphor for *minor;* hence, as minors, these people must remain within the custody of the state. Were minority, indigenous, and vulnerable sectors to acquiesce, the return to the logic of colonialism would be secured. In this respect, the term *minority* is brimming with a sense of stigma. It is a sign of displacement, a fissure. To counter this proposal, millenarian cultures uphold the right to think within alternative parameters without preempting their status of being modern. In other words, the adjective *Western* should be optional.

Now, the problem for us is how to entwine the discussion of civil society, the relationship between legitimacy and legislation, to millenarian cultures, Menchú's secrets, and her idea of the modern which is not Western. In search of a solution we must go back to the genealogy of the term *civil society* and ask if there is room within this liberal idea to harbor the concept of the non-Western modern. Is there a possibility of opening a space for indigenous and minority rights? For Charles Taylor, civil society is "a web of autonomous associations, independent of the state, which binds citizens together in matters of common concern, and by their mere existence or action could have an effect on public policy."[43] This way of looking at civil society presumes there is an implicit contract between civil society and the state; that is, there are forms of assembly that precede such a contract. For John Locke, in contrast, the primary organization is the community; society and civil society are fiduciary forms.

In Locke's classic formulation, community is a prepolitical (prestate) formation that precedes the formation of society and that exists before government. Community and society are, in fact, the preconditions of government. Whereas the community is a social formation for the enjoyment of our natural rights, government is a contractual relationship that takes humans out of the insecure state of nature and into the more secure terrain of a political society. Government is supreme, but it only has a fiduciary relation to society. It is a political agreement that can also be politically undone—hence the hope invested by and in the discussion of civil society, the prophetic character of the discussion Rorty pointed out in the case of feminism. By this logic, civil society is thereby preeminently political; it is, in fact, not distinct but synonymous with political society. However, if we examine the varieties of civil society, we find that there are societies that are not defined in terms of their political organizations or political constitution, societies where political authority is one among many, societies where subjective rights are predicated on a contractual notion of vassalage. There are three such models of civil society: the simplest is that of free associations that are not under the tutelage of the state—perhaps this is what today is called tribal, archaic, or prepolitical; the second, and more complex, is that where society structures itself and coordinates its actions through free association—Gramsci's idea of governance through popular fronts; the third is an ensemble of free associations that determine or inflect state policy —that is, the liberal model of democracy.

Within this expanded frame, we can find a place for Menchú's millenarian cultures, for what she is proposing is not a return to the past but rather a respect for the past within a modern political culture, respect that is understood in a multidirectional way—hence the meaning of "modern but not Western." Would it be fair, then, to think that Menchú wants an institutional and legal place for her culture within society, the organization of Maya institutions within civil society: that is, a place within liberalism? From my perspective, this is what she is aiming at, and this is where her political project aligns with multiculturalism as a political, liberal project. By foregrounding culture, specifically the Maya culture (whose past, but not its present, has already been recognized by multiple disciplines, from archaeologists and anthropologists to linguists and literary and cultural critics), she weaves together a new version of past and present. Her whole purpose is to ask people to recognize that living Mayas are still carriers of a time-honored legacy and that this legacy contributes to the pool of knowledge regarding society and nature. This is the rhetorical tenor of her discussion with environmentalists.

> Originary peoples have made a contribution to human thought concerning the defense of Mother Earth. Many environmentalist currents have expanded from this concept. It makes me profoundly happy that the conception of life of our people has taken on a larger scope at the global level. From 1989 until now, the world has again taken up the words of the indigenous peoples. . . . But as our words have become known in a positive way, they have also become known in a commercial fashion. Voluminous books have been published that try to usurp our thought system. . . . People no longer said, "These are the beliefs of the Yanomamis, these are the beliefs of

the Mayans, the Aztecs, the Aymara, these are the beliefs of the originary peoples of the Pacific, the Maori, these are the beliefs of the millennial cultures and therefore we respect them and we will make their beliefs ours in order to make them known to others." People simply say that they were brilliant indigenous minds that discovered the need for equilibrium.[44]

But she wants more. She wants political legitimacy, to have her culture recognized as the living community of Maya people and not as dead objects of study. This living community is made up of subjects who know and live their culture and therefore can speak authoritatively about it, who can generate knowledge about their own selves and culture. Her appeals to civil society move in this direction. Knowledge about themselves empowers the living Maya as citizen-subjects. Here is where her secrets are now located. No longer hidden, Menchú's Mayan knowledge is already relaying itself into the world.

What has transpired between the days when Menchú adamantly held on to her secrets and now, when she wants to give them away? What has occurred is no less than the political education of Rigoberta Menchú, culminating in her emergence as an entitled world political figure. Long gone are the days when Doris Sommer decided to become her accomplice and interpreted Menchú's secrets within the relations of power, speaking about particulars and universals and calling attention to the fact that readers must proceed with caution before the rhetoric of particularism, because not everything can be absorbed or translated, not everything can be grasped and interpreted. Sommer kept herself respectfully at arms' length and used Menchú's text to illustrate her ideas about minority literatures.[45] Sommer recommended caution when speaking about the particularisms of minority cultures. David Johnson and Scott Michaelson attributed the secrets to the invention of anthropologists who habitually exoticize indigenous peoples. They directed the discussion toward disciplines, knowledge, and power, at the same time underscoring an impasse in the logic of liberalism. David Stoll simply dismissed Menchú's information and called her a liar, and Mario Roberto Morales trespassed the threshold Sommer had guarded with such care to state that he knows better.

I will now take this discussion into the direction of legality and legitimacy and the perception of legitimacy and justice. Legality entails the discussion of *derechos de gentes* in the public sphere. Legitimacy is the legal recognition of her *creencias* as a valid episteme.

There are two decisive moves in the explanation of millenarian cultures that are useful to our discussion on legitimacy. One is Menchú's decision to speak about her secrets in public, the moment she shed all sense of shame and turned abjection into a tool of counterhegemony; the other is to avail ourselves of her secrets to discuss the social place of indigenous knowledges in reference to history. Ironically enough, what enables Menchú to enter the public sphere and reveal her secrets is the recognition that the preservation of the planet, of nature, of the earth is primordial. The green movement voices the concerns of indigenous people regarding nature. They uphold, and in so doing legitimize, the same ideas of nature defended by indigenous epistemologies throughout centuries. And although they seldom even footnote them, the convergence between ecological and indigenous thinking is remarkable. In fact, environmentalism is a fiduciary system to millenarian cultures, to the indigenous philosophies regarding the earth. Although this attitude may be interpreted as a way of usurping and plagiarizing others' ideas, one more instance of the lack of respect and recognition of the universal epistemic legacies owed to indigenous peoples, the ecological movement also empowers Menchú to give voice to her own vision of millenarian cultures. Is it not unbelievable that it takes an entire world movement and an apocalyptic vision for indigenous people's voices to be heard?

Thus *Rigoberta: La nieta de los Mayas* begins with the senses, with seeing and touching as forms of empathy and awareness, as forms of knowledge. Seeing is what humans do to humans, and through seeing she hopes empathy might be awakened. There is a hope that we can feel in our own bodies the violence inflicted upon other bodies because we partake of a common human nature. So, too, she hopes that the awakening of empathy between humans will also make us more receptive to the earth and its energies, to the gentle touch of rivers, and that these will teach us in turn to touch nature with a tender hand. Equilibrium is respect.

In a paper titled "Efectos de la impunidad en el sentido de Justicia," Luisa Cabrera explains some aspects of the difference between Maya and Western cultures and establishes the relationship between legality and legitimacy in Guatemala.[46] In total agreement with Menchú, but speaking in the language of the law, Cabrera argues that legally, Mayan culture has a collective character and stresses the relationship between community, people, and nature. Responsibility regarding liabilities and damages is shared. Communal and personal well-being is commensurable. Mayan thinking is communitarian, analogical, and holistic, in contrast to Western thinking, which is individual, analytical, and categorical. People, things, and nature are interrelated facets, and therefore violence does not only menace people; it constitutes a threat against the symbolic and material goods that provide cohesion and collective identity in Mayan communities.

In contrast to ethnic minorities that live disaggregated and isolated in cities, Mayan peoples constitute themselves from a vision of the cosmos and a well-articulated philosophy regarding the four elements (earth, wind, water, fire). People are synonymous with community, and community exists in an orderly and regulated relation to nature and cosmos. Community and land are the sources of social stability. Community is a group of individuals that need each other to live—Locke's sense of community as enjoyment. Mayan culture is holistic, because earth, soul, and stability are interchangeable. For Mayan culture, the earth carries a spiritual meaning and constitutes a collective patrimony; it is a source of energy and wealth. There is no lucrative, commercial, or material connotation given to the earth. The earth never partakes of the narratives of development Arturo Escobar criticizes.[47] The commercial and the spiritual visions of the earth are in opposition to each other and are the source of embattled relations, the origin "of war, cruelty, intolerance, racism, ignorance."[48] Thus, Cabrera's discussion of legitimacy as legality complements the words of Menchú.

Menchú ties abuses to the earth to social injustice and to the lack of respect for indigenous millenarian cultures. "Human beings need the Earth and the Earth needs human beings. The possibility of balanced coexistence on the Earth has been undermined. . . People on earth no longer remember that the Earth is our mother. They no longer remember what they owe to their community. They no longer remember that the Earth is the source of so much energy and so many riches. There has been a distancing . . . or simply, we have forgotten that the Earth exists and we don't remember that the Earth is a collective heritage."[49]

The human relationship with nature taught by Menchú's Mayan ancestors is now a forsaken legacy for most of us, saddled as we are with mandates of commercialism. In the Mayan view, history is tied to a holistic cosmogony where the earth is the collectivity, and one's sense of identity comes from being organically tied to it, of having kept the memory of it alive, jealously and zealously guarding it. Although cultures wear down with the passing of time, empathy with the past is not lost. Indigenous people still feel the live presence of ancestors and maintain the sense that there is a time for everything, for harvesting, for planting, for sharing. And this word, once it is passed on, is a commitment, a responsibility, honesty, and sensibility. Markets and governments are the opposite. They negate the existence of indigenous cultures, and when they recognize oppression, they transform it into a perception, a psychology. Hence the urgent need for rearticulating civil society and for indigenous peoples to organize their own societies within the civil space.

The Violent Text

SEPARATING THE SOCIAL
AND THE POLITICAL

I wish I had two hearts: one to deal with bad people and another to deal
with the good ones.

Interviewee in María Victoria Uribe Alarcón's *Limpiar la tierra*

I NOW MOVE FROM abstract liberal theories of the relationship between
civil society and the state to the concrete workings of Colombian governance.
This is a strategy to engage the propositions of social scientists in their efforts
to come to terms with situations that bear little or no resemblance to the refined abstractions of liberalism, where the state represents the condensation of
the relations of social forces, organizes the power bloc, and balances sectorial
relations to construct a popular national will that displaces class struggle through
the construction of a general interest and common sense. I am struck by the
enormous efforts scholars and analysts make to fit liberal concepts to illiberal
societies, basically "failed" states.[1] I am swayed by their arguments and their
genealogies: Colombia's failed state is a consequence of nineteenth-century
struggles for independence, when the two warring factions (liberal and conservative) vying for power failed to reach consensus on the type of governance

they wanted to institutionalize for the new republic. For certain, they failed to make the state the locus of national meaning, moral authority, and legitimacy. Incapable of debating their political ideas in a civil and public manner, they resorted to violence to eliminate opposition. Persuasion and debate were replaced by intimidation and silencing, and relentless and ruthless uses of force became the predominant form of politics. Extreme methods of inflicting pain, such as corporeal dismemberment, were practiced and displayed in the public arena to set an example through punishment, à la Foucault.[2] The internecine and protracted war waged by both groups against each other not only reveals the antagonistic character of their ideas on how to institutionalize power but also, and most gravely, set out the conditions of possibility for a cultural tradition of violence which established a seemingly irreparable rift between the social (civil society) and the political (the state). From its inception, the model of power established in Colombia contradicted any and all principles of liberalism; I wonder, therefore, what purpose using its categories serves.

I rehearse the arguments of social scientists, first, in order to demonstrate the difficulties implicit in reading illiberal and undemocratic societies against the background provided by the dominant model of liberalism.[3] Also, in counterposing the efforts of social scientists to untangle the intricate web of data which constitutes the structure of a failed state to the testimonials rendered by local, subaltern, and grassroots people— those who do not know or expect politics to operate as a complete or fully empowered form—I contribute to public debates on issues of governance. The use of liberal categories to read illiberal and undemocratic forms of power only serves to obscure and entangle the object of study, and testimonials provide invaluable data to discuss issues pertaining governance. Scholarship on Colombian society serves as a point of comparison for studying confrontations—local and translocal—that originate in areas whose social formation, organization, and unachieved forms of liberal states do not quite fit the liberal model. Such scholarship is also useful for interrogating the methods social scientists normally use to approach social phenomena.

A failed state is, tout court, an illiberal state, one that does not meet the horizon of liberal politics defined by liberalism. Liberalism's "regulative idea," in

Arditi's characterization, "is that political performances entail sovereign individuals casting their votes, political parties representing the people and competing for the right to shape the will of the state, and elected representatives deliberating on their behalf in legislative bodies in between elections. The state is neutral with regard to the competing conceptions of the good, government and elected officials are generally attentive to public opinion, relevant players abide by the rule of law, and external actors do not intervene in domestic politics."[4]

In Colombian bibliographies, things are much less tidy, and the most felicitous phrase to refer to the state of affairs, this failed state, is Daniel Pecaut's proposition of the separation of the social from the political. This phrase resonates in all Colombian bibliographies to the point of becoming a leitmotif. In this phrasing, I understand "the social" as an abstraction standing for the national community at large, and "the political" as the representation of bipartisan and oligarchic interests and governance—a failed, illiberal, and oligarchic *criollo* form of power. A state fails when it has not invested any time in imagining the type of epistemic surface over which to constitute a community encompassing all those who inhabit the governable space called nation so that the community, thus constituted, can formulate its aspirations of change as projects in a state they claim as their own.[5] In Colombia, the aspiration toward "the monopoly of organized violence," à la Max Weber, or to the construction of a "popular-national will," à la Antonio Gramsci, as Étienne Balibar seriously warns, are simply curtailed. Thus understood, the deepest problem facing Colombia, as a failed state, is how to imagine the concept of "people," meaning all those national individuals pertaining to a community. The challenge is how to construct the individual and historical identity within a field of common social values, norms, and collective symbols of behavior recognized by all within the historical frontiers. The notion of "people" takes as a frame of reference the subjection of one and all to the same law that interpellates individuals as subjects of law, in the construction of collective imaginaries. "A social formation only reproduces itself as a nation to the extent that, through a network of apparatuses and daily practices, the individual is instituted as homo nationalis from cradle to grave, at the same time as he or she is instituted as homo oeconomicus, politicus, religious."[6] A failed state constitutes communities based on difference and indifference.

Violence does not constitute nations, much less citizen-subjects. In practice, violence at best tempers, when it does not invalidate, even the descriptive possibilities of liberal concepts. The largest question is whether it is truly possible to bring persuasion and consent—or any other liberal category, for that matter—to bear on the relationships of power established today by the coloniality of power in postwork, postcivil societies. Narratives of violence radically root out this possibility.[7] Reading the literature on violence has provided a definite focus to this inquiry, namely the steadfast unmooring of civil society from the state.[8] Of particular relevance for our purpose are the imaginaries of nation provided by the close reading of highly obsolete forms of bipartisan politics that the universe of terror renders perplexing at best.[9] Testimonial voices speaking about violence in Colombia dramatically contrast with, say, Hegel's discussions on the state, which so neatly ordered the transition from natural, to civil, to political society. Here Hegel's assertion that the public nature of civil society was more ideological than actual (his major contribution to political philosophy is the generative linkage of labor first to civil and then to political society), followed by Marx's denunciation of public opinion as a mask for bourgeois class interest and his assertion that the public could not be claimed to be one with the nation, nor civil society one with society, are certainly more generative.[10]

However, one of the substantial roles played by narratives of violence in the formation-in-process of civil societies is to render transparent the often paradoxical and at best idealistic relationship between our forms of thinking about the social in relation to these two strong theoretical frames—Hegelian and Marxist—and their borders. Since the main testimonial texts examined in this study concern the representation of the nation through the hearts and minds of noncitizens, an engagement with serious issues of political science will be limited to the first part of this chapter, yet, since noncitizenship is related to failed, incomplete, or unachieved states, it is necessary to visit frequently the imaginaries of nationhood known to social scientists.[11]

READING ILLIBERAL AND UNDEMOCRATIC
SOCIETIES AGAINST THE GRAIN OF LIBERALISM

We begin by examining the propositions of Colombian social scientists regarding the central questions of violence as it relates to state formation. Social
scientists have typically addressed the relationships between violence, poverty,
social and economic inequity, and political and social exclusion as a structural
problem, and they have slated a series of tropes to organize the different
regimes of interpretation concerning violence. For the sake of simplification,
we will reduce them to three:[12] (1) social inequity and chronic, structural
poverty—often underscoring the argument of archaic and premodern social
structures; (2) the nature of the Colombian state—a failed or incomplete formation; and (3) the intolerance and intransigence with which culture handles
public affairs—lack of civil traditions.[13]

The first approach (social inequity and chronic, structural poverty), con-
vincing and dominant, explicates the sequence of violence by reference to land
and productivity, levels of development, patterns of capital accumulation, and
the generation of fast cash.[14] It is around land and the constitution of the
agricultural frontier that conflicts between rural workers, cattle ranchers, and
merchants—three of the principal productive actors of Colombian society—
revolve. In the last few years, it is around coca and emerald production that
these same actors recently reformatted their universe of mobility, meaning,
identity, and patterns of wealth accumulation.[15] As conflicts and social actors
move on historically (and they move fast and often), their ongoing interactions
scramble and bring the original parameters into crisis. Thus, in time, most
explanations of violence follow the route of warped and unplanned wealth-
production schemes.

The second approach (the nature of the Colombian state—a failed or incomplete formation) is closely related to the first. Fruitful patterns of production and accumulation, such as regional production of highly marketable goods
(e.g., coca, emeralds), which yield fast cash for a few, provide one explanation
for the violence overwhelming Colombian society at the end of the twentieth

century and account sufficiently for the convergence of other protagonists—the army, the guerrillas, and the paramilitary groups—into the same site. Practices of counterviolence have often been interpreted as "just wars" waged against structural violence. Although this is, on one level, a mode-of-production argument related to productivity, development, and capital accumulation, it also examines the structures from the point of view of political dominance and exclusion and dovetails approach number 3 in that it speaks directly about political struggles.

Point number 3 opens the gate for debating the nature of insurgency itself and raises the question of whether or not insurgents qualify as "revolutionary professionals." These forces subsequently multiply in a spate of armed forms, such as armies, guerrillas, and paramilitary groups, and their presence calls for an explication of differences and similarities, among them that between political and common criminals, insurgency and counterinsurgency, rebellion and repression. One of the major difficulties now is common knowledge—that today the guerrillas support themselves by kidnapping, extortion, and drug trafficking.

When considered as a totality, all the problems treated by social scientists boil down to the failed nature of the state. One of the most identifiable end points of this proposal is the problem of the leniency and inefficiency of the justice system, an all-encompassing and pervasive infirmity which leads to one of the unique dimensions of the conflict, back to the land and land tenure systems: namely, the concrete modes of territorial occupation and the types of social cohesion that these generate. All questions relate to how local powers within territories of violence articulate themselves with the nation and relate to political parties (and the kinds of social imaginaries or identities that arise from these articulations). Studies consistently call for in-depth analyses of the relation between violence and the rapid and unequal increase of wealth and point to the abysmal contrast between the poor and rich, within the context of a state authority that is systematically negligible.

In reading all these bibliographies, my sense is of a perennial intensification of conflicts that generates a psychology and ideology of total distrust, and radicalizes positions and repositioning.[16] Furthermore, my sense of the formula of the separation between the social and the political—the leitmotif organizing

Colombian scholarship on the failed state—is rendered plausible precisely by the dialectics of violence from above and counterviolence from below. The result is a permanent state of war and the coexistence of several simultaneous social projects, some for the rich (of Liberal or Conservative persuasion) and others for the poor. All evidence seems to indicate that these sundry social projects have successfully stalemated the process of state formation and that violence is the telltale sign of the continuing struggle between elite and subaltern national projects. One of the first lessons to draw from this research is that incomplete state formation not only subtends all kinds of primarily articulated social and cultural tensions but also produces, in the stage of high modernity, organized forms of confrontation and defense that are the effect of latent, historically hatched disarrays. Addressing early forms of confrontation at the beginning of the twentieth century, Isauro Yosa, Mayor Lister tells us,

> Around that time is when the Ley de Tierras [Land Law] was passed, the famous Law 200. . . . The Law was strict: it gave the landowner twenty-four hours to report an invasion of his estate. One had to get up early. Get up and go sow the land so that, when things were clarified, one could own the land. . . . The police arrived and asked, "Whose land is this?" We answered, "It belongs to all of us, there is no owner here." That is when the problem started. The landowners thundered in Bogotá. . . . It was unstoppable. There were more than a thousand settlers fighting for land that was not going to cost them a cent. The police arrived to remove us and we took it up with the town council. We reported the abuses and that is how we stopped them.[17]

I am swayed by the argument that violence is considered as essentially a political gesture that seeks power in those places where the oligarchic state cannot claim a monopoly of force or where it is unconcerned about redressing long-standing grievances. In the presence of failed states, we said above and repeat here, neither "the monopoly of organized violence," à la Max Weber, nor the construction of a "popular-national will," à la Antonio Gramsci, are possible, as Balibar claims. Struggles coalesce between other sites of power, which are conceived as rivalries, and these are qualified as premodern and archaic simply because they point to the absence of a civic tradition for discussing issues with words and its replacement by a tradition that discusses with machetes, knives, rifles, and machine guns. A differential state presence in a given territory, where society is left to fend for itself and abandoned to its own dynamics, produces alternate and varied forms of redress. Confronted with this situation, scholars, in an effort to be thorough and proactive, argue today for richer combinations of variables to explain the phenomena of regional violence in Colombia. Their greatest fear is regional contamination, an overbrimming of violence, which, like gangrene, could spread to the main cities, including the capital city itself. Their remedial hope is for the consolidation of the nation-state and the construction of a public space for the resolution of conflicts—an effort to which testimonial literature greatly contributes. A society that does not recognize itself in the state, that does not accept the state's mediation in its conflicts, and that is not capable of living with difference, will access violence (the philosophies of *desquite* and *tesoismo* that we will examine in the next chapter) as a form of redress. This situation denotes the existence of what Germán Palacio calls parastate formations, in which new actors take justice into their own hands and create alternate networks of power—leading scholars to believe that "the predominant model in Colombia is not that of private rebellion but that of civil war."[18] The greatest danger is the ossification of the present situation, a point of no return.

The Colombian lesson for the world is that an unachieved or failed state, read in terms of the rational development of democracy, or what Hegel called the common good, does not obtain, but that instead, within the frame of a failed state, movements of self-defense and social protest can turn into virtually all kinds of anarchic forms of resistance—not only those of the Leninist type, as Samir Amin argues.[19] If the crisis of the state implies that civil society is let loose and must fend for itself, all forms of unexpected banditry and terror can emerge. And if we add to this formula all kinds of "deviant" forms of production that generate rapid accumulations of wealth, we have not only the destruction of lives reported by Alfredo Molano but also the possibility of widespread terrorism. And that is why Luís Alberto Restrepo's solution of the formation of a broad-based national movement, a citizen's movement driven from below, is the only possible answer to the perennial state of crisis that gives rise to all forms of violence. This is perhaps a very good formula for the world at large, but I fear it is no longer feasible in Colombia for the reasons I set out below.[20]

Social scientists seem to leave the discussion of failed states and the violence they originate in a key of negativity. In listening to their arguments and claims, one thing remains transparent: these instances of violence are not expressions of the premodern and traditional, but rather modern and postmodern expressions of social conflicts on the underside of the failed state, if you will.[21] The wars of independence can, in fact, be interpreted as a modernizing impulse, a regional desire to partake in the world economy. Thus, if the series of excruciatingly mixed variables played out in the explanation of violence within liberal parameters renders all solutions to the conflicts moot, social scientists' assessments of the nature of the Colombian state, and the intolerance and intransigence with which public culture handles political affairs, hits the nail right on the head, as so do their observations on the absence of a civic tradition for discussing issues with words.[22]

LA VIOLENCIA

Louis-Ferdinand Celine, the twentieth century French writer, states, "In the beginning was emotion. The Word came later to replace emotion as the trot replaces the gallop. . . . Man has been removed from emotive poetry and forced into dialectic, that is, into gibberish, wouldn't you say?"[23] La Violencia in Colombia, properly speaking, is a period that runs roughly from 1946 to 1966.[24] It does not mean that violence in Colombia begins and ends with the period known as La Violencia. That only means that the topic or period known as La Violencia is our point of departure. In fact, the Commission for the Studies on Violence identifies four such stages: one in the nineteenth century, the second is La Violencia, the third overlapping stage runs from 1960 to 1970, and the fourth is located at the end of the 1970s and beyond. The first stage was part of an intraoligarchic struggle, a partisan tug of war between liberal and conservative parties. The second was led by popular leaders and was due, in large measure, to the tensions between the ideological program of the leadership and the military execution of partisan ideologies that produce anarchy, destabilization of power, and a marked fragmentation of the society. The third stage was inflected by the desire to replace existent forms of power with new ones. The fourth is characterized by a clash between the state, guerrillas, drug traffickers, and military and paramilitary forces. This last stage is a diffused form of violence, sometimes impossible to tell apart from political violence, and one that places armed struggle within an altogether new context. The main actors are guerrilleros, drug lords, and military and paramilitary forces, but the distinct ideological base of the guerrilleros has already begun to fray. I will not engage the first and the last moments of violence.[25] My takeoff point is the middle of the last century, and in so doing, I am honoring Daniel Pecaut's thesis that La Violencia serves as a horizon for all social actors in Colombia, including scholars, and that it is a founding trope, a point of reference for the history of people without history in Colombia—for the noncitizenry to imagine forms of citizenry.

The specific period known as La Violencia covers the years of 1946 to 1966. It is internally marked by Gustavo Rojas Pinilla's campaign of exterminating violence with violence in 1953, by the formation of the National Front —an oligarchic, bipartisan pact by which Liberals and Conservatives agreed to alternate and share power—in 1957, and by the organization of Cuban-inspired guerrilla groups—the Revolutionary Armed Forces of Colombia (FARC), the National Liberation Army (ELN), and the Popular Liberation Army (EPL) —in 1960.[26] The organization of the guerrilla groups in the 1960s, however, has been considered a watershed. It constitutes the emergence of a separate text signed by the unedited practices of the drug cartel and the *sicariato*—the practice of hiring juvenile hitmen, or *sicarios*. Yet, as with everything in Colombia's cascading history of violence, the social conflicts are so multiple and so inextricably articulated with each other that clear-cut divisions between one moment of violence and the next are only relatively established.

La Violencia marks a transition from civil offense to open insurrection. For Molano, it is "a microorganism embedded in the social core of Colombia. Scientists have struggled with its diagnosis and politicians have 'failed' in its prophylaxis."[27] For Ricardo Peñaranda, La Violencia "is the term that Colombians have adopted to describe the complex political and social phenomena—a mixture of official terror, partisan confrontation, political banditry, pillage, and peasant uprising—that the country endured for nearly twenty years."[28] For Restrepo, "the clash of contradictory violences generates only confusion, revulsion, and general repudiation. It does not stimulate a process of organization and confrontation between classes. There is no consensus in any sector, neither in the ruling classes nor in the subordinate classes, on what road the country should take"—neither a monopoly of organized violence nor the construction of a popular-national will. "No one dares to predict what the final results of various alternatives might be."[29] For Daniel Pecaut, the two prime characteristics of La Violencia are: first, the "immense destructuring of the old rural fabric and its preexisting social organization with the appearance of rural self-defense groups; and second, the consecration of the gap between the social and political orders."[30]

Considered from a structural point of view, La Violencia constitutes a landmark of Colombia's entrance into the modern world, with the clear signature of its particularity and difference and with a stance and wager on past and future models for reading the historical cases of national development. The split between the social and the political is precisely what distinguishes the Colombian model of modernity from other models, and more specifically from a model of modernization that is not made explicit in the bibliographies.[31] Political anarchy is the price it pays. The high tensions and imbalances between different social sectors and geographical regions is what modernity generates—a tendency that with the passing of years becomes dramatically radicalized. In this model, as Pecaut correctly argues, the social stakes of a rural population have nothing to do with the partisan struggles of the oligarchic *criollo* elite, and therefore the social conflicts involving rural actors unfold in different scenarios. These scenarios are conceived by social scientists as isolated and devoid of political expression, but my question is, isolated from what? I presume they are isolated from the idea of "nation" imagined by the *criollo* oligarchy and enshrined as the gap between the political country and the real country, an expression much trumpeted by the popular leader Jorge Eliécer

Gaitán, whose assassination marks the beginning of the period properly called La Violencia.

In sync with this radical depiction of violence, Pecaut's claim of the split between the social and the political considers that the isolated, fragmented, and resourceless rural masses (which is how the rural masses are described in the social science texts) are unable to "transform the pieces into a single episode"— i.e., a social revolution, a popular-national will—"that would portray them completely as protagonists of movements to modify the political and social structures of Colombia."[32] This observation notwithstanding, the rural masses and the Liberal and Conservative *criollo* oligarchy are thought of, perhaps unwittingly, as two distinct but equal political forces with the power to neutralize each other. Evidently, the protracted nature of the conflict in Colombia and the subsequent disorganization of the political to the point of anarchy are signs of the perdurability and intensity of the resistance, and hence power, of the rural masses. This resistance fissures the model—a fissure that paradoxically becomes a political variable. In this scenario, the idea of the disengagement of the social from the political points solely and uniquely to the lack of representation of the interests of the rural masses in a bipartisan regime that only represents the political interests of the *criollo* oligarchy, and the effect has been a large-scale social disorganization that has saturated the whole horizon of meaning signifying Colombia as a violent nation. In this light, the phenomenon known as La Violencia thus seems, absurdly, to have occurred outside the nation-state yet inside the national geography—geography becoming one of the variables useful to understanding the state's failure to represent the nation in its fullest sense as community, in the sense of constituting "the people"—a topographical representation of the divide between elite and subaltern historiographies.[33]

In the meantime, culturally, the social order was harnessed to traditional referents that bloomed unhindered under *criollo* oligarchic, bipartite political organization, and it was thus deprived of broad-based political participation and doomed to accept blind and undirected force to resolve its problems. Thenceforward, a Manichean imaginary prevailed, and political conflicts were interpreted uniquely within the frames of Christian fundamentalism—in terms of good vs. evil, true believers vs. heretics—making people wish for two hearts, one for dealing with good people and another for dealing with the bad.[34] In this regard, López de la Roche states,

> The Colombian people were educated, at least for half of the twentieth century, in an antonymic perception of reality, based on the dichotomies of "pious vs. impious," "true philosophies vs. false philosophies," "good vs. evil," and "truths vs. errors," which do not allow for possibilities of nuances and fail to grasp the diverse gamut of situations between these extremes. This has fostered oversimplification and facile ways of interpreting reality, as well as an inability to critically assimilate facts: we lack a tradition of healthy skepticism. We were not educated to doubt, but rather to form aprioristic and emotive definitions, to locate an idea comfortably in one of two extremes. This type of education has significantly hindered the acclimation of a spirit of tolerance and civilized coexistence with difference, an attitude of respect regarding dissent, and the recognition of the space of the Other.[35]

Although what divides urban and rural interests is completely a modern phenomenon, at the cultural level, what is being contested during La Violencia is not only the recomposition of bipartisan political order but also the hegemony of a Christian fundamentalism that is hindering the process of Colombian modernization. Testimonial literature provides a reading of the conflict from below, and by discussing the plight of subaltern social classes publicly, it contributes an alternative vision of violence as a force organized from above, exposing the way a failed state feels in the very marrow of one's bones. [36]

NATIONAL GEOGRAPHIES AND PROJECTS

Subaltern accounts of La Violencia do not have to contend with or explain the project of nation formation that is implicit in bipartisan historiographies, but they have to come to terms with the formation of self-defense groups, forces defined in opposition to big landowners, the army, and the state, and explain how the agrarian leagues of the 1930s eventually became an armed movement whose national counterhegemonic project combined agrarian reform with a military offensive under the expert leadership of the Communist Party. Obviously, this is a clearly different force, an altogether different story, and another type of national protagonism, one that speaks about the lay of the land, national geographies and projects.

In *Los años del tropel: Relatos de la violencia* and *Trochas y fusiles,* Alfredo Molano gathers the testimonials of people who lived through the years of La Violencia.[37] In his article "Violence and Land Colonization," he offers a very orderly account of places, protagonists, and overall dynamics of social, political, and economic action. His point of departure is Gustavo Rojas Pinilla's huge military offensive against the guerrillas during the years 1953–1957, during which people responded with the organization of peasant marches, a massive exodus toward the frontier, and the consequent regrouping of the guerrillas. La Violencia was then simultaneously a military and an economic offensive. The overarching force framing the narrative is the struggle between Liberals and Conservatives for the ideological hegemony of the nation and the control of the land. Consequently, elite historiographies organize the story around the trope of partisan politics—possibly the strongest and most generative ground of research. Subaltern narratives, like Molano's, focus instead on the splintering and polarization of the population, the formation of self-defense units that would eventually become the guerrilla group FARC, the opening up of the agrarian frontier, and the foundation of autonomous forms of production, so-called independent republics, which were "isolated areas in southeastern Cundinamarca and eastern Tolima where rural workers had taken possession of large estates and, under radical Liberal and Communist leaders, were seeking to maintain their gains by force of arms."[38] This was an armed type of colonization and, therefore, a counterforce that pressed against the hegemonic conflict fought between Liberals and Conservatives—although, as Pecaut correctly argues, the social stakes of a rural population have nothing to do with the partisan struggles of the oligarchic *criollo* elite or with social conflicts involving rural actors unfolding in different scenarios, resulting in misleading affiliations. Here is an instance that illustrates how Alfredo Molano's witnesses account for this divide:

> I am conservative but I have to admit that my party's members were the ones who added fuel to the fire. They took possession of farm after farm, forcing all of the liberals to flee, and those that did not flee were killed. The conservatives, who were

in the minority, received support from the police in order to evict all of those people. The police turned their uniforms inside out and did whatever they wanted. They arrived at the place the client had specified, they gave them a week or two to leave the property. Some left as soon as they could and left everything behind, others sold their land very cheaply. . . . And then other people started arriving, conservatives, because they were the only people that could remain there. Other liberals . . . they began to form gangs in order to fight with the police and defend themselves. . . . But also, groups of thugs that worked for the conservative party started forming.[39]

In 1946 and 1947, conflict had broken out in the areas of Cundinamarca and eastern Tolima, regions adjacent to the capital city of Bogotá, a center where one of the poles of power resides. The radius of action surrounded the capital city, located in the Andean region, and later spread out in concentric circles, eventually reaching, through the process of colonization and the opening of the agricultural frontier, areas as far as the Magdalena and Cauca river valleys to the north and south, and the Caquetá and Meta regions in the piedmont to the east.

Isauro Yosa, Mayor Lister, tells us how the military fronts began soon after April 9, 1948, the day Jorge Eliécer Gaitán was assassinated:

The dead were many and well known. The assassins were not. The police did not realize anything, as if everything were happening in a neighboring country. That is why we had to take up arms, because no one was responding. . . . I was the leader of the communists and the only one who had served in the military. I couldn't stab first and then jump. We had to face them. I sent my family to Chaparral and I went to the front, but there wasn't much that we could do because there were many attacks. Persecuted people started arriving at the *vereda* [a vereda is a rural subdivision of a municipality] of Chicala. We helped them, even though we didn't have anything more than spears and four crude blackpowder rifles [*chopos de fisto*]. How could we stop, what with the slaughter than was approaching from all sides, from house to house? . . . The first thing that we did was to build a headquarters and places for the families to hang their hammocks . . . in the Davis lands, above Río Blanco. We divided ourselves into several commissions defended by riflemen, which we named, in order to give them importance. . . . That's how the division that we called "Luis Carlos Prestes" was formed, named after a Brazilian communist that had been there but who nobody knew.[40]

The geographical spread of the conflict looks like a belt constricting the capital city and holding it in a virtual state of siege. By the 1970s and 1980s, the conflict had reached Antioquia, Caldas, and Huila, and the metaphor "independent republics" (which actually reinforces social scientists' hypotheses of failed or incomplete state formations) is now used to describe the areas taken by the guerrilla fronts organized by the FARC, whose presence in the territory was strong.

We must take into account that in Colombian sociopolitical narratives, land colonization and violence are simultaneous and intimately articulated processes; what varies are the tactics of the contenders. But who are the contenders? At each successive stage of frontier penetration, the contenders were the colonists, the cattle ranchers, the farmers, the army, and the state. Politically, they represented the live forces of the nation (the actors of a broad-based national citizen's movement driven from below, like the one that Restrepo proposes as a solution to the perennial state of crisis) that were organized either in the traditional forms offered by the parties—Liberal and Conservative—or in self-defense groups (Liberal or Communist). In time, self-defense groups became the basis of the guerrilla movement, and further on, part of the rank and file of drug lords. El Maestro, another interviewee, tells us,

> As a consequence of the way in which they pursued and assassinated people, liberal guerrilla groups started to appear. The liberals have more experience in this than we do, and they have been more organized. They have always had guerrilla groups. During the civil wars, the liberal party organized guerrilla groups, during the 1930s they organized guerrilla groups, when Rojas Pinilla [1953] returned, guerrilla groups were organized. . . . The liberals organized their guerrilla fighters from the top down, and that is why they have done a better job than us, because they have discipline and they are like an army.[41]

Economically, these rural actors represent subsistence economies versus commercial agriculture, and primitive and household methods of cultivating the land versus technological, market-oriented forms of production—two social projects in collision. The real tension was between two agrarian projects: one, a primitive, poorly and precariously financed agriculture that depends on soil fertility for its survival; the other, a very well financed and modern system of export agriculture. The former produces for the internal, local market; the latter for the external market. The corresponding forms of labor are, in the first case, family members and neighbors; and in the second, poorly paid laborers. It is easy to surmise that the offensive waged against the population responds to the aim of transforming subsistence agriculture and local-market farmers into farmworkers. This duality found its corollary in distinct forms and imaginaries of citizenship and nationhood that account for the separation between civil society and the state and that are represented in the forms of struggle undertaken during the period of La Violencia.

In this state of tension between labor and productive sectors, an already unachieved state favored modern forms of export agriculture, to the detriment of the smallholder colonists. When the colonists' forces could not be deterred, the army came in to settle the disputes between the parties, always siding with the big landholders. Had the state been in a position to decide in favor of the colonists, and had it worked out a system of credits and protection for the population at large, theoretically a more democratic form of modernization and development could have been established, and the social and the political in Colombia would have worked in tandem, thus achieving a fully realized liberal state. However, the political decision was contrary to the interest of the colonists, who represented the popular and subaltern interests—Balibar's "the people"—and the result was the radicalization of the struggle and a failed state.

During La Violencia, self-defense groups became guerrillas, and guerrilla fronts countered the army's offensive. But guerrillas were not only collective organizations of labor and self-defense. They were also social organizations that provided services denied to the colonists by the state. Further, their leaders engineered and provided a political plan that fostered a sense of purpose.[42] Where there was state support, the armed guerrillas tended to subside; where it was lacking, they increased. Moreover, the areas that were better defended by the guerillas were the sites of more violent aggression by the state. This logic carried all the way to the contemporary struggles over drug production that saw the further splintering between the social and the political. Molano's account of violence and land colonization leaves no doubt that the model is very conflictive, if only because the terms making it up are mutually exclusive, the parties highly intransigent, and the organizations very tightly articulated. The result is a great chain of violence that began in the 1940s and has endured to the present.

This violence was composite. To the civic, social, and economic violence we must add the epistemic violence and keep in mind that, in the course of two or at most three generations, Colombia's rural population has had to radically change its ideology and worldview and cope with a constant state of war. In practical terms, this means either bearing witness to or partaking in the massacres of neighbors and acquaintances. It also means altering identities: rural workers become subsistence farmers, subsistence farmers become guerrilla fighters and urban beggars or *sicarios*. This dramatic curve of change explains why some scholars insist that structural analysis is not sufficient to account for the effects of violence in the Colombian nation. They believe that the culture of violence needs to be thoroughly reexamined; the pressing question is what course to take.

We understand that originally the base force of the struggle was land, and the Liberal/Conservative conflict was one form through which the struggle was carried out. Stealing land from the colonists and expelling them from their settlements created a massive population exodus, a psychology of people always on the run—not a population of migrants but a population of drifters. The corollaries of this policy ought not to surprise the scholar. One is the colonists' absolute distrust of the state. For them, the state is not the neutral locus of authority and legitimacy, the structure that enables the common good, but rather an institution protecting an elite and partisan political arrangement. Innumerable times the witnesses provide testimony similar to this one: "The police and the army were the ones who armed the conservative guerrilla groups, everyone knew that. When Rojas Pinilla was the military leader in the Valley, all of these massacres occurred. He was the accomplice, the key to León María [the Condor]. One could not distinguish the conservative guerrillas from the detectives. . . . The conservative guerrillas got their weapons from the government in order to take care of Betania and Ceilán."[43]

It is in their struggles for the land, in defending their right to work, that we find the essence of the colonists' politics, the essence of their politics being to bear arms in self-defense, to look at family and friends as the only trustworthy people, and to consider their own labor as the only source of legitimacy.[44] This is one way of understanding the ethics of retaliation (*desquite* and *tesoismo*) and the danger of pushing people to their limits. At the beginning, the colonists' goal was not to overthrow the system but to defend their economic independence and political organization.

During the second wave of violence that takes place around the 1970s, the story varies considerably. Coca production was introduced, which offered colonists a way out of subsistence economies and a vehicle for capital accumulation.[45] For the guerrillas, coca production had a negative impact on the politicization and organization of the people, but political pragmatism prevailed, and the guerrillas became involved in the mass production of coca and the business of drug trafficking. So did the other actors: unemployed, underemployed, farmers, cattlemen, merchants, politicians, etc. The picture of the relationship between the political (state) and the social (civil society) becomes extremely complex and seemingly irreversible. The broken grammar of one witness interviewed by anthropologist María Clemencia Ramírez is a symptom of the new era:

> We live in a kind of poverty that has us so weighed down that we don't know what path to follow, and that is one of the principal reasons why the peasant, the young man or woman, takes the wrong path, because there you have the paramilitary groups, the guerrilla, and the army, and he or she can join any one of those groups. Then, who is the soldier? Who is the guerrilla fighter? Who is the paramilitary member? It is the guerrilla's brother or the soldier's brother is the guerrilla, or the cousin, or the nephew. Because of the poverty that we live in, we don't have any other choice we don't know what to do and so we need to join some group in order to survive. This is one of the points that we see that overwhelms us and that keeps us stuck in the armed conflict.[46]

This translation preserves the peasant oral syntax retained by Ramírez to underline the cultural position of the speaker and how difficult it is to untangle the present social field. Today, the military and paramilitary, the guerrillas, and the drug lords are the rulers of the land. Rural people do not know how to distinguish one from the other. Here is one person's narrative of this confusion:

> Contemporary massacres are perpetrated in small rural towns and isolated peasant homes. In these places, strangers dressed in camouflage uniforms suddenly appear and execute unarmed persons who, caught by surprise, are unable to defend themselves. . . . The fact that each armed group wears the same camouflage uniform only contributes to the terror. "All of the uniforms are the same," said a terrified peasant incapable of differentiating the armed men that cross his *vereda* sowing death and terror. "Today there is confusion in this country. Today it's not only the army that uses that type of clothing. Years ago it was only the army that one saw wearing camouflage uniforms. Not today. Everyone dresses the same and that's where one gets confused and doesn't know what to do. To a peasant, all of the uniforms are the same."[47]

Their common enemy is the state and all the international forces that support it. The relationships among these groups are always violent.

Until the 1980s, the guerrillas controlled the land through blood and fire and provided an optimal environment for the production of coca. While the hegemony of the guerrillas over the drug lords prevailed, and the guerrillas had a monopoly on arms, they prohibited the collection and the payment of taxes in *bazuco*—a crudely processed type of coca. There was a certain order. But when the drug mafia broke the agreement and organized its own forces to fight the guerrillas, bedlam broke out, to the point that today it is difficult to analyze Colombia's balance of forces in terms of previous arrangements and articulations. It is futile to inquire about the roles of the police, the army, the guerrilla, and the drug traffickers. Molano fears that the relations between them are so tangled that a *chulavita* experience of violence might repeat itself in Colombia—*chulavita* being a reference to the repressive, armed, conservative group active during La Violencia.

Constituting Subaltern Subjectivities, Disclosing Acts of Violence

On some, they performed the "tie cut" . . . they pulled out his tongue and left it hanging out, like a tie; on others, they performed the "flannel cut," and the head was left hanging; one girl was found naked with a breast in her mouth, another was found with her father's penis in her mouth. . . . a pregnant woman's belly was opened up, knifing the twins she was carrying. Her tormentors then placed a cat inside her and watched as she died, torn apart from the inside by the desperate claws of the cat.

> Alfredo Molano, *Los años del tropel*

SOCIAL SCIENTISTS succeeded in laying out the variables conditioning the structure of Colombian society, focusing on land and land-tenure patterns and highlighting the concept of the agrarian frontier to underscore the chaotic nature of the social and point to the inchoate form of the political. Invoking Fabio López de la Roche's argument that the fundamentalist Christian view serves as the umbrella or atmosphere to this historical moment provides a brief but significant comment on the cultural parameters subtending this mode-of-production model. I now shift from high to subaltern forms of culture in an effort to get my readers to move past the gentle custom of paying lip service to subaltern people's voices, offering a chance to grasp the power of the embodied, place-based, self-referenced speaker. Grasping systemic violence through affect, an alternative that is present in testimonial literature, seriously interrupts the abstract generalization of social science and brings political hermeneutics to a critical halt.

In *Los años del tropel: Relatos de la violencia*, Alfredo Molano's collection of testimonial texts, six protagonists relate the story of events that transpired during the years of La Violencia (1946–1966). Although each story is attributed to a single speaker, Molano uses the device of a collective narrator to convey the gathered, combined testimonies of numerous persons he interviewed in regions affected by La Violencia, thus providing a seamlessly articulated narrative.[1] The story told is one of violence, sadism, and the utter degradation of the rural landscape that otherwise might have become the site of a strong, farm-based communitarianism that could have offered Colombia a different path to economic development and political modern democracy.[2] Instead, thousands of people were massacred, and thousands more were made into a spectacle with the purpose of terrorizing everyone. Blood-related crimes were multiply articulated and carried emotional, political, and economic messages.

Looking at these stories not only from the point of view of liberal ideologies and politics but also from the standpoint of subject formation and subjectivity, Molano's work invites a differential reading.[3] The absolute lack of political, rational, or logical explanation for the events, the lack of suitable language to grasp it, the lack of a logical frame to enclose it, is appalling.[4] Violence defies and renders questionable the same epistemological frames that have been used to read it. Only Julia Kristeva's concepts of psychosis and the abject, and Arditi's use of symptom, in the Freudian sense, to read liberalism at its edges, approximately help me read the events. "In psychosis," Kristeva states, "the symbolic legislation is eliminated in favor of the arbitrary drive, void of meaning and communication." Psychosis, a state of turmoil characterized by the loss of all referentiality, brings to history the presence of trauma and its importance in constituting subjects, including those of "failed citizenship."[5] In symptom, Arditi writes, the repressed, a traumatic experience, "is not simply exterior to the ego but also internal to it"—an internal periphery "designed to capture the peculiar status of an outside that belongs, but not properly so . . . a region where the distinction between inside and outside is a matter of dispute and cannot be thought outside a polemic."6

DISTRESSED SUBJECTIVITIES

Efraín Barón, one of the composite narrators in Molano's *Los años del tropel,* describes the experience of witnessing:

> Everyone went to see them: mutilated, their throats cut wide open, hanged, with their tongues hanging out. They had pulled out the heart of one of them and only a hollow chest was visible; many other men had their penises yanked off, not cut off but yanked off. Some women had their vaginas pulled out. A very well-to-do man in the region had been minced into pieces and left like that, in pieces, inside a bag. That is what I saw that afternoon. I don't know if they were liberals or conservatives because you didn't know who was who, but seeing those corpses made you want to scream. They were not satisfied just to kill them, but rather after they were dead they killed them again. Somebody told me that they ripped them apart to kill them twice, to kill death itself.7

In *Los años del tropel,* the syntax and narrative delivery of the interviewees registers the heartbeat of a distressed regional, if not national, subjectivity. History is narrated as a personal experience, drawn from the archives of the living, the direct sufferers of the event, not from books, as we can see from the testimonial of Efraín Barón quoted above. I wish to concentrate on three discursive traits of this damaged consciousness as it expresses itself: one is the emphasis on being and identity; the second is trauma, the obsessive repetition of the same events and how they occurred; and the third is the anxiety over the representation of sadism.

Most of the stories begin with a political formula of self: "I am," "he is," "they are," and their opposite, "I am not," "I have never been . . ." The primary identity of the subject is not social, but rather political. The protagonists define themselves in political terms, as in, "I am a Conservative" or "I am a Liberal." Later, these epithets will multiply into trails of unending synonyms, as in "He is a *pájaro, chulavita, godo, chusmero*"—all synonyms for repressive conservative figures—or "He is brave, a victim, and even a hero." This politically inflected ontological map is inseparable from a regional map that precisely locates events —Tuluá, Betania, Ibangué, Cajamarca, Armenia, Ceilán, Antioquia, Caldas, Boyacá. Thus, self and region are enjoined and form an indissoluble, inter-dependent bond whose obliteration and break-up is recorded in the texts collected by Molano.

The decomposition of the body politic is mirrored in a narrativized distressed self that bounces between Conservatism and Liberalism, until it reaches the status of full-fledged social degeneracy, or perhaps converts from Liberal to Communist guerrilla. Over time, matters are infinitely complicated by the involution of guerrilla into those who are labeled criminals (a trope circulated through the narratives of the failed state), or the real overlapping of functions between the social actors, making Ranajit Guha's difference between criminal and rebel indistinct.[8] For a long time, however, and long before the organization of self-defense groups, political criminality constitutes itself as a travesty of authority. The political itself becomes the generator of social chaos. Conservative and Liberal witnesses coincide in their disgust for the atrocities committed against their own faction, as well as against the population at large. Self-awareness sometimes manifests as remorse, an ontology desirous of resistance and change; this is a way of affirming self in the face of adversity and against all odds. Predictably, however, a series of notable transmutations and permutations of being and identity ensue, but all of them convey, in their movement, a panorama of closures in succession. The illness is social and prescient; nobody is spared. Here, Ana Julia recalls an incident that reveals this sentiment:

> One day some children were playing in a little park that is near a school; they were all children, sons and daughters of families that had sought asylum. They were playing with slingshots. All of a sudden a police officer arrived and took the slingshot away from one of them and kicked him. . . . Some of the kids tried to defend the boy. Then the police threatened them with their revolvers. These guys got angry . . . and started throwing rocks. One of the rocks that they threw hit one on the back and

the police officer stops short. He fired, but he was so dumb that he only shot the ground. When the kids heard the shots, they got even angrier and started using the slingshots on them. The poor guy didn't know where to look, or how to defend himself. . . . He tried to run to one side and they caught him there; he fought back and ran to the other side and came face to face with the slingshots . . . They kept at it, attacking him again and again as if he were an animal that they had found on the mountain . . . ! Half-dead, he tried to defend himself, but how could he? . . . That night the curfew is put into effect and the police get revenge. Through the cracks in the windows, you could see them marching out the liberals with the butts of their revolvers, they dragged them out of their houses and beat them up and down the street so that the people would learn. They grabbed one guy . . . and tied him with a rope to a car and dragged him all around the town and left him thrown in front of the hospital. . . . The boy was already a cadaver; they left him there just as a joke, to be cruel.[9]

The stories deftly undress the power of horror. The repetition of words, the simplicity of style, the redundant thematization of events, alongside an abundance of grounding idiomatic expressions—*volado, berraco, berriondo* (all synonyms of brave)—highlight the excess that lies beneath the text's calm surface: namely, that which precedes and exceeds meaning, trauma. Terror is terror; murder is murder—a tautology, but perpetually dissatisfying and self-referential signs point to the not yet fully semanticized drive to hurt. Sadism, but mainly its effects, underscores a unique blend of social and political collapses that ensnare us in all kinds of predicative riddles and elisions. The sole reliable unit they narrate is the family. It is no wonder, then, that family affairs are the only visible thread left by the political.

Paradoxically, what is left hanging over this recurrent displacement of ontologies and geographies is a bare shell of a distressed self whose gashed consciousness is certain of the past but uncertain of the present (and more so of the future), inhabiting a world without telos. In the interstices of this predication, what is sought after is not easily nameable. The words *assassin, murderer, blood,* and *cruelty* clearly leave the speaking subject uncathected—incapable of emotional connection—and dissatisfied with what he or she is aiming to articulate. There is an obvious sense that words don't approximate, let alone capture, the object, that anxiety is present not only in the repetition of the same words—

to massacre, to assassinate, to burn, to sow terror—but also in the repetition of the same acts that underscore trauma. One of these acts is encapsulated in the term *el boleteo* (ticketing), which refers to the practice of "writing anonymous letters to peasants with Liberal sympathies, threatening them so they won't vote, and then forcing them to abandon their farms."[10] Gabriel García Márquez wrote about this process in *La mala hora*.[11] But in fiction, real events are bleached clean. Not so in the testimonials, where the logic of narrativized events dovetails the logic of rearranging the whole regional economic structure.

Writing anonymous letters is just one device of terror chronicled by Molano's interviewees. Another is the practice of *recalzar* or *voltiar*—"refitting" or "turncoating" people who agree to change (or are coerced into changing) their political identities in order to have their lives spared. As José Amador testifies:

> The Conservative party gave some Liberals . . . the opportunity to renounce their liberal ideas and become Conservatives. I did not think that it was a bad situation because one was Liberal or Conservative without knowing why, one only knew that his father belonged to a certain party and one chose to follow the same line of thinking. Now, with the 'refitting,' each person consciously chose what was best for him, because what was best for him was to stay alive. That is why I supported the 'refitting.'
>
> If a guy agreed to become *godo* [conservative] they didn't force him off the land or kill him, but later he was forced to sign a bill of exchange for a made-up debt. The *pájaros* negotiated these bills of exchange at the bar for a lesser price to get the cash. Those who were buying were not *pájaros,* but anybody, a merchant, a small businessman. But since the peasant could not pay the debt, they took his land."[12]

The Conservatives also organized an office, the Conservative Directory, to make the change of political identity official. Efraín Barón recalls:

> The client came to the office and said: "I want to be a Conservative." Then a clerk took a deposition stating, "I, so and so, resign from the Liberal Party and join the Conservative Party, and I agree to vote for its candidates, glory be to Christ and the Fatherland." The guy signed in front of two witnesses . . . who also signed the deposition. . . . They came in scared and left as if their balls had been cut off. Then on the eve of an election, Conservative loyalists, brandishing revolvers and copies of the writ of refitting, would contact the new converts and encourage their presence at the polls.[13]

Activities such as these usually indicate a lowering of the threshold of peasant resistance toward Conservative terrorism. Terror has a way of compelling recognition. Identity is primarily political in this situation, because it is in and through politics that one lives or dies, that one eats or starves, that one has self-respect or lives in perpetual humiliation. In Colombia, politics is a domain interpenetrated by robbery, mutilation, deceit, and murder with impunity. There is no sense of justice whatsoever.[14] Political ontologies and a sharp political awareness make us take notice of deviant notions of authority, but also of very distressed and utterly traumatized subjectivities.

In *Los años del tropel,* it is the Conservative speakers who have the luxury of feeling remorse for and disagreement with the activities of their fellow Conservatives. Under Molano's editorship, the text is clearly sympathetic to the Liberals. Conservatives are represented as the perpetrators of violence and deft performers of sadism. The Liberal self, by contrast, is presented as a questioning, radically critical, and interrogating consciousness. Often this conflicted self is traceable to an earlier labor identity. José Amador states forcefully: "I am a working man and that is why my clothes are drenched in sweat and my hands are rough." José is a man full of bravado, a male chauvinist whose metamorphosis into a frightened, "limp" man with "shaking legs" is one of the most compelling testimonies in the book. José tells the reader who he is and what he is, but he also states who and what he is not: "I have not stolen cattle, I have not resisted the law, I have not offended anybody." Thus, a labor identity merges with a political identity, a self that cries out for citizenship and claims a legal status for himself. "The thing is that I haven't given a cent to these gentlemen. They asked me for money and I haven't given in, that's the problem. Then what is the matter here? Where is the protection of the authority? How do things stand, Mr. Mayor? Are these gentlemen thieves or policemen? . . . And tell me, major, what is the charge against me? . . . No sir, things are not like that, we still have the law here."[15]

This claim to law, which is also a claim for citizenship rights, is one of the many that are reiterated obsessively throughout the text. Let us remember, at this point, that citizenship cannot be reduced to a periodical exercise of suffrage rights. . . . Citizenship is a form of entitlement, and a condition that implicitly recognizes both the diversity of those who exercise it and the variety of modes and domains where that exercise takes place. Indeed, citizenship transformed the modern history of subjection by conceiving the subject as a site of resistance to subjection. As Balibar notes . . . the citizen ceases to designate simply the ones who is called before the law, the citizen also becomes . . . the one who makes the law or declares it to be valid . . . . Citizenship . . . provides us with a format to think about resistance to subjection.[16]

The rhetorical interrogation of the system of governance belies a condition of statelessness, a denunciation of the abuses of authority (or the absence of authority), a sense of the fusion of authority and criminality, the existence of a criminal, failed state, and possibly an early form of state terrorism—another lesson to learn. The genealogy of this shaken national ontological condition reaches back to the Bogotazo, the assassination of Jorge Eliécer Gaitán on April 8, 1948, as it is reiteratively stated in the text. Many of Molano's witnesses recalled Gaitán's promises with optimism, and for them the Bogotazo signified a dramatic and drastic closure, the end of any possibilities of being a citizen, of enjoying social tranquility and peace in their nation. In spite of the fact that El Maestro is a Conservative, he tells us:

> I went to many of Gaitán's political acts, and there were many conservatives there, all of the people loved him even though he was a Liberal. . . . I think that many conservatives voted for Gaitán under the table and I think that if they hadn't killed him, he would have ended the political parties in Colombia and avoided the violence. Gaitán had a doctrine, he had discipline for his party. But what did the Conservative party have? A poor excuse for a discourse by Laureano Gómes in Medellín in which he called on the youth to maintain power through violence, or a small plan that they drew up in Cali that said the same thing as always about family and the fatherland. No, the people loved Gaitán tremendously. If he had won the election, the Conservative party and even the Liberal party would have been left without followers and those followers were the ones who killed in Betania and in Ceilán.[17]

Gaitán's assassination was the last straw that broke the promise of pact between the elite and subaltern classes in the form of a national popular bloc— Luís Alberto Restrepo's solution of the formation of a broad-based national movement, a citizen's movement driven from below as the only possible answer to the perennial state of crisis that gives rise to all forms of violence.[18] After Gaitán's death, chaos broke out, and the fabric of society was irreparably frayed. The death of the only leader who could have led the nation opened the gates of destruction, and a series of arbitrary and cruel acts ensued. From then on, identity and being hinged on who struck whom first.

As can be gathered from José Amador's life experience, in the Colombia of Molano's interviewees, any act of communication could endanger a person's identity and being. A simple bodily movement or gesture could be interpreted as taking a position for or against something, or read as an act of aggression and turned into action. A sideways glance, "giving the evil eye," and nonverbal expressions in general are sufficient reasons to persecute, terrorize, and dispose of people. Speaking triggers the possibility of harsh aggression, retaliation, and its escalation. If there is rumor that something will happen, it is immediately followed by mobilizations that escalate the conflict. Keeping oneself alive is contingent on the likelihood of first strike. An aggressive or a frightened being is the result of organized crime, massacres, and butchery. This new self is the only way to confront the brutality mustered by the coalition between "civil" police and Conservative forces, the so-called *pájaros* and *chulavitas,* led by the feared caudillo El Condor. "I remember," El Maestro states, "that in one of these gatherings in which we talked about taking care of things quickly, as if we were flying, that the nickname *pájaro* was mentioned. To do something like a bird is to do them flying, in the moment, and that is how they were done."[19] These murderers, according to the narrator José Amador, were "pure criminals that had been sprung from prison; they did not forgive anyone and almost all of them were paid to carry out their misdeeds [*tropelías*]." Many people suffered from the violence: "They severed their heads, cut off a hand or their ears to present as proof and to keep count of the debts to the leader that paid them. The bags of heads could be seen on top of the draft animals so that these bastards could cash in their daily pay."[20]

All of this boils down to a confrontation between organized crime and organized defense. Self-identity is contingent on what side of the spectrum people are on: they can be criminals, victims, or *guerrilleros.* The reality subtending all these acts is that the government wanted to disorganize the people, to confuse them after Gaitán's assassination. Colombian popular identity, as political agency, had to be annihilated—a clear case of necropolitics, in Achille Mbembe's sense.[21] In desperation, one of the witnesses makes this account: "When the government realized it was screwed, what did it do? They released the criminals from prison and hid them in the army. Naturally, the criminals, thieves, the inmates, when they saw themselves free and saw the streets cleared of authority, began to rob and kill and people followed them, and this is how the attack on the presidential palace was forgotten, the revolution was forgotten. . . . That was the mistake. It was calculated very well by the government to disorganize the people, who wanted to avenge Gaitán."[22]

Individualism, as an exoderm of being and identity, was not a possibility in Colombia at this time. There was no way to assert one's own beliefs without being imperiled. Any trifling particular became a pretext to perform something sinister. The text is full of instances of the use of cruelty to eliminate people. Often it all begins with a false accusation. For example, somebody is accused of stealing, and an order is issued to capture this person. This action terrorizes the individual, his family, and everyone else in town; once terror is achieved, the exodus begins. El Maestro tells us, "The ideal situation, for me, was to sustain the power of the Conservative party by scaring the liberals but not killing them. That's what the party had to do in order to not fall from power because in actuality the liberals were the majority and if they had voted, Laureano would not have gotten the presidency."[23] Entire communities took flight, and their abandoned property and products of their labor was transferred to the hands of the government. Farmers became "gypsies" and "nomads." Their identity was an oxymoron: peasants without land, people adrift, strangers in their own lands—"an outside that belongs, but not properly so . . . a region where the distinction between inside and outside is a matter of dispute and cannot be thought outside a polemic."

In the course of time, the elucidation of these cases becomes practically impossible. Researchers are ensnarled in a series of accusations and counter-accusations that garble the events and obstruct even poetic justice. Who is telling the truth, the accused or the accusers? All of them seem to be victims and victimizers, although if we are to take into account the descriptions of witnesses, to be a Conservative is to be endowed with the power of horror, whereas to be Liberal means to be always on the run—"an outside that belongs, but not properly so." However, the point of the narrative is not to figure out who is telling the truth. The real important event is the enforced alteration of personality, the perpetration and maintenance of trauma. The process begins with threats, followed by the praxis of bravura, followed by the transgression of legal norms visible in *el boleteo* and *el cambeo,* followed by sadism, followed by real killings. No warning is handed out before the reckoning is delivered. The body, riddled with bullets, diced by machetes, or stabbed with a knife, becomes the last receptacle of politics—the place where the political punishes the disbelievers. Sadism highlights the logic of a practice, together with its drama. This is not selective violence, but rather an all-out war—a "dirty war." Yet it is specifically focused on the body and in escalating cruelty to the point of bringing joy to those who inflict it—the perversity of jouissance. It is in the enjoining of pain, humiliation, or subjection with pleasure that the perversion of sadism lies.[24] Full satisfaction is entirely conditional on the maltreatment and debasement of others, albeit open or closed forms of political sadism always occur in the name of some elevated doctrine or ideology. In Colombia, "Conservatism is the defender of Church and family, the only goods one really has because the rest is vanity. God is the true support in the other life, and the family is in this one."[25]

The narrative of sadism spreads like a connective tissue throughout Molano's testimonies. First, there are naïve reports on killings and a simple description of weapons—sticks, pistols, knives. It escalates through references to the forms and manners of killing, followed by the effects of killings, descriptions of the sites of slaughter, and meticulous descriptions of the body parts affected—all delivered in a flat, clinical language.[26] The dissonance between content and tone makes the reader feel uneasy. Obviously meaning must be located beyond, suggesting that a more sophisticated apparatus is required to fully apprehend meaning, to untangle all the horror implicit in these abject acts. Perhaps an image, a photograph, a film, or a very refined and well-wrought poetic language can convey the meaning of helplessly watching dear ones tortured or killed at the hands of a criminal: a baby tossed into the air and caught by the sharp blade of a bayonet or a rusted knife, an infant being drowned by pouring boiling soup into her mouth; a young daughter being defiled by a rapist so many times that her parents choked on their own dehydrated throats while witnessing the attack.[27]

Ears, skulls, noses, bellies, throats, testicles, penises, breasts, fingers, anuses —anything related to sexuality is maimed, tampered with, and violated, and then displayed so that the theater of death is perpetually performed for the living. The quivering, skinned, burnt, maimed bodies are piled up, one on top of the other, in the city, by the hillside, tossed into the river, taken to the morgue, left in the street. The real aim, we are told, is not to kill but to terrorize, to perform the power of horror; to drastically, and perhaps irretrievably, sunder the social fabric of the national regions; to reformat labor and land-tenure patterns; to alter the structure of subjectivity until critical consciousness is transformed into a dirty and disposable rag—until there is no possibility of a return to ethics and meaning. How to avert the gaze and not see a voter's finger cut off and stuck into the man's anus? How to ignore the penis or breast inside the man's or the woman's mouth? What to do when testicles are thrown to dogs, when people are minced to pieces, when bones are crushed one by one, when people suck a dead man's or woman's blood?[28] "When a friend of mine, who was among those who came to Ceilán, saw the massacre, all that violence, he returned to Tuluá, vomiting the whole way, and he remained in that condition for three months more. He vomited everything he ate, he was at the brink of death because his stomach rejected everything."[29] These events, this consciousness, these emotions close the drama of the countryside during La Violencia. Nausea, terror, paralysis, shaking legs, exhausted will, shattered nerves and bones will be replaced by anomie, the desensitized personalities of urban children, the *sicarios,* in the 1980s.[30] That is, in Mbembe's words, the essence of sovereignty as necropolitics.[31]

CONSTITUTING SUBJECTIVITIES OF SELF-DEFENSE AND RESPECT

In speaking of Doña Hermilda, Alonzo Salazar reports, "Peasants remember her as proud, with an upright demeanor, commanding and with a fierce spirit; they defined her affectionately as a general of three suns."[32] If the biggest problem of interpretation encountered in the above section was the reading of insurgency as criminality and of accounting for sadism politically in Molano's text, the problem presented in this section is much more arduous. It requires us to consider that in the transition from modern (La Violencia) to postmodern (the *sicariato*) forms of violence, we must entertain the notion that the stabbing of people in public is a means of constituting the subjectivities of self-respect, and that gunning them down is a form of labor. Here, I take the narrations of self of two generations—Doña Azucena's and Antonio's, mother and son—to illustrate this transition and rehearse the philosophies of *desquite* and *tesoismo* that inform the constitution of self-respect. I also follow their reasoning in explaining criminality as a form of labor. In setting out my agenda, my purpose is to second Alonso Salazar's efforts to discuss these hard and controversial issues in public, in an attempt to contribute to public cultural debates worldwide and to help him catapult this issue to the transnational public arena. If, during La Violencia, the world was turned upside down by the difficulties of coping with violence written in the very flesh and bones of rural people and their relentless displacement to the frontier ("an outside that belongs, but not properly so"), a real interpretative impasse ensues when this modern form of aggression becomes thoroughly postmodernized and new and more belligerent and drastic styles of assault get culturally institutionalized in the urban space by drug lords and the *sicariato*. If we argue that criminality is a means of gaining self-respect and carving out a living within the realities of modern "failed states," then could it not be argued that the same holds for organized crime, rogue states, and international terrorism: that is, that these constitute a means of gaining self-respect and carving out a living? I am dismayed at the lack of hermeneutical resources for analyzing these new social configurations—for understanding rogue states, organized crime, and international terrorism, among others —so much are our ways of thinking, even on its edges and internal peripheries, preinhabited by liberal parameters. My only guiding lights are Samir Amin's claim that subjective desperation leads to forms of response not precisely of the Leninist type, and Masao Miyoshi, who submits that "ours . . . is not an age of postcolonialism but of intensified colonialism, even though it is under an unfamiliar guise."[33] In the previous section I was content with having psycho-analytical categories as background tools to read sadism; now my burden is to find ways of proving criminality as a unique form of political mobilization.

ALONSO Salazar's testimonial text *Born to Die in Medellín,* serves as a vehicle to pass from one proscenium of violence to another, from La Violencia to the *sicariato;* from the 1960s to the 1980s, from forms of resistance employed by rural peasants to those employed by gangs in the city of Medellín, and from conflicts waged in the name of political party affiliations to the chaotic pinball violence of drug lords, gangs, police, and paramilitary and guerrilla groups in ever-shifting configurations.[34] Salazar sets us right up in the midst of a post-modern scene constituted by testimonials from the city of Medellín. I want to argue, first, that reading this urban staging of violence against the grain bears witness to the transition from modern to postmodern forms of self-defense, re-sistance, and labor. Second, this drastic restructuration of the urban landscape also comprises forms of popular mobilization in which subjectivities of self-defense, respect, and labor are constituted—a phenomenon of identity for-mation that is not unrelated to that of workers in the cities of Bogotá and Cali before La Violencia (as far-fetched as this may seem). Third, we are definitely amidst a sequel to the situation in the 1960s countryside, as the colonists who had opened up the agricultural frontier have now transferred back into the heart of the city.

Our discussion will focus on *Born to Die,* a text composed from a series of interviews undertaken between 1989 and 1990. The characters interviewed are seven: Antonio, Doña Azucena, Don Rafael, Ángel, Julián, Mario, and the priest. The story of the *sicarios* (child contract killers like Antonio) is a story that begins toward the end with a conversation between Salazar and Antonio, as Antonio lies dying at the San Vicente de Paul hospital for the poor and wounded. Other conversations occur at other public institutions, such as the prison, or in public spaces such as the *comunas* (poor neighborhoods). These are narratives of physically and emotionally famished boys driven to despera-tion, and they simultaneously constitute the essence of a debate about the rea-sons to argue for a life outside reason, or on its edge: that is, articulated by a different type of logic. They are long exposés of disaffected youth with one direct interlocutor, the educated journalist, and many other indirect interlocutors, such as the first-world readership, like us, in our public institutions and communities in externment, far away from the scene of the *comunas* on the northern hills of Medellín. The witnesses speak to Salazar, who then tells us their stories in writing so that we listen, and we listen so that we can retell. Thus, their stand is known, heard, and discussed; their bid for social justice is made; their life experience comes to be part of our discussion of public culture in various public spheres in the hope of persuading us of their plight.

The stage is a city that is simultaneously represented as the city of eternal spring and as the murder capital of the world. Medellín is the Manchester of an industrial drug empire, the city that generates the largest contemporary surplus capital from the production of cocaine. In this way, the primordial moment and place of early capitalism is being compared to another moment and place of late or high capitalism. Medellín is also the youth capital of the world, as well as the *sicario* capital of the world. Murder is a job, and a well-paid one at that. But whatever the point of the spectrum, it has at its core an element of class conflict: "The Medellin cartel leaders can be seen as genuine products of the local culture, people of mainly humble origins who showed remarkable imagination and self-confidence in building a successful business empire out of nothing."[35] This is the story of a class that has been built up and how it came to constitute itself as a new power.

Unlike Alfredo Molano, Salazar does not make explicit his methodology in gathering the data, but he does tell us that he has protected the real identity of these young men by changing their names and places of birth, and that he has edited their testimonials in some parts to lend clarity and coherence to their accounts, while always preserving style and language. Yet, *Born to Die* expresses a strong civic concern and pursues an ethical aim. The author's intention is to publicly discuss the problem of young children becoming *sicarios* while giving the same youths a chance to speak for and about themselves, thus encouraging scholars to reflect on what makes the delinquency of children possible and to demand a public and political solution to the problem. Salazar has long had an interest in documenting violence in Colombia, as his other publications attest.[36]

Chapter 6 of *Born to Die* contains one of the important theoretical moments of the text, which helps us unravel the question of self-constitution and respect. About the philosophies of *desquite,* Salazar says:

> Many years ago the poet Gonzalo Arango wrote the following lines on the death of Desquite, a Liberal bandit leader during La Violencia in the 1950s: "I place this rose of blood in one of the eight bullet holes that they shot in the brigand's body. One of the shots killed an innocent man who never had the chance to be one. The other seven killed the assassin he had become . . . and I asked over his grave dug in the mountain: Is there no way that Colombia, instead of killing all her sons, can make them worthy of living? If Colombia cannot reply to my question, then I prophesy this misfortune: Desquite will be born again, and the earth will be watered once more with blood, pain and tears.[37]

Salazar speaks figuratively about the philosophy of *desquite,* which he connects with a return to "primitivism" and "tribalism," in order to "offer the gods human sacrifices." Salazar draws a simile with Kamikaze culture pilots and Shiite terrorists, in that these figures also are "young people who are willing to die in action."[38] This philosophy answers questions about Salazar's own philosophy, his methodology, and his message, and explains why he has put the burden of data collection of crime upon himself. At the same time, it speaks directly to a postmodern constitution of self, to be discussed here via the self-narrations of mother and son, Doña Azucena and Antonio.

The testimonials in *Born to Die* expose the culture of *desquite* practiced by youth in all its aspects to the public eye. The fact that *desquite* was turned into the name of a person, Desquite, implies the constitution of self as revengeful —that is what *desquite* means in Spanish, an eye-for-an-eye philosophy. Salazar's hypothesis of "cultural intermixing"—that is, the intermixing produced by the emergence of gangs as the effect of globalization on low-life culture and punk culture (echoing at the level of self-formation the hybrid cultures produced by the market so well studied by Néstor García Canclini, or the hybrid social by Benjamin Arditi)—underscores a refurbishing of the philosophy of *desquite*. The intermixing or hybrid is historically produced, and it is a blend of old (Antioquia's tradition) and new violence, or the residual of past times (the modern at its edge) that comes to bear on new ones. This intermixed and hybrid culture is the culture of death that zeroes in on the ephemeral sense of time and a life of very short *durée*. From the old this hybrid takes the philosophy of *desquite*, and from the new the consumption of goods young *sicarios* take to an extreme. The culture of death demands a profile of high visibility: to be very brave (*berraco, berriondo*, and *teso*, hence *tesoismo*), conspicuous consumption of goods, and sets of well-established critical performances the young boys learn from the North American movie industry. In *Born to Die* young *sicarios* report on their desire to emulate the behavior of actors such as Chuck Norris, Black Cobra, Commando, or Stallone. *Tesoismo* and a conspicuous display of market goods and well-publicized brands structure the essence of self-respect. The film industry and the prison are the two universities of evil. Criminal training is provided by fiction, and brand names are props for constructing self-esteem.

But what, then, is the distinction between old modern and new postmodern forms of violence? Clearly one difference is that subaltern struggles have intensified and deepened; their air and tone of urgency now stretch to the limits of despair and self-respect inflected by globalization and constituted by trivia and mass culture. The extent and depth of the struggle can be gauged by the age of the participants, their values, and their degree of involvement, by a philosophy of disdain and of "who gives a royal fuck," given that we have been born to die.[39] To say things forthrightly, many of them are very young adults, even children, who are prepared to kill and to die for a pair of Reebok sneakers and who consider gunning down people a form of labor and *tesoismo*. A film like *Las vendedoras de Rosas* by Víctor Gaviria graphically illustrates this phenomenon, as do the books *La virgen de los sicarios* (Our Lady of the Assassins), *Rosario Tijeras*, and others.[40] In *La virgen de los sicarios*, the young *sicario* asks the older man for several objects, including Reebok sneakers, Nike shirts, a refrigerator for his mother, a stereo, a television, and a Mini UZI that he exchanges for sex and affection.

Unlike the conceptions of the body related by María Victoria Uribe during La Violencia, where the body was conceived as an aggregate of parts proceeding from animals and the classificatory system in use was that of the peasants, for the *sicarios* the body is a very temporary abode and an ephemeral source of joy and pride, the only place where desire is manifested. It is no longer a body described within the contexts of hunting and meat processing, of forms of killing animals, or of the practices and beliefs associated with illness and health—the rituals of death played out by different organs, for instance, the heart or the head. It is a body schooled by the film industry. "We get videos of people like Chuck Norris, Black Cobra, Commando, or Stallone, and watch how they handle their weapons, how they cover each other, how they get away. We watch the films and discuss tactics."[41] It is a body already profoundly intercepted and crossed over by the uncertainty, flimsiness, and frailty of the virtual modern/ postmodern. This is a body that wears labels and displays labels in public— for labels, totally fetishized and reified, embedded in the flesh so to speak, are simultaneously a source of prestige, a sign of status at the local level, and the showcase for the absolute triumph and epiphany of the global postmodern. The body of a good *teso,* I daresay, is the surface upon which all the glitter of industrial labels flashes. A *teso* lives in style: "The young boys walk by in their glowing T-shirts: bright red, orange, green, yellow; they wear medallions round their necks, on their ankles; all of them are in Reebocks [*sic*] or Nikes."[42] In *La virgen de los sicarios,* the young man's body is already morphing into the postmodern cyborg, a virtual body whose props are, on the one hand, the turbocharged motorcycle, and on the other, the Mini UZI.[43] Refrigerators, typewriters, mass-produced devices—like silence and utopian dreams of pleasant Macondo villages —mark the modern horizon for the older generation: for the mothers, for the aging grammarian who is the proto-agon of *La virgen de los sicarios,* for the existentialist intellectual whose grasp of the postmodern is flawed, if not negligible. Old gadgets and old dreams belong to the domestic sphere; expensive audio systems, electronic regalia, and machine guns belong to the public sphere, the domain of young *sicarios.*

There is more to the body of the *sicario* than surface and carriage, more than the accoutrements and style he enshrouds himself in, more than his muscular ability to keep watch or walk in control. In the opening scene of Salazar's *Born to Die,* the depth and quality of this body, a *teso* body, is invoked in the ritual of drinking cat's blood mixed with wine, an animistic rite. For a cat "climbs the walls, leaps nonchalantly from fence to fence, walks on the silent pads of its paws across rooftops, vanishes effortlessly into the shadows of the night." To climb, to leap, to walk silently, to vanish in the air, to become a shadow—all are symbolic virtues conveyed to the drinker of "cat's blood [a Third World Batman/Superman], full of the urge to pounce unerringly on its prey. Blood that conjures up strange energies, that speeds the brain."[44] As I read this passage, I cannot help but think of the gimmicks and special effects used by advertising and commercial films to achieve the fantastic simulations and contagious transformations that animate street children today.

An imaginary of kids—sometimes as young as eleven years old, never reaching their mid-twenties; beings imbued with animal-like qualities—is projected onto the postmodern real screen, where it mixes with another imaginary of metaheroes projected by the globalized power of Hollywood and Hong Kong. On the home front, these kids wage a war on undefined boundaries that transect their small worlds, their territorialities, their *comunas;* kids like Antonio—"only twenty . . . .[with] a skinny body, a face drained of color, dark eyes sunk in huge sockets . . . a calm voice, searching inside himself, as if taking stock for reasons of his own"—tell their stories, their own stories, to us. They are born to die. Death, no longer layered by the role played by different organs, like the heart or the head, no longer performed by one single cut that directly affects the heart or the head (the part of the body that the *cuadrilleros* are most concerned with and toward which they direct their blows), but a quick and fast one, generally inflicted by a shot directed always toward the zone of the thorax, which puts in evidence modern notions of anatomy.[45] Antonio states, "I don't care about dying, we were all born to die. But I want to die quickly, without all this pain and loneliness," without "this feeling that my body and my mind are being torn apart. Having to stare death in the face all day long, grinning and beckoning at me, but not daring to come any closer." The change in the imaginary of the body and the philosophy of death is mirrored in the shift of weaponry from the premodern cutting weapons—knives, scissors, blades—used during La Violencia to the modern and postmodern guns and submachine guns—"T-55s, 32-shot mini Uzis, 9mm Ingrands"—preferred by the *sicarios.*[46]

Organizationally, this latest popular mobilization differs significantly from those that came before. Early twentieth-century movements were more classically organized along party and trade-union lines, whereas those of the 1980s follow the format of brotherhoods and *comunas.* Former organizational lines of self-defense (trade unions and political parties) were more dialogical and underlain with the possibility of constructing popular blocs and common-front politics—Restrepo's dream of a broad-based national movement, a citizen's movement driven from below as the only possible answer to the perennial state of crisis that gives rise to all forms of violence. The new ones, in contrast, are closed structures whose codes borrow primarily from forms of solidarity based on proximity and blood—a response to the politics of *desquite* and *tesoismo,* despondency and despair. Gangs are organizations that spring up in neighborhoods and are composed mainly of friends, children that play together, hang out at corners, and grow together. Gangs provide affection, a place to go, a sense of territoriality and identity. But when gang members survive to become adults, they join larger crime networks that extend beyond the *comuna* into the city. Despite these differences, the 1980s type of violence is represented by those who practice it as a form of organized labor, one that promotes social identity and a sense of pride. Actually, their identity and self-respect is constituted by the mixing of new forms of self-defense with new forms of labor, thus also contributing to the formation of the hybrid. In Antonio's words, "Killing is our business really, we do other jobs, but mostly we're hired to kill people. . . . We charge according to who we have to hit: if he's important, we charge more. We're putting our lives, our freedom, our guns on the line. . . . We don't care who we have to give it to, we know it has to be done, that's all there is to it. . . . It's all the same to us, we've done our job, that's all."[47]

As we can gather from the above quote, for *sicarios,* gunning people down is a form of labor. The prices charged, the varieties of customers, the cost of production, all are figured in economic terms, subject to the laws of supply and demand. Actually, this formula is one that must be economically and socially reckoned with, given that it not only provides individual livelihoods, sustains families, and creates social bonds but also, and more importantly, accounts for the primary accumulation of capital that subtends varied forms of global power and terror. So far, scholarship has neatly ordered them under the rubric of lawlessness and studied them as forms of criminality. Children's testimonials ask for less conventional forms of analysis.

CONTINUITY between the modern and the postmodern moments of violence is also embodied through the *sicarios* themselves, through their legacy. Many have parents or grandparents who experienced La Violencia directly, and many of their family members were among the colonists who opened up the agricultural frontier. A redolence from that period pervades Salazar's text; one of the most compelling parts is the testimonial rendered by Doña Azucena, the mother of the young murderer Antonio—a woman "tough as nails."[48] I want to move now to her narrative to establish the nexus between the two periods and discuss the constitution of subjectivities of self-respect through the philosophies of *tesoismo* and *desquite,* which she illustrates more directly. What strikes me most about Doña Azucena's testimonial, which later will be reinforced by the testimonial of Don Rafael and others, is the constitution of a new subjectivity that comes together in the word *teso. Teso* conveys a sense of "the real"—"real" bravery, or "real" men and women. The word is thus invested with a symbolic power that inspires respect; it invokes a sense of reliability and trust and thus constitutes a point of departure for a subjectivity that will organize the new universe of meaning in the city of Medellín during the 1980s.

In Doña Azucena's biography, there are two key moments to her development as a *tesa.* The first occurs in her childhood: a personal confrontation between the young Azucena and her schoolteacher. The second occurs possibly in her youth: a political confrontation between Azucena and the police. In the first confrontation, misinterpretation and misjudgment trigger violent reaction; in the second, the clear-cut arbitrariness of the police triggers her outraged intervention. Let us try to understand the first incident. The schoolteacher sends young Azucena to pick up some roses and asks her to snip the thorns off. Azucena faithfully complies with the request but overlooks one thorn left on the stem. When the teacher pricks her finger, she becomes angry and slaps Azucena in the face; in exchange, the young Azucena promptly slashes at her with the knife.

This aberrant reaction is no less than an impulse of self-defense honed by legacies of abusive authority. The hyperbolic nature of her response is proportional to the depth of Doña Azucena's injured psychic self—a measure of the intensity of the long history of crushing aggravations experienced by peasants. We must recognize, hard as it may be, that transgressing people's human and civil rights can unleash violent responses, as violent and harsh as the ones that have been inflicted on them. Recounting the episode gives Doña Azucena the opportunity to reflect on her memories and to explain her action as attributable to her quick temper, to deflect historical humiliation onto psychological and personal terrain, and to rationalize her behavior reductively as a case of self-defense: "I've never let anyone put anything over on me." Her narrative of self mirrors her son Antonio's when he states "I was born with this violent streak." Azucena confides that her children "were born as rebellious as [her]," but that Antonio has been "the wildest."[49] I concede that psychology is rendered sufficient to explain the social.

In the second confrontation, all psychological mediation is withdrawn and the political predominates. The incident takes place during La Violencia, during the period of struggles between Liberals and Conservatives, which is constantly evoked in *sicario* and drug texts. In this episode, the mounted police are preparing to arrest Don Polo as he lays out the floor for his dwelling in a new shantytown settlement in Medellín called Barrio Popular. Don Polo's crime is simply to try to build part of his house. Doña Azucena, a member of the small community, comes to the defense of Don Polo and his rights. She intervenes in an effort to make the police acknowledge their error, even if only grudgingly: "You can't take him if you haven't got an arrest warrant." Her aim is to prevent an injustice, as she tells us: "I was really angry by then, and I thought well, if I'm going to die then so be it, may God forgive me all my sins but this injustice shouldn't be allowed to happen."[50] The legal authority invoked by Azucena is bleached out by overexposure, yet the residual outline pieced together from her recollections clearly underscores that the clash between colonists and the police often follows inexact and procedurally arbitrary applications of the law. Can we gauge now how far we are from a state that is "neutral with regard to the competing conceptions of the good," where "government and elected officials are generally attentive to public opinion, relevant players abide by the rule of law, and external actors do not intervene in domestic politics"?[51]

Though Doña Azucena is reacting to two different situations of injustice —the abusive action of a teacher, on the one hand, and the unfair actions of the police on the other—common to both cases is the absence of any instance of appeal. Here we are far from the horizon of liberal politics, in the less tidy arena of the practice of liberal states that make it imperative to contest the notion of politics as the art of the possible and replace it with the idea of disruption of consensus—as Arditi advises. Therefore, Doña Azucena disavows abusive authority directly, taking justice into her own hands. Her personality and sense of being are invested in an adamant will to resist, to be respected, to protect herself and her children, but also to present a bid for social justice. A realization that the law is "always out to get the poor" feeds her determination to resist, even at the risk of being targeted herself.[52] Is not citizenship, too, a form of entitlement, and a site of resistance to subjection and not only a periodical exercise of suffrage rights? Such determination is the primal moment of becoming a "real" being, a *tesa*—someone willing to put their own physical well-being at risk constantly as a means of gaining respect. The days of identity formation based on political allegiance to a party are long gone. The lessons and wider implications of Doña Azucena's story are, first, that respect is a key word for inscribing being and identity of self and others; it is at the core of constructing a new kind of subjectivity. Second, terror and terrorisms are primarily experienced psychologically, embedded in the flesh, and not politically.[53] The third and most important lesson is that respect is the absolute condition for the organic construction of common fronts (a fusion of the psychological and the political); these common fronts represent the only possible way out of terror and the abject—as Restrepo advises, a proposal that, in principle, I totally concur with.[54]

The presence of the trope of respect and self-respect, as well as the performances by which respect is obtained, take us to blood-related forms of legitimacy, to the familiar and the tribal, where *tribal* does not signify a retrogressive return to the archaic and premodern but a postmodern phenomenon, what Carlos Vilas calls "taking justice in one's own hands," arising in the social field of the failed state.[55] Violent struggles for self-respect are signs of unachieved structures of meaning and power, symptomatic of postmodern tensions between the social and the political. Succinctly put, resistance, bravery, and respect, in that order, constitute the trinity underpinning the new peripheral, postmodern forms of subjectivity that are encompassed by the word *teso*.[56] Not for one moment do I want to consider treating this form of subjectivity from the point of view of law and order, nor do I want to argue that it is a manifestation or representation of criminality. I want to explain Doña Azucena's exceedingly violent behavior in the two instances related above as clear evidence of the processes of a failed state. If citizens take justice in their own hands, if citizenship is an entitlement and a site of resistance to subjection and not only a periodical exercise of suffrage rights, the corollary is that the system is not delivering the proper services to its constituency. Social scientists call this structural lack of capacity a "failed state." This failure of the state accounts for the discrepancy between popular demands for protection and justice and the state's inability to provide these things promptly and efficiently, and explicates the various forms of anarchy that it produces and reproduces.[57]

IN her study *Limpiar la tierra: Guerra y poder entre esmeralderos*, María Victoria Uribe argues that violence can be explained in terms of the absence of a public space in which to mediate, negotiate, and resolve social conflicts.[58] The corollary of this absence is the precipitation of scores of "freelance" actions for which social actors need resiliency and courage—*tesoismo*. The result is to expose the private and the intimate to the public, thus fusing spheres that for liberal philosophies must be kept asunder. Acting out the intimate and private in public gives the false appearance that violence erupts only from personal conflicts, not from social or political ones. However, once conflicts begin, their psychological effects, their symptoms, spread throughout the whole social field via networks of relatives, neighbors, and friends, before disappearing easily into the folds of popular concealment. Though conflicts often surface in the form of personal aggravation and aggression (as with Doña Azucena and her teacher), it is clear that long-standing social and historical grievances are the subjacent causes.

The ethos sublated in this formation is a kind of social association, which comes up among people driven to desperation, where direct blood ties and family alliances are in command and where face-to-face resolution of conflict is the rule.[59] In failed states, direct injury runs counter to fair and reasonable play; it hits the community in its guts and must be confronted head-on—Doña Azucena gashing her teacher's flesh. In Uribe's study, I take the opening metaphor of the two hearts—one for dealing with good people and another for dealing with the bad ones—to signify an internal, emotional, schizophrenic tear, a limit to the current state of affairs: liberalism at its limiting edges. It expresses at least a desire to disentangle two forms of sensibility that tear a person apart. There is little doubt that larger issues lie below the surface of personalism and revenge.

In a 1978 article entitled "El bipartidismo como encubridor de la venganza de la sangre," Uribe's purpose was to explore the mutilation of the body as an expressive tactic of disciplining the enemy during the armed conflicts between Liberals and Conservatives and to show the consequences for the social soul created by the absence of public space for debating issues.[60] The purpose of *Born to Die* is to bring some of the agents of violence in Medellín into the realm of public discussion; the journalist acts as a conduit for those who otherwise would not have access to the printed page, who otherwise would continue to express themselves only through bullets. Bullets presently constitute the *sicarios'* only means of expressing their identity and exercising their will, embodying Michael Warner's idea of counterpublics discussed in chapter 2: namely, those that depend more heavily on performance spaces than on print. Theirs is a politics of pent-up anger and death that is as alluring as it is hopeless. As one of Alonso Salazar's witness's claims, this is a choice they did not make.

MOLANO'S testimonials render it evident that affect is the entry point by which ethics steals into the politics of the social text, a point at which criminality turns into rebellion as an exemplary case of *fanshen*—the turning of consciousness upside down, the reading of texts against the grain.[61] These accounts of violence start with the premise that the narrated is not solely a political event that can be read against theoretical proposition such as the "just war" alone, but rather elements of a troubled subjectivity that cannot be grasped by liberal frames of analysis alone; it instead must be relocated in psychoanalysis, where the symbolic has value and private and public indistinctly merge.[62]

Testimonial literature asks us to reconsider disciplinary divides, to validate the oral over the written, to accept elliptical, discontinuous, and fragmentary stories. It asks us to realize that the interviewees' voices impel a reading of history as story, as a symptom of the repressed that always returns, and to assume that the literary persona, the "I" and its narrative, are true and faithful—arguments beautifully rehearsed in works on trauma, like Shoshana Feldman's and Nora Strejilevich's.[63] Testimonial literature is that space which bears witness to the inchoate, irrational, and disjointed, a space that incites us to read La Violencia differently. It repeatedly expresses the theoretical break to fit these events and assure us that there is only the emotional, visceral recall of what transpired. Its purpose is to collect data, "to reenact the tragedy in depth for the reader."[64] Hence, it uses techniques comparable to autobiography, a genre that registers the "shock not merely institutional but profoundly symbolic, administered by [violence] to meaning and the identity of transcendental reason."[65] This is a genre that draws attention to the semiotic break produced by a condition of statelessness, "the strangeness of a land that was being left alone," and of "a country in which power was absent, a country exhibiting the sociological symptom of a political transition" where "political institutions in crisis no longer provide the symbolic identity of power and people."[66] In this place "they destroyed everything, killed innocent people, fair people, good people, they respected nothing, nothing, nothing. The river became a river of blood and they didn't do anything."[67]

Thus, a trust in bringing together life, word, world, and history is vested more in literature than in sociological and historical accounts—alas! We are to be swayed by the rhythm of tragedy, by the bruised ego becoming the true measurement of history, and by history itself, a narrative no longer contingent on the centralizing and regulating role of the state (à la Hegel) but, paradoxically, on its absence and a yearning for it.[68] Revenge, the philosophy of *desquite* and *tesoísmo* examined above, the power of horror, and a failed state all concur in bringing about the loss of affect, the impossibility of justice, and the eradication of all forms of solidarity for a "speaking subject with no object of signification and/or no object of love."[69]

CRIMINAL HEROISM, POPULIST BANDITRY, BODY-BUILDING POLITICS

In his 2001 book *La parábola de Pablo,* Alonso Salazar discusses the generative openness of the Colombian state at the end of the twentieth century. Of Pablo Escobar—the legendary head of the Medellín cartel who surrendered to authorities, only to continue his criminal activities in prison, and who eventually escaped, finally to be killed by Colombian security forces in 1993—Salazar says:

> [he] was a man with the demeanor of a statesman . . . He finished a war in ten minutes. He seemed to be a man who could fit the country in his head. To go to Moravia, the famous hill where people lived on top of garbage heaps, to take them to a neighborhood with all sorts of comforts, was a political deed that everybody in the country had to acknowledge. Pablo did not have the appearance of a bad man. He was good-natured; he seemed . . . [to be] a *bacán.* . . . People came by the thousands to hear him speak at events. . . . He said, "I rode a bus for 28 years, and because of that, I am one of you, I am from here, consider me one of your own. I come here because the economic conditions have changed, and I come to share with you what is mine, to share with you the right that we Colombians have to live a dignified life."[70]

If the state is conceived as the condensation of the relations of social forces, the unstable equilibrium of compromises it represents was never achieved in Colombia. Undoubtedly, this process cannot be put on the shoulders of the untamable genie of Pablo Escobar, who is at best an example of "populist banditry"; nor can it be attributed to the steadily rising violence of the drug cartel per se. These are wrong flags to raise. There are deeper causes that this sensationalism occludes, the most important being the set of alternative temporalities and carryovers that first inflect and then subsequently deflect the articulation of the social forces into one single locus of condensation. When looking at the singular and the particular, such as the case of Colombia, to disregard old temporalities makes us incur logical contradictions, establish comparisons that never meet, or keep excedents that are always held out in the imaginary parallelisms we establish. These excedents are always so rich and specific that leaving or setting them apart detracts from the task that is being researched at the time. What is left out is erased, or so much taken out of focus that its blurred stance dims until it falls into literature and poetry. Poetic justice, in fact, is the only way of reading criminal heroism as body-building politics.

I have stated that the distinct mark of Colombian history, the grain defining its discourse of nation formation, the particularity that defies the generalizing impulse, is violence. Violence is handsomely acknowledged and given primacy by all Colombian scholars, but this violence radiates in many different directions, and so violence is a word that remarkably concentrates the meaning and memory of these older legacies collapsed today in the master narrative of the drug cartel. So strong is the presence of the trope, so hyperbolic its expression, that it is truly very hard to overstate the case.

Pablo Escobar and the *sicariato* represent the latest or most contemporary stage or moment of a failed state. For me, this phenomenon undergirds the stern resistance of the poor and effectively deters the coalescence of another *criollo* oligarchic social contract, as well as the condensation of traditional models of class domination and, ultimately the consolidation of the Colombian state as the locus of meaning, authority, and legitimacy. For these reasons, and more so for the lessons it brings to the current state of affairs, we must take the *sicariato* to heart. To put it bluntly, violence is the indicator of the unsettling experience of the societal crisis of hegemony. Politics, wherever its locus, must reckon with this force, whose fluctuations of tone and address are everywhere and which, like it or not, no orthodox proposition, classical and liberal, can bring to closure.

If the role of the state is to organize the power bloc, to balance the relations among its various sectors, to displace the class struggle through the construction of a general interest (nation, morality, common sense)—that is, to achieve "the monopoly of organized violence" or construct a popular-national will—then the Colombian state has simply fallen short and failed. If this is true, then we are thrown back from politics and history to the terrain of theory, the moment at which both are narrativized as logic, and to the old question of the splitting of the social from the political (in Pecaut) and of the political from the real country (in Gaitán). It would be advisable here to heed Dipesh Chakrabarty's warning about the way the secular social sciences mistranslate the singular by reinscribing it into a generalist language whose built-in frame of reference is Western.[71] In this manner, the social sciences erase the particular and colonize reality, turning it into a mirror of the Western gaze. Hence, one of our most urgent tasks is to engage the tensions between structure (understood as the socioeconomic and historical conditions of Colombia) and practices (what people can actually do, given the structure in which they were born) played out on the terrain of culture, always keeping in mind that the world is so plural that no particular can represent the whole. When the singular is remarked, the comparativist stance is rendered positively problematic.

The following example throws light on the case. In 1981, the M-19 guerrilla movement kidnapped María Nieves Ochoa, sister of Jorge Luis Ochoa, a drug mafia kingpin. It is the Colombian military that informed the mafia of María Nieves's abduction, and it is the kingpins who, in response to the kidnapping, formed a paramilitary organization MAS (Muerte a Secuestradores/Death to Kidnappers). To pressure the M-19 to return María Nieves, MAS acted sometimes as an independent paramilitary brigade and sometimes in coalition with the army and its allies in neighboring states—mainly Venezuela and Panama.[72] In the process, it becomes clear that these groups represent three equal forces in the nation, and if there is to be a national state formation, it stands to reason that these are the forces that must be reckoned with, the forces that must coalesce for a solid state to exist. What are the constituencies politically and symbolically represented by these three forces? Roughly speaking, the visible, legalistic, and failing liberal state represents the older oligarchy whose National Front pact, firmed up in 1958, effectively ended in 1974. The M-19 guerrillas represent the populist (perhaps popular) fraction of the liberal bourgeoisie, disengaged from the state. The drug lords represent a nexus of landless, displaced rural people (small farmers perhaps) and petty-bourgeois entrepreneurs, the latter of whom become the handlers of the new money.

However, throughout the texts comprising this story, class factions are traversed by all kinds of subfactions, splits, and alliances. It all seems as if a new hegemony is constructively underway, with the paramilitary groups, fragments of the old oligarchy, and the drug lords as the main participants.[73] To this picture we must also factor in the presence of the global megastate, one which seems to have a bearing on the articulations at the heart of the local state. This megastate has come to represent the global interests of the multinational corporations, which are not out of the picture in this story of the weakening of the power articulation at the local level, and therefore deeply enmeshed in the dilemma as well. All these forces together will have a strong say in the formation of the new hegemony, the continuation of violence, or the balkanization of the territory into smaller units. In the following section, my focus is the popular imagery woven around the figure of Pablo Escobar.

REINVENTING THE POPULAR HEROIC

The story of Pablo Escobar is narrated within the paradigmatical codes of a late or postromantic populism. In *La parábola de Pablo,* Alonso Salazar does not want to tell Pablo's story within a narrative of law and order, of criminality and illness, of development and progress, but as a memory remembered and retold by a number of invisible witnesses.[74] He relates how Pablo's image lives on in the popular national imaginary, how in Pablo Escobar the popular heroic is reinvented. To this end, Salazar devises a character named Arcángel, a man who represents those who remember Pablo but who want to remain anonymous. Thus, the name stands for those who collectively piece together Pablo's presence in the minds of the people. Arcángel is not only an interesting narrative device but also a telltale sign that the story continues to live in the memory of living participants, all of which take the same name of Arcángel. Arcángel stands for the people, the popular masses, and anonymity. They keep vigil at Pablo's graveyard, and their presence underscores the existing political currency of Pablo's deeds. Clearly, the scores have not been settled, and the condensation of meaning and politics has not been obtained.

Pablo's image, in death, symbolically looms large over the living; the further removed from his time, the more powerful it becomes. Here we are in the presence of the construction of a myth and the reinstating of enchantment to history. Pablo acquires the supernatural power that Chakrabarty describes as proper to spirits and their agency. He is under his own spell and inhabits "a world that is marvelously real."[75] In this manner, the testimonial, as a genre, reverts back from secular to enchanted narration. Subaltern texts often follow this pattern, but can Pablo Escobar and his story be classified as subaltern? Born poor, during his life, Pablo became rich but extraditable. He was a man without a country, without a place. When he was young, his parents had to move from place to place within Colombia; as an adult, he had to live clandestinely within the same country he called his own. But what is most handsomely attractive about Pablo's postmortem representation, one that ties in the question of culture to the discussion of the failed state, is his alliance with the poor—a kind of neopopulism if you will. Pablo Escobar reinvents the popular heroic.[76]

In Salazar's text, Pablo Escobar is portrayed as a paradigmatic figure—an intrepid fighter, a jovial leader, and a prominent person. In many ways, Pablo is the sign that condenses what in others is disperse. He is simultaneously the landless peasant, the liberal leader, the guerrilla fighter, and a solid and magnificent entrepreneur. In Molano's testimonials, a number of characters acquire aspects of the popular heroic without quite achieving that rank—men like Manuel Marulanda and Jacobo Arenas. Pablo gathers together a loose set of latent predicates and provides the culmination to a series of struggles—possibilities that derive from the beginning of the last century. Yet the legacies of most of these former heroic figures circulated only within the particular geographies of Colombia. Pablo, on the other hand, transcends region and nation and projects himself globally. In this respect, he is one of the first postmodern, transnational, and global Latin American popular heroes. However, looking at him from a dominant standpoint, Pablo is viewed globally as the contemporary incarnation of Laureano Gómez's local figure of the basilisk. The basilisk is Gómez's representation of the Liberal Party as the enemy: "the Liberal party . . . an amorphous, unformed, contradictory mass. Our basilisk walks with feet of confusion and insecurity, with legs of abuse and violence, with an immense oligarchic stomach, with a chest of fury, with Masonic arms and a small, diminutive, communist head that, nonetheless, is the head."[77]

As a representation of the popular heroic, Pablo's biography is grounded in the quintessential myth in Colombia, which is that of being a *paisa*, a person from Antioquia. *Paisas* are renowned for their entrepreneurship, for being good businessmen. In fact, as the myth goes, being a *paisa* and an entrepreneur comes to be one and the same. These are the long and decisive strides that are to underscore Pablo's capacity as a businessman, as a builder of capital. In this manner, Pablo adds meaning to the generic rags-to-riches myth of the region, and the myth adds meaning to Pablo. Now, the irony is that this capitalist entrepreneur grew up hearing stories about the revolution in Cuba, about Fidel, and about Father Camilo Torres in Colombia. Pablo's early environment was filled with words relative to liberation that provided Pablo with an anti-imperialist and anti-oligarchic discourse. Furthermore, Pablo was born in 1949, a year after Jorge Eliécer Gaitán was assassinated, and therefore grew up during La Violencia. Thus the liberationist discourse is layered over the discourse on violence, which in turn is layered over the discourse on financial and entrepreneurial leadership. It is from the convergence of these three discourses that the idea of the popular heroic, much expected in Colombia, came to be embodied in Pablo—the basilisk-demon, the *teso's teso.*

The split of the social from the political is at the heart of subaltern narratives, and although they are constructed within the master code of secular histories and universal political theories in a particular mode that is contrived, they are built within a particular historicized memory of uninterrupted violation and aggression. In this regard, they partake of other subaltern histories. Thus, Pablo's image mixes well with a series of representations of the popular heroic borrowed from other central and peripheral areas such as Italy and the United States—El Padrino (The Godfather) and Bonnie and Clyde are two examples. Pablo's story intersects with stories of enchanted history, and his image is a crossover between a Hollywood construction of pop-culture heroes, comic strip heroes, and fictional heroes in the style of García Márquez. Pablo is a postmodern Buendía. It is this overlap that translates the world of violence into the world of heroism and leadership and the world of corruption and mafia leadership into the world of entrepreneurship. Pablo, as an icon, fills a need, closes a gap in the national and international fantasies of the poor, and becomes the most precious object of desire, a quintessential role model through and through.

What I am proposing here is not to translate enchantment into the secular language of political theory, into something universal that is intelligible only through the guarded parameters of disciplines, but to notice the deficit, the lost residues that are left out when we do so. Pablo's story is a particular story that must be understood as a particular story. Of this particularity, I want to preserve the way it circulates in the public sphere, nationally and globally, and to contrast the story lines of the different discourses making it up, as well as to gauge their impact in these different public spheres. For the problem of the complex of discourses making up Pablo's popular iconography is not solely the shadow provided by the afflicted, the disposable, and the drifters who constitute its backdrop, but also the *sicarios* that it invokes, and the idea of the mafia kingpins whose work comes to impinge on the discussions of civil society, public sphere, and the state. That is why I believe that the themes chosen to debate these matters—being a *paisa* and an entrepreneur—are very important at regional, local, and national levels, in contrast to the meaning these very same themes acquire at the international, global level.

As a paradigmatic figure of the terror of the popular (Gómez's basilisk), Pablo takes his place in the new lineup, where figures representing legal forms of opposition are indistinguishable from those representing illegal ones. Here, Gaitán's figure can be substituted for that of Pablo, and, in turn, Pablo for the likes of Osama bin Laden and Saddam Hussein. Here the metaphor of the mythic basilisk as a composite of species is a cogent and arresting image that synthesizes the global fear of the popular; the idea is that the popular cannot accumulate capital, cannot become one with the rich, and cannot be rich. Hence, extreme forms of figuration, such as that provided by the basilisk, represent hyperheterodoxy or hybridity to provoke an equally extreme reaction of terror and fear. What is multiply articulated cannot be easily assimilated by Western sensibilities or epistemes. Thus, whereas locally the discourse making up Pablo's image in Colombia's public sphere is one of heroism mixed with entrepreneurship, globally the discourse is one of criminality. It triggers a state of high alert.

Nationally, there are several associated tales that contribute to the enthrallment of Pablo's myth as it rolls along in the public sphere. One of them relates to his grandfather, Don Roberto. This vignette is narrated in the style of high literature, and Don Roberto is made into a folk hero who lives in the magic world of the real marvelous made popular by García Márquez. He is the kinsman of Arcadio, Aureliano Buendía, and Melquíades. According to a testimonial of Doña Hermilda, Pablo's mother, Don Roberto used to sell whiskey that he transported through the backcountry in a coffin, surrounded by people dressed in black pretending to be attendants at a burial. They, in fact, buried the coffin carrying the whiskey, but in the middle of the night they would disinter it, get the whiskey out, and package it in eggshells previously emptied of their content. This story in itself is so unreal and charming, so full of inventiveness, that we cannot help but adore Pablo's grandfather and see in him the origin of Pablo's entrepreneurial drive—another Buendía.[78]

Later, the grandfather gets wind that his scheme has been betrayed, and so he prepares for the inevitable encounter with the police. But instead of starting a vendetta and soiling the text with blood, he puts some rocks inside the coffin. When the police open the coffin, they realize that it is filled with stones. As a result, Don Roberto is immediately diagnosed as mad. It is the old man's ingenuity, his candor in relation to the means and manners of making money, which captures the imagination of a public who repeats his stories with zest. If he made it, everybody can make it. The vignette is constructed on the power of poetic justice tied to the possibilities of business and making money. The illegal acts narrated by the story are stripped of prohibition, turning the system upside down on the basis of Don Roberto's delightful ingenuity. Though he reputedly performed these acts in the past, when he was a young man, the stories are retold with Don Roberto as an old man, as "Pablo's grandpa." The juxtaposition of legal/illegal, young/old, poor/rich adds gusto and interest to the narrative, which the popular counterpublics enjoy. All that is illegal and criminal is bowdlerized in the text. At another level, Don Roberto's story is the story of the capital *boliche,* of the thwarted development of capital and entrepreneurship in Colombia, of the impossibility of capital accumulation and capitalist development in the periphery. Thus the grandfather story intersects with other stories of global markets and economies, but not with their cultural publics.[79]

Another great story is that of Alfredo Gómez, El Padrino, Pablo's mentor. Alfredo Gómez, the great capo of contraband, serves as the bridge that helps Pablo cross the borders between premodern and global capitalism; between a folkloric trickster discourse and a fundamentalist demonic one; between Robin Hood and the devil. It is while both men are in prison that Pablo witnesses how the elder *traqueto* of marihuana and cocaine negotiates with powerful political figures. With an acute sense of opportunity and great intelligence he studies how this man conducts business. Salazar tells us that it is from prison that Pablo graduates with his expertise in politics and business: "Pablo observed his teacher without missing one detail: he learned his way of making money and spending it, of being inflexible but charitable, and of deciding other people's fates. And he learned that money was used to bribe judges, police officers, and politicians."[80] Having begun at the bottom, working as a bodyguard, as a *mosca* (the man in charge of moving ahead of a convoy to buy off the authorities), Pablo then became a *traqueto* himself, a pioneer in terrestrial piracy, automobile theft, bank robbery, a gunman—like Clyde Barrow or Pretty Boy Floyd, right? He even collaborated in inventing a new tactic: the "motorcycle murder"—his legacy to the *sicariato.*

Pablo, like his underworld mentor, moved within legitimate circles with an amazing freedom. He was part of the national Colombian mafia, groups of *traquetos* and bandits, magic and emergent—*magic* is a word made up of mafioso and *milagroso.* There is, then, a kind of national pride that makes Pablo the instance of respectability and upward mobility anywhere. In the minds of the poor, "narcotraffic favored the insurrection of plebian sectors that played a leading role in the profound transformation of Medellín and of the country, which a writer has called a revolution without philosophers." Out of these *milagrosos* and *emergentes* "hot money served to form momentary economic groups that took over the traditional enterprises of the country. . . . The new bandits, bored in their own abundance, said 'let's go steal cars, look for enemies.' . . . Everything was exhibited, especially death. Crazed, they killed many people just because they were thieves; just because they were addicts; just on a whim; after that, they killed each other in revenge, because of incorrect accounts, and later on they killed authorities and the opposition until they achieved total domination."[81]

Two further observations ensue from the preceding discussion. One concerns the constitution of Pablo (and of all masculinities like his—the brave ones or *tesos*) as an ideal type, a self whose performance of august opulence and munificence factors into the sublimation of frustration experienced by the disposable, the drifters, the homeless, the resentful, the afflicted. Pablo is the icon that stands for liberation, the promise of shedding the negativity these people have internalized about themselves over time. He is judged for what he is, rather than what he is not. Pablo is the negation of the negation realized through money and thereby stands as an example and embodies the possibility of transcendence and positivity. The second is related to governability, discussions in the public sphere, and investments in the market of cultural capital. Pablo epitomizes the ungovernable. Not because he is brave, artful, and cunning, but because he has accumulated money, and money is power. Globally, all things being equal, Pablo's stories should circulate within the financial discourse of Fortune 500.

Insofar as Pablo's impact is concerned, we already pointed out that he has joined the global pantheon of evil ones—Osama and Saddam are his peers. But locally, in Salazar's work, we are told that "elemental men," "simple people," "country people," the archangels of the world, those who speak and recycle Pablo's image, not only convert him into a patron saint, but also into the Ego-Ideal (in the Freudian sense of the good and moral self to which we all aspire). For these people, Pablo is "a king without a crown," "the champion of mimesis," "the most alive dead man in all of Colombia."[82] Pablo inspires curiosity and admiration. At his graveside, people petition for concrete charitable acts, the same acts for which he was known in life: provisions of shelter and money, the payment of debts. Nationally, his powers are always inscribed within a financial apparatus that obtains immediate yields. Thus, Pablo, as a stable and miraculous feature of the cultural landscape, is both a representation of the Ego ideal at the local level and a postmodern international outlaw—an enigma sustained by his legendary silence and hermeticism—a man of many faces.

So, what was Pablo's true persona? Locally it was one of hope mixed with entrepreneurship—the two national discourses framing him. In this light, Pablo's figure is the backdrop for a discussion of the constitution of marginal or subjugated subjectivities in the public sphere—above all, what it means to be a man, a person, and a citizen subject. The poor projected and continue to project onto him the illusion of being—to be someone, to achieve something. But Pablo also stands for what the U.S. Drug Enforcement Agency considers a psychopath, an evil man, an egocentric maniac, the da Vinci of crime—that is, the international basilisk-demon who joins the necropolis of the despicable and portentously abject. This negativity not withstanding, Pablo also projects himself as a great man, a leader, an expert in negotiations, and a politician. Salazar assures us that Pablo exuded leadership: "a frontal leadership, desirous of adrenaline, sunk in the mud, brave in battle, a thrower of rocks and Molotov bombs . . . he wanted to be a leftist but wealthy." He is described as having been shy, unencumbered, and unassuming in his youth, but towering above his companions because he had "a calm spirit, strong character, and an occult vanity."[83] In his prime, he is remembered as a man of progress, surrounded by bodyguards, distant, but with a triumphant aura. But what matters now is what he has become: the symbolic capital of the popular heroic. The profiles of the popular bandit and the leader dovetail, for both embody qualities associated with bearers of social justice. And the composite political leader/poetic bandit enters and is nourished within a popular imaginary that includes heroes high and low, national and transnational: the Lone Ranger, Zorro, Santo, alongside the Untouchables, Bonnie and Clyde, Pancho Villa, Al Capone— exceptional characters who are born once in a century.

We are grappling here with no less than the transition to late modernity and postmodernity. Therefore, issues relative to land and land tenure, political alliances, and parties from the early part of the century come to be replaced in late modernity by money—the universal signifier. In all these stories, money comes to constitute one, if not the definitive, difference, because it is a sign of success crossed over by a multiplicity of axes of meaning. Money signifies the entrance into a space of discussion and a circle of power. Money is also the clearest evidence of having employed a correct strategy. At a more popular level, money can also be used or invested wisely, and in Pablo what is dangerously underwritten is a more democratic use of profit—a social-democratic style of wealth redistribution in a neoliberal arena. Insofar as Pablo's use of his money benefits the poor, his figure substitutes for that of the welfare state. Pablo's distribution of money is the concrete result of his vision and power; it is not charity, but a social investment. It is also a political investment that comes back in the form of veneration and, more importantly, respect—a type of admiration that brings him up to the level of a benefactor, a leader, and after his death, a patron saint.

I end this story with a myth: it is said that Pablo's style of doing business always involved trust in the honor and the word of people. He never asked for anything in writing. Cutting deals through oral agreements, a communal aspect of premodern culture recycled by Pablo, stands as a synecdoche for a very attractive human environment, a populist utopia in the style of Macondo, a community of people where large families—mothers, fathers, grandmothers, brothers—live in harmony, where best friends and faithful companions are in surplus. It is this ideal of sociality and communality that lives on in the minds of the poor. Perhaps we can keep a primitive and archaic image of Pablo symbolically, as a talisman for keeping in mind the many references to peasant and premodern ideologies that inform Colombian scholarship on violence, and as a memento for recalling that things past make up the utopias and terrors of the present and future.

Feminicidio, or the Serial Killings of Women

LABOR SHIFTS AND DISEMPOWERED
SUBJECTS AT THE BORDER

To depoliticize a nation is not simply to convince all its citizens of the futility of concerning themselves with public affairs, of the inexorable nature of the decision-making process, since no sort of collective pressure can be brought to bear on it. . . . It is also to deprive an entire country of the possibility of making moral choices, of the possibility of expressing its indignation.

> Carlos Monsiváis

FEMINICIDIO IS THE TERM used to refer to the serial killing of women. *Feminicidio* in Ciudad Juárez (a Mexican border city opposite El Paso, Texas) is a daunting marker of the shift from modern to postmodern forms of labor. Some of the women killed are workers at the *maquilas,* one of the newest forms of labor organization that high-tech, corporate capitalism has devised. Given that *feminicidio* is at the center of this postmodern border scene, the pathology of the serial killer is the most salient and facile explanation for this social trauma. However, texts on the subject indicate that the figure of the serial killer circulated by the media masks the underlying effects of both the kind of work that is *maquila* labor and the havoc wrought by women's emancipation through labor.[1]

Unstable conditions and high-voltage tensions are produced by the simultaneous articulations of all kinds of rough borders, as well as the difficulties they bring to well-established parameters of analysis. I use the term *border* to signify flexible domains, areas that can be disrupted, hermeneutic and epistemological "free zones," as well as transit areas or arenas that do not impinge upon or are unencumbered by all kinds of ties. A border is an anonymous place, a place with no trace, a territory deeply imbued with transactions and transitions; it is hunted down by the law (political and disciplinarian) and shadowed by the subterranean "natural"—that is, the world of needs (Hegel) or the geographies of primordial, instinctual, and archaic desires (Freud). Nothing at a border can be warranted, no sharp wedge driven into it, no cogent argument worked out to explain it. Everything at the border is lopsided. Borders are places that harbor all kinds of unaccustomed activities.

Maquila work and gender are two endpoints of a dreadfully tangled twine that threads through all kinds of border complexities, including the epistemological. In the messy affair that the relationship between woman and labor exposes, there are other sets of relationships that can serve as ground to unravel how the killing of women is staged. These sets of relationships include those between countries (governability is one of the main issues here), between what is legal and what is not (legitimate and illegitimate forms of labor are successfully played out in border scenes), between one culture and another (financially investing and receiving cultures are implicated here), and between the state and civil society (as provided by the Hegelian theoretical master code or model). But whatever ground we choose to unravel these violent texts, and whatever type of hermeneutic terminology we access for our analysis, the fact remains that the event of killing women in Juárez—like killing indigenous people in Guatemala or rural people in Colombia—throws normativity in disarray and makes it impossible to think through or think past already well-established, yet worn-out, parameters of analysis.

The truth is that the important concepts to grapple with within this border scenario are gender and labor. The reconfiguration of these two spheres has muddied the epistemological waters. The burden of this and the subsequent chapter is to explain why women are at the center of all these conjoining borders, how their deaths intersect legal, illegal, formal, and informal types of labor, and how they come to be part of the unconventional traffic of stolen goods, drugs, and the migration of industries and people that characterizes today's social theater. These renderings seek to lay bare the networks of decision making and power brokering.

In order to pull apart the knotted threads of this giant tangle, I take as a point of departure the relationship between civil society, labor, and the state established by liberal political theories—I use Hegel's ideas as a master model or code—simply because they constitute the background underlining the analysis of the murder of women in Juárez. Postcolonial social, political, and cultural texts in Latin America are cut out against the background of liberal categories such as civil society, the public sphere, and the state (or political society). My burden is to make sense of a critical analysis that simultaneously invokes and rejects the intervention of these categories in positing the Mexican state (as the locus of the political) and holding this state accountable for *feminicidio*. For that I use Michael Hardt's article "The Withering of Civil Society." He first sets up the master model responsible for establishing the mediation of labor in the constitution of political societies in all its cogency and neatness, and then reviews the significant interventions of Western thinkers (Gramsci, Foucault, and Deleuze) that bring the concept of civil society to a critical point. My intention, in following Hardt's lead, is to understand how Western models and countermodels of analysis for reading the political postmodern in the West do or do not help me to read *feminicidio* in Mexico and to gauge how much the social practices of illiberal states veer from these models. I notice that, in sync with Western criticism of Hegel's concept of the public sphere, testimonials about women in Juárez engage the question of labor, particularly *maquila*, to heighten the disintegration of social bonds and expose the frail nature of Mexican political society, thus also bringing the Hegelian master model to a halt. The real challenge now is to figure out what other epistemological frames scholars can access to understand social phenomena. These are some of the questions raised by *feminicidio*.

Concerned about the critical situation of civil societies under high capitalism, Hardt draws a map of the concept and offers four distinct moments: Hegel's, Gramsci's, Foucault's, and Deleuze's.[2] This map provides us with an opportunity to understand how the concept of civil society operates within all these models. In Hegel, the key moment is the articulation of society, labor, and the state. His tripartite model moves from natural society (a society of needs) to civil society (a society organized through the category of labor) to political society (a society where all needs and conflicts are resolved).[3] This curve traces a path from irrationality and unrelated self-interest to rationality, order, and related self-interest. Civil society is thus the happy medium between natural and political society: it "takes the natural human systems of needs and particular self-interests, puts them in relation with each other through the capitalist social institutions of production and exchange, and thus . . . poses a terrain in which the State can realize the universal interest of society in 'the actuality of the ethical Idea.'"[4]

Hardt offers three approximations to civil society: in the first it is the society of labor, in the second it is "specifically the society of abstract labor," and in the third it "is the society of the organization of abstract labor."[5] Civil society teaches us the necessity of transcendence: the subsumption of the particular into more organized and systematized forms of labor. All of the institutions in civil society contribute to this end. The transition from concrete to abstract labor is the process by which the singular is transformed into the universal and the self-seeking nature of labor and of individual needs is taken over by the state. It is presumed that as the representation of the universal, the state stands for the fullness of the community and is the place where all social movement and conflict end and the "ethical Idea" is realized.

This big logical and historical event, when natural becomes civil and civil, political is a "rational" movement; rationality implies, after Habermas, the protocols and procedures of discussion allowed within capitalist societies. In political society, civil society gains "a more complex economic definition, due at least in part to the progressive spread and maturation of capitalism." Civil and political societies are thus cognates of bourgeois society. In fact, Hegel's use of the term *bourgeois society* for the English term *civil society* discloses the mutual interdependence of bourgeois society, philosophy, and political theory. In comparison, Gramsci's model constitutes a bona fide parenthesis. His genius consists in reversing Hegel's model by making the state elements exist, as Hardt characterizes it, "only as subordinated agents of civil society's hegemony."[6] He actually recommends the withering of the state in favor of civil society.

Foucault, in Hardt's estimation, takes Hegel's model to its limits. His organizing category is not labor but education. Social institutions "educate" citizens, "creating within them the universal desire that are in line with the state." The state is not there to solve social conflicts, but to dissolve and diffuse them. Political society is control society—not a transcendent singularity but governmentality. "The rule of the governmental state is characterized by its immanence to the population through a multiplicity of forms," by the active intervention of the state in "managing individuals, goods, and wealth, as can be done within a family, like a good father who knows how to direct his wife, his children, and his servants." Thus understood, civil society is the site of the modern economy, "the site for the production of goods, desires, individual and collective identities . . . of the institutional dialectic of social forces, of the social dialectic that gives rise to and underwrites the State." There is no divide between civil and political society—they have become one. The state is society; society, the state.[7]

Finally, Hardt argues, Deleuze takes Hegel's and Foucault's ideas to their ultimate conclusions and speaks about a society of control. In Deleuze's model, all the institutions of civil society are in crisis, and their disintegration is creating a social void where there is no law, order, or sense.

This genealogy of civil society as recited by Hardt—from Hegel's model of idealistic rule, which holds the state as the locus where antagonisms dissolve, to Foucault's disciplinary regimes of governmentality, to Deleuze's idea of society as the crumbling tunnels of a mole—is useful for my work, in that it helps me understand the crisis of liberal concepts that render them inoperative even in and for Western societies. What troubles me most is not the concept of civil society, but rather the mediation between civil and political societies operated by the concept of labor. This mediation subtends the Hegelian model and comes to bear directly in my understanding of *feminicidio*. My question is, how does the *maquila* organization of labor come to inflect the nature of

Mexican political society? Does it enable the transition from civil into political society? Does *maquila* labor trace a path from irrationality, disorder, and unrelated self-interest to rationality, order, and related self-interest? Is it "a process whereby particular differences, foreign to the universal, are negated and preserved in unity"? Does it subsume the particular (individual, subjective, self-seeking) into more organized and systematized forms of labor? Does it embody the "representation of the universal where the state stands for the fullness of the community, the place where all social movement and conflict end"?[8] Is the Mexican state the actuality of the ethical Idea?

Reading Juárez against this grain yields a flat "no" to these questions and leads us to conclude that, were we to use these theoretical modes of thinking, the three societies—natural, civil, and political—seem to concur in Juárez. So too do the models of governance—Hegelian idealism, Foucauldian governmentality, and Deleuze's disintegration. In invoking Hegel (as well as discussing other adjustments to liberal thinking), my aim is not to adopt his imagined historical script but rather to expose its maladjustments when applied to illiberal societies. My quibble is, most of all, with analyses that take the liberal model for granted, never once reflecting on its implications. My burden resides in avoiding the use, myself, of these categories whose use I so much warn other analysts against.

THE CULTURAL TEXT AND POLITICAL SOCIETY

All the facts pertaining to the murder of women in Ciudad Juárez document the aporetic character of the relationship between the cultural text and political society. Cultural analysts interrogate the nature of the state by denouncing its indifference to *feminicidio,* yet they simultaneously demand that justice be served to the bereaved families of these women and that protection be given to all the nation's citizens. Thus, while they rebuff the state, they hold it accountable to the well-being of the community. This untenable position simultaneously demonstrates belief and disbelief in the political and a positioning of culture within political society that still enjoins a belief in civil society as the area where one stands up for and defends the natural rights of people.

Among the important theoretical options that emerge from these positionings are: (1) that in response to the events, and to indict the political authorities, cultural texts takes on the responsibility of elucidating what has transpired; (2) that cultural texts ask for justice by speaking in favor of a disenfranchised and abandoned citizenry, pleading for the instatement of a state of law lest society revert to a state of generalized mayhem and ungovernability—i.e., "natural society" as the absence of state in the master model—in which each and every citizen must fend for himself or herself within the public sphere; (3) that cultural texts intervene critically by underscoring that all claims for justice spill over to areas far from the purview of the local and national public spheres, far beyond the reach of the Mexican state; (4) and that there are intricate relations between "legal" and "illegal" forms of labor pointing to an intensified colonial reorganization of the world, as Masao Miyoshi claimed.[9]

Taking labor (*maquila*) as a point of departure, a point cultural texts bring up as a major contribution to political theory is that political societies globally are all implicated in *feminicidio,* that if in the master model labor organizes society, in our case study labor disorganizes it, precisely due to "the progressive spread and maturation of capitalism."[10] Seen under this light, Hegelian principles become parochial and Hegel's theory of labor as mediating from less to more organized forms of the social. That which is so neatly organized for Western Europe is turned upside down in that it fails to firm up the political ground globally. Although Foucault's proposal of governmentality (a blend of control and authoritarianism) addresses the nature of distinct environments and underlines their specificities, here it is more helpful.[11] For him, in high-tech, postmodern societies (France), politics has reached a degree of permeability and saturation, to the point of erasing the divide between civil and political societies—one has collapsed over the other. The state is an authoritarian apparatus serving to regulate antagonistic social forces, and the institutions of civil society constitute "the paradigmatic terrain for the disciplinary deployment of power."[12] Foucault's addenda imperil liberal parameters of analysis entirely from within.

I view the Mexican state similarly, although it presents different sets of variables. Here the idea of governmentality, as the collapse of the civil and political societies, does not so much invoke a totalitarian control of antagonistic social forces as the merging of the criminal and the political. *Feminicidio* is a clear symptom of this merge, a springboard that serves to help us understand the manner in which political society is harnessed to criminal society, partakes in it, and is the beneficiary of all kinds of labor—legal (*maquila*) and illegal (traffics—of drugs, people, organs, and pleasure). Thus, *feminicidio* also highlights the limits of liberal parameters to explain phenomena worldwide and points to the ungovernable nature of the global—here ungovernability stands for the flip side of Foucault's governmentality, the form politics take in our environments, undoubtedly a model closer to Deleuze's metaphor of the social and political as the crumbling tunnels of a mole. Our task now is to think about the concrete forms and manners by which *maquila* labor obstructs the passage from civil to political society and how this logic constitutes the nature and character of the global postmodern in Ciudad Juárez and communities like it.

I see cultural analysts of *feminicidio* as taking on the burden of exposing and denouncing the obvious participation of the political—law-and-order institutions, including the police, the justice department, the governors, and even the national executive—in the disheveling of the social, thus highlighting the aporetic that runs against the grain of the theoretical master model. What the cultural texts ultimately demonstrate is the collapse of political and criminal societies, and they do so by examining the question of impunity and relating impunity to labor. This relationship underlies the generalized social mayhem. Taking seriously the general proof of impunity of the criminals responsible for *feminicidio* denounced by the cultural text—and by impunity they mean to protect, cover, stand for, and act on in the name of the criminals and their actions—it is only logical to conclude that, in Mexico, political society is criminal and grossly in contradiction with the common good. This is so obvious— so much a *verité de La Palice*—that I wonder about the utility of this concept, as well as of the liberal model to speak about the social in Juárez. However, my answer is that the cultural texts use the liberal frame, as I argued in previous chapters Rigoberta Menchú did, either to push the borders and seams of liberalism and make it more inclusive or to demonstrate the aporetical nature of the model, liberalism's internal edges, by setting liberal theoretical concepts against the common practices of the Mexican state, thus ascertaining that this society is, according to studies of *feminicidio,* politically criminal.

A direct corollary of this proposition, as absurd and tautological as it might be, is that in Mexico, political society stands for the well-being of the criminals. Once we accept this proposition as plausible, the next step is to ascertain the intimate relationship between legalized investment (*maquilas,* the highest expression of abstract forms of labor in Mexico) and a criminal state, or the connection between abstract labor and political society on a global scale. The connection between these two areas is precisely the domain of what the cultural texts denounce as a cover-up. The mystery that the documents identify is precisely this occluded and obscured area in which political society (the Mexican state) and transnational investment—legal and illegal—dovetail. The only way of unraveling the mystery is to come to an understanding of the networks of power connecting illegal forms of labor—that is, "traffics"—and the *maquila.* At this moment the master model collapses. If the concept of civil society was severely impaired in the Foucauldian model due to totalitarian forms of control in informative societies, the concept of labor as a mediating agency between less and more complex forms of social organization for the common good does not obtain in Juárez, and ungovernability takes hold of the story.

Every one of the cultural texts leads us in whole or in part to the *maquilas,* which are the most organized form of labor devised by high capitalism. To cite Margo Glantz, one of the most respected cultural voices in Mexico, "the murdering of women in Ciudad Juárez would not be possible if *maquilas* did not exist." She continues, saying that *maquilas* are part of that "traffic of bodies that border towns favor: in that traffic are included *braceros* and women that migrate from the rural zones to obtain work in the border town that is associated with the traffic of drugs, prostitution, gangs, and sects."[13] Members of the Mexican Commission for the Defense and Promotion of Human Rights (CMPDH) admit that "the majority of the victims were women and girls between 15 and 25 years of age, almost all migrants and workers of the *maquila* industry, small stores or students."[14] The "Manifesto" quoted below states,

The homicides of almost 300 workers are directly related to the grisly working conditions that exist in the *maquila* industry of the border with the United States, a situation that is allowed and protected by the local government. Such transnational industry has subjected female labor, and male too, to a new type of slavery or brutal exploitation, daily working hours of 16 to 18 hours, without a contract, medical in-surance, pension plan, compensation, retirement, accident insurance, violating the Federal Law of Labor and the Constitution itself, submitting laborers to being fired if pregnant and to a permanent sexual harassment. . . . There are signs that some *maquilas,* in a veiled manner, provide women for the white slave trade, organ traf-ficking, and snuff films.[15]

Sergio González, the most authorized voice in this matter, states, "women live under high risk. Propelled by the need to work, they try to evade poverty and the hostilities surrounding them. But in the city's shantytown, gangs and drug addicts abound. A great part of the victims of homicide in Ciudad Juárez were workers, and were abducted in transit from their house to their work and vice versa."[16] Based on this evidence, we ought to conclude that the state of law does not exist in Juárez. The evidence also suggests that the whole system is im-plicated in the matter and that the responsibility reaches even the high levels of the presidency.

Taking these hypotheses to heart, the rearticulation of gender by labor—both legal and illegal—also renders ridiculous all kinds of moral explanations of *feminicidio* in Juárez, such as the following: "Much has been said about the dead women of Ciudad Juárez. That they were workers with a double life, stu-dents of doubtful reputation, young girls badly cared for by their families, bar-tenders with dangerous affiliations. It has also been said that they carried on high-risk lifestyles, that they knew their assailants, that they dress inappropri-ately, that they were not born in Juárez or simply that they had bad luck in being in the wrong place at the wrong time."[17]

To think that personal style or family foibles and misdemeanors account for *feminicidio* is a stark choice. To accuse women of provoking men, having hormonal problems, belonging to the "weaker sex," being attacked by family members, or being sex workers is trivial and flawed reasoning, as well as deeply unnerving. These accusations provide a traditional explanation for the massive killing of women and naturalize social and cultural phenomena. They are at-tempts to push the problem back into the private and personal as a way of dismissing its political nature and treating the pervasive problem as something incidental and particular. We all know that domestic violence is also political;

it endorses the putative right of men's ownership of women's bodies—one that leans heavily on male entitlements and presumes women's unmanageable emotional states of being. However, my claim is that public violence is a phenomenon of an altogether different nature: it reveals a socio-psychopathology that ultimately claims ownership of the social body at large, and that, as in the case of *feminicidio,* deeply enjoys the maiming, torturing, killing, and kidnapping of women. Whereas in domestic violence the relationship is reputedly one to one, in public violence there exists a concurrence of organized groups and all kinds of public institutions. Domestic violence begins at home and ends up, in the best of cases, in the hospital or health centers and in the worst at the morgue, while public violence occurs everywhere and is brought to an end in a dumping ground. Worse still, public violence denotes the exercise of extreme forms of collective cruelty and mutilation, the sharing of psychotic (this is what "demonic" means in this context) sets of values by the group participants, and the existence of a cultural economy and stylistics of death that boast great sophistication in their execution, desire shortcutting around social prohibitions that give these groups amplitude outside the socially prescribed codes.

To make this distinction between domestic and public violence is not to condone one and condemn the other. It is simply to establish the critical difference between them. What follows is a quote from the document presented by José Antonio Parra, a criminologist under contract by Cuidad Juárez's State Judicial Police (PJE), to the Judicial Police, linking both domestic and public violence and making one contingent upon the other. Reflecting on family values in relation to state and labor values, Parra states:

> There is a break of the nuclear family and a lack of respect for it that implies that if there is no respect towards the mother or the sister (the women) within the family, there will be none within the external social environment in which the individual develops. . . . This combination of factors, attitudes, and ways of doing things, added to the social environment of the border, *has permitted the clash of people with criminal profiles with women's desires to change their behavior and advance in their own development; adding this to a possible lack or fracture of the family values of the victimizer and occasionally those of the victim,* takes us to the tragic events that since 1995 worry and concern the society of Juárez.[18]

The disjointed relation between public and domestic violence and the association Parra establishes between disturbed men and working women underscore political analysis in the cultural text.

LABOR, CRIME, AND GOVERNANCE

One of the most difficult tasks confronting public interest in *feminicidio* in Ciudad Juárez is to prove the liaison between crime, labor, and government. The legal field is so impervious to the scrutiny and scope of public vision, and the relationship between "the real," the philosophical, and the ideological is masked to such an extent, that getting back down to bedrock seems impossible. However, the evidence is so clear and palpable that it cannot be rebutted. What swings the door wide open to the impervious and the masked are the maimed bodies of women that time and again appear in the public space. The frequency of their appearances, the spectral character of the carriers of crime and bodies, the perversity of their mutilations, the age and profile of the abducted, tortured, and murdered drives the essence of power into the open.

To insist on finding out the exact number of women murdered, their ages and social ranks, and the circumstances of their deaths is a way of contributing to the process of criminal investigation. However, the numbers are so high and the count is so confusing that it is easy to lose all sense of perspective. This process entails the awareness of a serious and perhaps irreparable tear of the social fabric, one that forces into the open all the complexities of illegal businesses, the so-called black markets or traffics that must remain underground. The coalescence of criminal and political society and their appropriation of the public sphere is a tall order. This situation is very similar to what Foucault describes in the case of highly developed societies: namely, the collapsing of the political and the civil into each other, producing a cancellation of the latter by the former.

To illustrate this situation with numbers, it is enough to remember that at the close of the twentieth century, four hundred urban gangs roamed Ciudad Juárez. This is a formidable force, one that demands a serious revision of the balance of forces between the police (part and parcel of the political sphere) and crime. A serious and extensive revision of these two forces will begin with the realization that even for a well-organized and well-funded police force, the gangs comprise serious contenders. In fact, the coexistence of these two forces in plain sight jams public activities and brings all possible negotiations or consensual agreements on safety to an impasse. For all intents and purposes, these are high-risk conditions for any society, as Juárez presents a public atmosphere laden with tension and an environment of guerrilla warfare, which only approaches the scope of war, gangs, or mafia and cowboy films.[19]

These tensions concern everyone, but they have turned particularly noxious to young, poor, brown-skinned women (the patent profiles affirmed by the murderers). They experience this tension to a tremendous degree because they are the ones to put their bodies forth into the public space. This menace has reached such an extent that women must take care not to tempt or demean men when they walk down the street, so as not to provoke them, or, as Carlos Monsiváis avows in a provocative and sneering manner, to be ready to walk the streets disembodied. True, misogyny reaches far back in time, and it is precisely one of the many cultural aspects under investigation in the hope of ending this crisis in Juárez. I will address this question further on. Here it suffices to say that society must reckon with the fact that young, poor, brown women cannot walk the streets to go to school or work without being imperiled. Therefore, although the hypothesis of a serial killer can serve as an explanation for these serial cases of murdered women, I find it more productive and cogent to entertain a more macrohypothesis that involves the synchronization of the economic and the political, without denying the psychological impact this relationship brings to bear on the social psyche.

In order to have a sense of how pressing this question is, let us review some numbers. *El silencio* presents 137 cases, of which 52 represent women who remained unidentified. In only 38 of the cases has the murderer been identified and punished. However, the number of missing women reported in 1998 was 500, of which only 350 were located. This leads me to surmise that the number of missing women who are never even reported is higher and that a greater percentage of cases are not even reported or investigated. The authors of *El silencio* report the number of cases that are not investigated on a monthly basis to be around 30. However, an individual from the justice department has admitted that there are 6 cases of missing women reported daily. This amounts to the astounding number of 180 women a month. Of these cases, 10 percent are never heard from again. There is no information as to whether the missing women are locals, women recently migrated, or if they disappear in one state and reappear in another, as 60,000 migrants are estimated to arrive in Juárez every year.[20] The most vulnerable sector of this group of migrants is women between thirteen and eighteen years of age—thirty seems to be the age limit of the victims. Family members identified the majority of bodies by recognizing fragments of garments the victims were wearing. Most of the women are reported to have disappeared between the hours of 3:00 and 5:00 p.m., near the cathedral or its surrounding areas, within a radius of four kilometers of the *maquilas* or around kilometer 5 of the road to Casas Grades, the Eje Villa Juan Gabriel, and the Perimetral Carlos Amaya. It seems some of them knew each other, lived nearby, and worked in the same *maquila*. In all cases the profile of the victim contradicts the profile of the femme fatale. Most of the bodies are left in empty lots, uninhabited zones, rivers, canals, roads, garbage dumps, parks, cemeteries, and cotton fields—all places where they will eventually be found. Most were strangled, burned, asphyxiated, mutilated, bled to death, wounded in the thorax, and overall suffered multiple traumas.

The messages written on the bodies of women reveal many of the psychic traits of the perpetrators, "the grisly mixture of a human predator, sexual beast, superior mind, and elegant gesture of a person who considers murder one more of the fine arts."[21] They deploy the psychopathologies of a sick society. The idea is that the bodies of women are written texts or signs that the underground uses to communicate with one another. The mutilations are unequivocal evidences of the hatred towards women and the texts reporting them, a criss-crossing of eroticism, art, and death—yes, I said eroticism, art, and death. Actually, the attention given to these cases represents the emergence of and warning against a common and everyday type of criminality, one which rewinds the logic of the master models, taking civil society back into natural society, the society of needs and brutality, where the state is absent but which is now characterized by a fast-forward movement of those human groups now subjected to the pressures of high-tech and organized capital.

Here is where the transition predicted in Hegel's model between civil and political society is interrupted in Ciudad Juárez. If political society is the expression of abstract labor and the social bond that delivers the common good, labor in Juárez is that which facilitates or allows for the criminal saturation of the public and drives a wedge between the formal and the real society. I subscribe to Alfredo Limas's thesis that *maquilas maquilan lo social*: that is, *maquilas* produce the social. The vectors or indicators of this production are rendered evident in the set of transformations shaped by *maquilas*. *Maquilas* produce migrations, demographic saturation, urban restructuring, reordering of gender relations, sociocultural segregations, and overall disorder. The investment of capital in the form of *maquilas* does reconfigure the public space, but it makes no provisions for urban development, hence bringing a socialization of labor reminiscent of Dickens to coexist alongside cybernetic robotization. In this manner, the earliest and latest versions of industrialization coalesce. All evidence suggests that corporate capitalism enables the concurrence of the natural and political in the social—Miyosi's intense colonialism—and nurtures the return of the specific primary and archaic brutalities of high tech to the societal.

The outcome of this labor process—sometimes referred to as neoslavery— is not only low salaries without medical insurance or other employment benefits of any kind, which creates a reverse of the common good for the well-being of capital, but also a youth without telos, who are desperate and disenchanted and whose only form of employment outside the *maquila* is the participation in all types of informal, violent, and criminal forms of economies—the traffic of stolen goods, dead or alive. It is not useful to dwell on all the moral explanations that governmental institutions have provided to interpret this phenomenon or to cloud the issue by appealing to the role of the family in the education and protection of children. Here we are engaging familial forms that are both informal and completely neglected by the law. The state's effacement of the pain and mourning of the bereaved mothers, fathers, and siblings in these cases is sufficient to verify that the government has no interest in these families and that without social support, morality is an empty proposition. Furthermore, this moral drift is severely questioned when confronted with poor women's lack of opportunities. They simply do not enjoy the benefits provided by social institutions to citizens. To defend themselves they have only their own physical selves, their bodies and muscle power, and it is their vulnerable flesh that turns them into perishable, disposable beings, at times living only zoological forms of existence—just take a look at the shantytowns—more proper to natural than to civil or political societies. These are temporal ways of life that exist under constant pressure and danger, excluded from all kinds of high-tech enchantment.

More than anything else, this is the true hothouse or proving ground of the coalescence of well-organized crime, well-organized capital, and a well-organized state—a Mexican variation of Foucault's governmentality. *Maquilas* represent real governance. They are stronger than the local state or national government. *Maquilas* represent occupied territory, an appropriated space, a hermeneutical border. They stand for the mechanisms articulating all the black markets (traffics) into a totality that brings together hope and disenchantment, labor and unemployment, human and biological survival, real and perverse pleasure. This is an atmosphere that pervades the whole of the social body, including the streets, places of entertainment, transportation means, small businesses, and hidden traffics. Social and public spaces are sinister and inhabited by legal (*maquila*) and illegal (drugs, organs, prostitution) forms of labor. Diana Washington has described the situation very accurately:

> Up to this moment the public knows very little about the two lines of inquiry that exist in relation to the serial killings of Ciudad Juárez. The paths that these lines follow come from high-ranking authorities. Also, and deplorably, there is the possibility that the Mexican authorities in charge of these cases will not follow them up. Why? Maybe because they cannot, they do not want to, or because they are forbidden by higher authorities. . . . The group that operates in Ciudad Juárez consists of various men. Collectively, they represent millions of dollars, own great enterprises, and have connections with organized crime and with important politicians that are near the president.[22]

To speak about the state more bluntly, the Mexican Institute of Studies of Organized Criminality has stated that "fundamentally, crime is organized from the State, protected by the State, defended by the State against victims' demands —society—to bring to a close the aggressions of delinquent groups. In fact, Mexican 'mafias' inhabit the very heart of the State."[23] Thus, a serious reflection on *maquila* labor brings up all kinds of major and serious issues, such as government and governmentalities, development, bodies, and mentalities. The question has been raised as to whether or not this is a form of democracy or a transnational oligarchic system.

CRIME, PLEASURE, HEALTH, SERVICES, AND JOY

The public display of women's bodies are garishly overlaid with messages. The first messages denote the convergence of traditional misogynist interpretations of gender alongside its reconfiguration by *maquila* labor. In traditional idioms, women are considered as frail and in need of male protection. In order to be properly protected, they owe obedience, respect, and gratitude to the male in charge—they must fit a profile that strikes a proper balance between fear, subservience, and service. To stay on course, they are to be demure, remain at home, and tend to family affairs in all the service areas, by providing physical and emotional nourishment, a clean environment, and fast and proper pleasure upon request. Thus, the private and intimate place is in tune with the ideologies and rules established by private property. Theoretically, complying with all these mandates, however, does not guarantee the physical well-being of women at home, since the particular intricacies of male (and female) fantasies and dreads are never explicitly written into the contract but are rendered operative on a daily basis, and sometimes made visible in domestic violence. Working outside the home, however, introduces women to a different set of rules and norms than those governing the private arena and asks for a reconfiguration of misogynist ideologies.

Ana Bergareche states that patriarchal ideology is transmitted via all available forms of media, but the growing autonomy of women has severely challenged the sexual economies of male chauvinism in only one generation. What is untenable and unbearable to the patriarchy in this situation is the destruction of male fantasies, and with them, Renata Salecl will venture, that of male identities. This is a risky proposition for women because in the male fantasy she is turned into something dirty—garbage, debris, and something that deeply and definitively endangers the masculine order—and therefore she has to be disciplined through punishment and turned into an example individually and collectively. Hence the messages that are sent to different mafia interest groups are also sent to the population at large. The problem here is the interlacing of love and hate, lust and crime, art and murder, the natural and the political— examples of which will be provided in the last chapter of this book. Here is where my analysis of *feminicidio* does an about-face and confronts the natural head on. "Natural" here, then, is understood not only in the sense of natural, human, survival—which is the Hegelian sense—but also in the politics of desire, with emphasis on the natural as the primitive and archaic outlined by Freud. I will elaborate more on this further on. Sexual crimes are a social warning to everyone, an act of power and discipline, a sign of masculine, brutal, natural, social, and political power, and an invasion of the public space—when not a complete takeover. Thus women's bodies are multiply articulated and plurally narrated, and misogynist perversion fully takes flight. A woman's body under high-tech corporate capitalism is a heteroglossic, polymorphic sign of labor and tenacity, a cyborg arm, a factory, an instrument of biological reproduction, and the ideal site for the demonstration of social resentment, perverse eroticism, and jouissance.

It is within our purview to speak about the wrenching breakdown of masculinism that the serial murder of women in Juárez reveals, because they raise the stakes considerably. The manner in which these female bodies transmit messages lies in the way they are laid out for public consumption: their eyes blinded so they cannot see, their mouths gagged so they cannot speak, their sexual organs destroyed so they cannot feel.[24] The reading of the positions is multistranded and inevitably linked to violence and perverse eroticism. In fact, the scenes are deeply unnerving and make the hairs of our necks stand up. However, we are simultaneously presented with a stark choice: to either see and read about them, or to choose not to. Clearly, we cannot forgo the experience.

Thus we read on. First, we get acquainted with the profiles: young, brown, slender, long hair, wearing jeans and a T-shirt, poor. That is, women whose families truly cannot defend them are made the victims of crimes. Along with the physical and socioeconomic profile, we are presented with the place where they can be abducted from: usually the street; on their way to work or to school; but the possibility also exists at meeting points such as small businesses, mainly shoe stores, dance halls, and even bars. However, the inclusion of bars is a decoy to make women into cardboard cutouts, a continuation of misogynist discourses. Subsequently, there are the descriptions and, in some instances, the pictures of the positions in which they were found:

> The body was laying prone, the head oriented towards the north, the right arm tucked under the abdomen and the left arm half flexed alongside; the legs were spread. Dead by strangulation is confirmed. She had her hair tied with a brown rubber band. The body still wore a white T-shirt with the logo "California. The Golden State" across the front. The garment was wrapped around on top of the breasts, as was the white brassiere. Under the body, a green pair of jeans with blood stains and corpse fauna was found. On the left, at in the vicinity of the thigh, there was a shoe without shoelaces and a pair of white underwear. Except the shoe, which had a label reading "3 Brothers," none of the pieces of garments had visible brand labels.[25]

I have included this long description because it contains elements that are common to a majority of the bodies' descriptions.

The lucrative industry of extermination follows organized schemes or ritual patterns that stunt the imagination and force us to tackle the problem head on. Organized schemes reveal that the victim is generally abducted from the street as criminals dart toward her and subdue her by force while she is waiting for a bus or simply walking on the sidewalk. Signs of struggle reveal that she resisted when she was accosted from behind, a fact that negates the misogynist excuse of provocation or teasing on the part of the woman. In the majority of cases, the act of murder itself seems to occur through suffocation or strangulation: either by choking the victim, asphyxiating and smothering her until the life is squeezed out of her, or by twisting her neck until it breaks. This may or not happen at the moment of abduction itself, depending mainly on whether she resists or defends herself. Some of the bodies have one or both nipples severed. They seemed to have been bitten off and yanked out with the mouth. Either before or after their death, the women are cut and slashed with pointed and sharp objects that mutilate the bodies to the point of making them unidentifiable. Tying limbs in the back or front is another sign that reveals the pleasure of leaving the woman defenseless, and many victims have been raped from the front and the back, as the rips, shreds, and torn body parts so seem to indicate. After that they are either thrown into the public space, buried, burned, incinerated, or disappeared using a mixture of lime and chemical substances that leaves no trace of their existence as it disintegrates all organic matter. The style revealed in the tampering with their bodies—the cuts, slashes, marks, positions in which the bodies are left, and the positioning of their clothing—underscores a style and points in the direction of the same or like perpetrators or organized groups of some kind. Most are found in a state of decomposition that indicates that their dead bodies were kept for a time in a different place from where they were eventually found. In some cases, it seems that their bodies were kept in a refrigerator.

What does this all tell us about the perpetrator and about the society and its political organization? One point that carries over concerns the identities of the murderers. They have been identified as Abdel Latif Sharif, a member of the "Los Choferes" gang; Sergio Armendariz, alias "El Diablo," the leader of "Los Rebeldes"; "El Chacal," also known under the pseudonyms of "El Tolteca" and "El Drácula." We also have their proper names: Antonio Navarrete, Francisco Minjarez, Alejandro Máynez, also known as Armando Martínez, and his cousin Melchor Máynez. And then, there is the commanding presence of the drug cartels and their capos—among them Amado Carrillo Fuentes, the Cartel de Juárez capo with connections in Chile, Argentina, Colombia, and the United States. Some of these people seem to be scapegoats, merely names to fabricate a story; some are part of the very lucrative industry of death. But their pseudonyms make us suspicious of satanic rituals. At the very least, their aim is to frighten everyone that surrounds them.

One of the central questions is: how is it possible that all of the people mentioned above know the stories, names, and trades of everyone else? Are they the anchoring thinkers, are they acquainted with the story because all of them belong to the underground industries, or because the police dropped stories and names during interrogation and when the accused reproduce them, they incriminate themselves? None of that is clear, except that those truly implicated do not actually work so illegally. In the struggles among the cartels, evidence of the alliances between army generals comes out right into the open. The film *Traffic* thrives on the exposure of all these types of connections, as well as on leaving others covered up.[26] A methodological cue was provided by a very efficient operation undertaken in which narco burial grounds, cemeteries, and alliances were localized within a radius that encompassed Rancho Tiradores del Norte, Rancho La Campana, Rancho Santa Elena, and Rancho Santa Rosalía. The evidence found unmistakably lays out the issues and paves the way for the understanding of *feminicidio*. Several bodies were found around these properties, and they confirmed the suspicions of orgies, kidnappings, and executions in which both the police and the narcos participated. The contrast these cemeteries offer with the determined search of the victims' parents is astounding. Whereas in the ranchos everything bespeaks opulence and degradation, and even satanic rituals that seal the pact among the implicated with blood, the Xeroxed posters on the buses and on the city lampposts where the distressed families denounce the disappearance of their dear daughters and siblings underscore the poverty of resources, the sorrow of the aggrieved families. The astonishing difference between the two political economies, those of the parents and those of narcos, occurs over an irreparable social fracture.

One of the main conclusions to draw from this analysis is that liberal categories are not only insufficient for analyzing the new set of variables offered by the repositioning of women within the new forms of labor or to explain how new forms of labor inflect the social and the political; they also cannot account for the relationship between the global and the local, processes all of which are seriously implicated in the understanding of *feminicidio*. And although most of the cultural analyses are written against the background of liberal categories—liberal categories are in command in modern Latin American societies after the nineteenth-century movements of independence and institutionalization of republican forms of governance—the master code fails to deliver what it promises: namely, the transition between civil and political society mediated by abstract labor. However, the critical repositioning of these very ideas suggested by Foucault and Deleuze (Gramsci's proposition was a perishable and gentle, left-leaning, social democratic parenthesis) is more generative, in that it looks as if, in both cases (in the case of Juárez, as in Foucault's and Deleuze's) civil society (civility and civilization) is either jeopardized or eliminated and the possibilities of the mediation of liberal categories in the explication of the social is rendered otiose.

The Perverse Heterosexual

THE NUMBER OF articles, books, films, pictures, paintings, and theatrical productions concerning the women assassinated in Ciudad Juárez grows steadily.[1] This is due not only to the bemusing and menacing nature of this massive event that bewilders scholars but also to the intuition that it constitutes a symptom of overriding importance of events to come and constitutes one of the patterns of governmentality in the postmodern world. Without packing everything into a convenient catchall explanation, it can be said that evidence of this menace can be found in the murders of women in other areas of Mexico, such as Baja California, Nuevo León, Guanajuato, Tamaulipas, Oaxaca, Sonora, and Guerrero, as well as in other countries, including Guatemala. I want to call attention to the massive production of literature on the subject so as to highlight the place of culture and its function, and to focus on one particular text, *El silencio que la voz de todas quiebra: Mujeres y víctimas de Ciudad Juárez,* which has been the singular object of praise in Ciudad Juárez (*Huesos en el desierto,* by Sergio González, being the undisputed authority on the subject in the view of most national scholars).[2]

Among all the texts written on *feminicidio, El silencio* is particularly praise-worthy on a local level. I do not know quite how to explain this local impulse, but I assume it is due to several factors. For one, the text underscores the intellectual commitment of the local intelligentsia in Juárez. The presumption is that those who live in the area know more about it or have better access to information on the subject matter than do researchers elsewhere. Another reason is that the local intellectual encounters more risks by writing about this subject than researchers in other places, like myself, who are relatively outside the direct sphere of influence of the drug lords. There is a threat hanging over all those who investigate *feminicidio* in Juárez. A case in point is that of González himself and of all the individuals he mentions in his book. Silence also means silencing, and vulnerability is not only a sign of commitment but also of authenticity and authority. Many researchers of violence have paid with their own lives for diving headfirst into these murky waters.

As part of the public debate, *El silencio* constitutes a piece of evidence of the empathy that a group of women writers manifests for the murdered and enters a plea to intervene and document this matter of public interest that exposes the unprotected lives of some social sectors under the governmental regimes of *maquila*-style "democracies." Thus, the text lays bare the close-knit relationship between public, private, and intimate. The intent of the text is to retrieve, for the heteropathic postcollective memory—that is, the indirect cultural memory—small bits and pieces of the lives of the young and unprotected women who have been murdered, alongside the testimonials of their mothers' affect.[3] The text reveals sufficient evidence of the fissure between the family and the state that is produced by the powerful mediation of money and private property expressed by the *maquilas.* I want to underscore the gratuitous forms of death, together with social defenselessness and the improbability of finding the culprits, as reasons that trigger cultural action. The women writers' collective is not invested in finding the offenders but in providing the documentation that places the burden for finding them on the state. The social impact of this text resides in its enactment of knowledge that directly impinges on state affairs and interpellates the state regarding the butchery of young women at the hands of invisible and yet unpunished agents.[4] Thus, *El silencio* is a text tenaciously invested in unraveling the garbled state speech marring the investigation on *feminicidio.*

The women of the writing collective unabatedly work towards breaking the silence. In this very word, *silence,* we find an indictment that connects directly with certain aspects of the investigation: namely, to expose and defy the stark operational mode of state institutions and their procedures. The discourse of the law shows itself to be bankrupt and worn out by its turning a blind eye, the word of the state soils the investigation, and there is the grim insinuation of a conspiracy, an area of darkness that takes the form of blaming the victim. It is clear that the writers are denouncing the deleterious nature of the state and its tendency to cover up crimes. Hence, it is imperative to combat the circulating hypothesis of the culpability of the murdered, who, to repeat Carlos Monsiváis's irony, in order to avoid being murdered must walk in the street "without bodies."[5]

To understand the stunning connection between words, lies, and power, it is necessary to insist on the nature of the confrontation between civil society and the state and to grasp the nature of the Mexican state today, ensnarled in the horns of a dilemma. It is precisely the nature of the state that is in question, and more specifically the grisly relationship between state and labor, which is evident in the *maquilas* and drug lords. How these spheres are articulated is a mystery that may never be unraveled because, as the Center for Investigation of National Security (CISEN) states, "the structure that supports corruption can establish relations of complicity with powerful groups or with enemies of the State, coming to constitute themselves into a power parallel to government"[6]— as it is in Colombia.

Hence, to break this particular silence, the particular objective of the writing collective is to summon the presence of the murdered and speak in their favor. This is presented as a worthwhile project, one in which women ought not to falter. The identification with the murdered and the edifying and clarifying tone of the text come to bear on the meaning of "saving the dignity" of the women—one of the nonmaterial, unmeasurable quantities and intangible goods that justice consists of, as Iris Marion Young specifies in her work.[7] Seven scorned girls are selected as examples; these seven are rehumanized and their visages and aspirations reconstructed. The women writers put forth the thesis of a double blow, one physical and the other moral; a reason for which the physical presence of the murdered through photographs is reinstated in the cultural text. The girls are visible and present to the reader in the here and now. Through this physical reconstruction, they simultaneously retrieve the multiple contexts—social, personal, and intimate—in which the girls lived. The threat is presented as being multiply articulated. The issue is related to a human drama, and what they want is to review the case. Thus, to those who prefer the device of writing, writing offers the special advantage of identifying consciousness with their own political ideas and norms.

The unfaltering reconstruction of the environment begins by rehearsing the crime scene and the conditions of criminality right at the heart of labor. We then visit Lote Bravo, Lomas de Poleo, and Cerro Bola, González's "geographies of danger," zones of the marginal poor and recently employed by the *maquila*. In their desolation, these *lotes, lomas,* and *cerros* reproduce the image of the desert where there is nothing but garbage dumps and a roving silence, a place far from the city, where structures like Target and Wal-Mart rise up. The combination of nothingness with garbage with late capitalist industry underpins the contrast between life and labor. Postmodernity has fully descended upon the people of Juárez.

The story begins with the finding of human remains and is shot through with bones, skulls, and shreds of dry flesh. The tragedy is that murdered women become hard data and statistics and that human drama is just fodder to theoretical mills. The first reaction these findings provoke is indignation, then awe in the face of impunity, and after that, the desire to find the culprits. But nobody has seen anything. There are no witnesses, accomplices, or fingerprints—nothing! The cases are consummated facts, and the judicial system just takes notice of them: between 1993 and 1998, 137 women were murdered. The crimes are never resolved or investigated; they are simply reported. The public record takes on the style of ellipses, informing on the multiple gaps of information. None of the records are trustworthy. Time and again the reports are confusing, incomplete, garbled; the irregularity of their narratives and languages are predictable and their hypotheses untenable. The files and their data are incongruous and always show signs of tampering.

Incorporating the terms of politics in recognition of the importance of the state, in *El silencia* the women of the writers' collective do not recoil from the idea of a well-organized state, a state apparatus where justice will be rendered through the use of autopsies, forensic investigation, and expert opinions. All this reveals the constraints of complex fantasies about a well-constituted state and its power that are nourished by the hidden genealogies of liberal philosophies—Hegel's in the first place—when not by more prosaic and mundane vulgarizations, of such ideas aired in movies, CourtTV, or CSI television shows, in which the state is idealized and presented as a solid bastion against criminality and the primary instance galvanizing protection of the community. The absence of such an ideal version of the state in real-life experience provokes indignation, and discredit falls upon the state. Neither in Juárez, nor in Colombia or Guatemala, does the state have the monopoly of force; but in Juárez, as in Guatemala, there seems to be a common front between organized crime and the state. The dazzling absence of such a responsible institution—or the coalition between organized crime and the state—considerably raises the stakes and precludes or deters from the possibility of clarifying the crimes. The women of the writing collective bemoan the fact that there is no way of demanding precision in the data and its collection. To come to grips with an investigation of this nature is to walk right into the domain of the abject; it is to reenact the crime and not just to read about it in the media. Digging into the crime scenes takes us to the relationship between murdering women and sexuality, an aspect I will examine later in this chapter.

CULTURAL INTERVENTION IN PUBLIC LIFE

Feminists philosophers have declared that the biggest tension in modern thought is the separation of the public and private spheres. There is no place where this scission proves more defective that in Juárez. *El silencio,* a cultural text produced locally, not only hits the state internally but also erases the distinction between public, private, and political, moves towards the intimate, and unveils the predicament of a defenseless maternity that is besieged by *maquila* forms of labor, by the cultures of profits and markets, and by perverse forms of sexuality that constitute the exercise of power of a terminally wounded masculinity.[8] What is the effect and political impact of this type of cultural intervention? One answer is that this cultural text intervenes in public life by expressing the consensual opinions, complaints, and unhappiness of a concerned and disturbed literate citizenry that speaks in favor of people who have been totally stripped of all protection. Thus, the voices of other women support the young murdered women and their relatives, cover them with the mantle of maternal affect, and constitute writing in a forceful instance of the right to speak.

El silencio is a poetic, public discussion of the plight of poor women that articulates their public and private lives and marks the need for political action. The express purpose of the women's writing collective intervention is to explicitly reinstate the dignity of the murdered, who have been accused of having provoked their own deaths. The technologies of gender contribute to this task by throwing their academic and theoretical weight over these bodies to highlight how gender constitutes the politics of state exceptionalism, parenthetical democracy, and sovereignty as necropolitics.[9] It is simply wrong to override the juridical personality of the deceased. Therefore, the writers' intent is to rehumanize the young girls whose remains sometimes do not even allow for a reconstruction of their true semblance. This is only possible after death as a postmemory gesture, following Marianne Hirsch, in the testimonials of affect that their mothers extend to the truncated dreams of the murdered. These imaginary narratives clarify, deepen, humanize, and reposition women. It is in testimonials that they are excised from the criminal section of sensationalist newspapers and relocated in the intimate and affective narratives of subjectivity. The reconstruction of life and dreams bypasses complicity and negligence.

The writers of *El silencio* locate themselves in multiple positions: as researchers, accusers, detectives, and writers. They reconstruct the environment of the crimes and lay bare the essentials: not only the social, personal, and intimate intricacies of defenseless maternities, but also migrations, working schedules, and the realities of *maquila* labor. The introduction to the text lays out its method and offers a thumbnail sketch of the investigation. By way of juxtaposed presentations, the writers move in between personal and impersonal data, the specifics of the crimes, and life itself with its small actions and stories. Given that they are also concerned with the accuracy of data, serious archival work documents the concurrence of public institutions in the cover-up of the women's murders. Their reconstruction of facts takes on the function of supplement— to offer documentation to commemorate the lives of the deceased. The gross neglect of the organizations in charge of solving the cases does not pass unnoticed. *El silencio* speaks loudly and clearly about the criminality of the state.

From the above we can infer that, as a form of labor, the writing of cultural texts still commands credence and serves to disclose previously undisclosed and unknown pathways. It does not recoil from certain topics and is determined to visit issues that go to the heart of ungovernability. Cultural texts articulate the unspeakable or that which big media enterprises silence, and they straighten out the sensationalism of cheap news-media rags. Cultural production is still a sign of the partial functioning of the public sphere and civil society, and its interpretations are important in the critical revision of the political, if only because they underscore areas where consensus has not been reached and, more importantly, where disenchantment can turn into ungovernability and a relapse into natural society.

In the case of *feminicidio,* the authors of cultural texts present a common front by carrying the struggle against a mass event that can reach the whole of the community and spread beyond its borders. I have been arguing that the mass murder of women, *feminicidio,* is related to labor in all of its formal, informal, concrete, abstract, legal, and illegal forms, and that as a social event, the mass murder of women calls into question the orderly categories (some of which have already lapsed into either dogma or common sense) with which we are accustomed to reading social realities. So the authors of cultural texts have taken it upon themselves to narrate the different ways of perceiving mass crimes, and even of illustrating labor as the performance of mass crime, spreading all throughout the social body.

In a text like *El silencio,* we notice the series of strategies that organize multiple narratives of murder. This is not a text bound to begin with caveats, but rather one bent on wresting the evidence away from disqualifying and scathingly dismissive explanations. It is one that incorporates hard data, testimonials from the relatives of the murdered women, pictures, the names of each of the young girls, the contexts in which they were found, the causes of death, when each disappeared and when each was found, who is the presumed murderer, and the state of the investigation. The innocence of the murdered looms large in their views, and the writers deem it essential to lay out before us how political society is a network of points and affinities, nothing short of a litany of pollutions and impurities that mar justice.

The first two outstanding themes of *El silencio* are silence versus the desire to speak. And we ask: what type of silence do the writers have in mind, and what is the type of voice that can break it? The question springs from the fact that there is no silence in this text. On the contrary, it is full of voices and information. Silence, as I take it, is then the telling metaphor not of what has been suppressed but of what has been misspoken, of what has been stated incorrectly, of what those with power choose not to reveal. Silence is also the unheard voice. It is the voice without impact or resonance, the voice that is only noise, whisper, sound without signification, enunciation without content. After seeing the number of graphics and statistics, numbers that constitute the armor of the text, we can surmise that silence refers to the relation between words, language, and the law. Or is it rather that silence is a metaphor of the law that speaks in tongues?

That is, silence is not silence as we understand it ordinarily, but rather a metaphor for a dissonance, a misspoken word, lies. To break the silence, then, signifies the clarification of the language of the law and, with it, the censuring of the behavior of the institutions that it represents. To interfere with the word of the law is to break the silence and to contradict the government with the multiple voices of the bereaved. To break the silence does not mean then that other voices do not exist, but that a contradistinction can be established with them. Silence speaks to the position of the government and of justice regarding *feminicidio,* whereas the voices in the text belong to all of those speaking against it—there included the writers of the collective, together with the voices of the relatives that speak for the missing and murdered girls. Although all the voices together break the silence, the voice that I want to focus on here is the voice of the writers, because they are the ones who stand in the place of culture and against the state, for civil and against political society—in the sense proposed by Gramsci. After all, I am reading this type of investigation as a confrontation between the cultural, procitizen text and the legal, countercitizen texts, as a confrontation between the civil society and the state. The format of the text and its strategy constitute the breaking point of a silence that is rather a form of complicity, but complicity with or among whom?

From the very beginning, the burden of the text is a deliberation on method. The overall strategy is to move the reader from impersonal data and the characteristics of crime, to human life and rights expressed in the small aspirations, dreams, and desires of the murdered women. If the first move needs the archives to verify the data, the second leans on the ages of the missing and murdered women and the testimonials of their lives. In fact, the ages of the young girls are remarkable—some were only thirteen when their lives were brutally cut off. In documenting the facts, the writers verify the concurrence of institutions of civil society and the state in *feminicidio,* alongside the social vulnerability of the families. By dint of appeal, the authors articulate public and private spheres, which they call the two lines of thought, whose relationship they will make patent. However, it is hard to pry apart the two spheres, because both bring their weight to bear on the case. Life in general, public and private, is vulnerable, impoverished, always in a state of natural danger; public institutions are always deaf and mute to its cry. This vulnerability is what anchors the case to labor—*maquila* and traffics. One must never forget that most of the murdered women live in desolated places; in order to go to work they must get up at dawn to catch a bus, and they return to their homes at midnight. Thus, their daily movements occur under the shadow of danger, and they contend with overwhelming odds, occupying areas that Sergio González describes as the "geographies of danger."

Intellectuals concerned with the cases, as well as the families of the murdered women, offer some hypotheses as to how the abductions took place. They presume the abductions occurred at ordinary places, for example, at a shoe store where the assassinated women worked or went looking for a job, or simply visited to buy shoes. Many of the women were last seen near a shoe store or told their parents they were going to one. We can infer that these types of stores are meeting points or contact zones, borders, and that fake job advertisements or recommendations lure women there. The real advantage that such an establishment affords for criminal activities is that it is a public, inconspicuous type of small business that can have flexible working hours and go bankrupt without attracting anybody's attention. Thus, the places where contacts are obtained are mobile, changing, and unobtrusive. Shoe stores figure prominently in abduction narratives, but they also do in crime scenes, drawing particular attention not only to the cowboy style of dressing identified with a particular social sector, that of *'cheros* (rancheros) or *vaqueritos,* but also to the fetishism of shoes that underlies many of the crimes.[10] Shoes actually figure prominently in these narratives and can be read as signatures in a text.

Another recurrent supposition implicates bus drivers, if only because they transport workers from their neighborhoods to the *maquilas.* Buses run from very early in the morning to very late at night, putting drivers in an ideal position to kidnap women. They can act under the protection of twilight and have a good alibi in their work schedules. It is easy to surmise that drivers act as liaisons for the criminals. The same holds true for shoe-store employees, and both shoe-store employees and bus drivers are points of entry to the crimes in the bibliographies. Here we are already identifying an entire social sector of lower-middle-class workers who have a point of entry to the class, rank, and age of the murdered and missing.

The last supposition points directly to the labor center itself, the *maquila.* Parents always factor in the working hours of the murdered girls with regards to the circumstances of their assassination. This implicates, at the very least, the lower administrative echelons of the *maquila* in the crimes, because they are the ones that decide the time a woman reports for or leaves work. The record shows that in some instances, when the murdered woman and her family members worked the same shift, her schedule was changed with the presumed objective of isolating her at work and leaving her to fend for herself while she was there.

Three working sectors are thus directly implicated in *feminicidio:* bus drivers, small business employees, and the lower administrative rungs of the *maquila.* Here is where the track reaches a dead end. The young women and their families' testimonials reach this border of the night, of the city, of labor.

After that, a gigantic hermeneutical obscurity opens up. Nothing in their lives explains why they vanish; nothing can be constituted into a reasonable pre- or postabduction narrative. There are only series of interpretative hypotheses and suspicions. The most important hypothesis refers to a profile that is for purchase—young, poor, brown, slender, long hair, and of pleasant disposition. Their physical appearance and their labor data are all the information left before these women enter into nothingness. Before the abduction, everything is normal, quotidian: they go to work, ride a bus, go shopping. There is nothing unusual in their daily routines. Therefore, the abduction is a rupture, something rare, a case of estrangement that opens to all kinds of speculations. On the other side of this speculation is the state, the institutional bodies of law and order, the police, the judiciary system, local and regional states, and national and transnational governments. Everyday life is on one side of the border, and the state is on the other. In the midst, there exists a troubled public and civil sphere.

This details the practices of those who establish crime and of those who drive women to and from work. Here I cannot help but remember that one of the putative gangs involved in the murders are "Los Choferes," a gang that takes its name from bus drivers, from "*rutas*," the name given to public transportation in Juárez. It would not be too swift a conclusion to presume the collaboration between schedulers and drivers; the twin positions provide a valuable warrant that accounts for the disappearance of women. But where they take them and what they do with them is a matter of total conjecture. My argument is that the young women and girls walk right into the twilight zone set up adroitly by industries of crime: drug traffic, the production of pornographic and snuff films, traffic of human flesh and organs inside or across the borders that rise in the shadows of *maquila* labor.

According to this hypothesis, the organization of labor is deeply implicated in these criminal acts, and it is the localization of crime at the heart of legal labor that warrants the invulnerability of the criminals. Has it reached this point yet? Yes, it certainly has. Political society and the development of capitalism with its current form of labor in the abstract, represented by the *maquila,* is the actual form of articulation of the state or political society that rules over the community as a totality—not the collapse of civil and political societies, but rather that of crime and politics. The most frustrating factor for elucidating the link between crime and politics consists in the difficulty of proving the direct link between legal and illegal forms of labor; yet we cannot disprove it either, and that is the space taken up by culture to debate the cases. In fact, after a long and serious investigation, Sergio González has summed it up by saying:

> Above all, the existence of hundreds of serial homicides against women in Ciudad Juárez, Chihuahua, is patent, a fact that seem to implicate, as Robert K. Ressler proposes, the participation of one or two serial killers, aside from common criminals. It perhaps could be the product of a sacrificial orgy of a misogynous bent whose victims are searched out and selected systemically (in streets, factories, commercial establishments, schools) within a context of protections or omission from Mexican authorities during the last decade. In particular, this protection comes from its police force, judicial functionaries that count on the support of a group of businessmen of the highest economic and criminal power all over the country. The general motive in question refers to a homicidal rite of sexual content that serves to coalesce, fraternize, and guarantee the silence of those who belong to the secret: a very influential mafia. The particular motive is perhaps a nonmotive, as Robert K. Ressler asserts: "the serial killer kills to kill, he does not usually have a particular motive." The guilty are free, and the innocent people are in jail.[11]

GAZING AT CUT-AND-DRIED BODIES OF WOMEN

To end this chapter, I veer away from state politics into the politics of subjectivities and subject formation and read the representation of murdered women in Juárez through the lens of psychoanalytic and scopic theories of vision, whose burden has been to explain enjoyment in the performances of horror and pornography. I consider the possibilities of psychoanalytic analysis where murder, sexual pleasure, and perverse heterosexual masculinities coalesce as a supplement to liberal interpretations of public affairs and as an indicator of the limits of liberalism. What I try to accomplish with this very explosive material,

which requires a great deal of carefulness, is to put my readers in the three uncomfortable positions underscored by Renata Salecl's study of Jenny Holzer re-
viewed below: namely, that of the victim, that of the witness, and that of the
murderer, thus rounding out the material explored by *El silencio*.

My meandering here through the fields of Lacanian psychoanalysis has
to do with the fact that I could not find a way of connecting the behavior of
rapist-murderers to impunity, which is the loose end left by the women's collective of *El silencio*. I needed to relate the limits of liberalism, if not to a theory,
at least to an understanding of the subject produced by and performing under
such a situation of limits. The idea that perfectly sane (civil) human beings,
sheltered under the umbrella of *maquila* labor and covered by a criminal state,
performed atrocious forms of rape, torture, and murder did not square with
me. The aesthetic composition of the pictures taken of murdered women
found in the desert, the pleasure that both the murderer and we distantanced
onlookers experience in gazing at them—this gave me an opportunity not
only to reflect on the morbid satisfaction of looking at actual cut-and-dried
human bodies, but also an entrance into the realm of works relating lust and
murder, primal desire and primal fear—for me, a daunting marker of the shift
from modern to postmodern forms of labor. Renata Salecl's study of Jenny
Holzer examined below is one of them.

The pleasure of horror and pornography allow me to extrapolate Salecl's
reading of the Lacanian notion of the Big Other as a waning authority to that
of a withering liberal state. Her notion of choice as related to psychosis was also
useful in explaining the predicament of subjects encountering limiting situations and epistemological disorders that obfuscate. Putting together the concepts of a waning Big Other, a withering state, and psychosis and psychotic
behavior opened a way into the hearts and minds of rapist and torturing killers.
There is no question that a criminal society deeply disturbs the subject, who
sees him/herself either permanently in a double bind or cast adrift in a free-for-
all situation. Taking the risk of viewing the representation of murdered and
tortured women as art opened the gates to the psychology of the perpetrators,
whose own desire so much troubled the women's writing collective of *El silencio,* who looked at them solely from the point of view of state politics. It is in

this context that I consider Lacanian psychoanalysis an addenda to the crisis of liberalism.

A close look at a famous and very controversial picture of one of the women murdered in Juárez, taken by Jaime Bailleres, can serve as an example.[12] In that picture we cannot tell with any degree of certainty the gender of the representation. We cannot tell if it is the seared face of a man or of a woman. In my first looking at it, this was the head of a woman. In my mind, I could bring her to life and recompose her image. Over the charred head, I reconstructed a bundle of tight curls. In her eyes, I saw a heavy coat of mascara. The purple color of her full lips recalled the tones of dark lipstick. The oval face and the light striking her right cheek turned death by torture into something beautiful. And the multicolored scarf of earth tones, wrapped around her neck, established a contrast with the light that enhances the beauty of horror. This was in part my own work and in part that of the photographer, Jaime Bailleres, whose angle of vision lures me to look at this cut-and-dried face with the eyes of aesthetics. Viewing it with her murderer's eyes, I surmised that in the posture of this parched head and in her opened eyes and mouth agape he might have seen the spasm of orgasm rather than the wince of pain in her coming face-to-face with the horror of her imminent death.

Although the comparison of murder and art is very polemical in the case of *feminicidio,* in looking at this picture it is impossible to erase the aesthetic intention and visual pleasure of the photographs, of the medium itself, and of our gazing eyes that find themselves caught in a bind.[13] Do we enjoy the pictures or reject the social environment they represent? Charles Bowden has remarked on the tension between aesthetics and crime in the following, often-misread, quote. Speaking about the power of the above image he writes,

> Jaime Bailleres has projected a beautiful black carved mask on the screen. The head is tilted and the face smooth with craftsmanship. The hair is long and black. It takes a moment for me to get past this beauty and realize the face is not a mask. She is a sixteen-year-old girl and they found her in the park by the Puente Libre linking Juárez to El Paso, Texas. . . . The skin has blackened in the sun, the face has contracted as if mummified. She was kidnapped, raped, murdered. Jaime explains that the newspaper refused to publish this photograph. The reason for this decision is

very loud: the lips of the girl pull back, revealing her clean white teeth. Sound pours forth from her mouth. She is screaming and screaming and screaming.[14]

This is, I gather, the predicament of what the postmodern calls the aesthetic sublime, which is the convergence in the same time and place of intense sensations of beauty and extreme fear.[15] This is also the power of the visual image, what André Bazin observes as the obscenity of unbearable truths, such as those we have been studying here.[16] Freud expressed the extrapolation of contradictory but equally intensive feelings in the word *unheimlich,* "the name for everything that ought to have remained . . . secret and hidden but has come to light," a representation of the unconscious and the emergence of the repressed, which has to be factored in in *feminicidio* as the trauma of a wounded masculinity that kills.[17] Julia Kristeva speaks about the *unheimlich* as the power of horror and the sense of the abject, a bodily sensation of revulsion, coupled with a strong desire for something the subject lacks.[18] Stephen Greenblatt compares the sensation with the power of a heart attack, as did Homi Bhabha in his theorizing of the postcolonial subject.[19] All of these concepts convey the experiences of first encounters with the new, strange, and unfamiliar; all express the mixture of desire and revulsion, craving and panic to know that accompanies the first sight and feelings that pervades the visual images of *feminicidio.* The following long and rough passage in Bowden conveys, I believe, the meaning of all these concepts underlining abject social practices:

I want to know about *over there.* I want to know the smell of the streets at 2 a.m., the taste of the whore under the streetlight, the greasy feel of the juice rolling down my chin from the taco bought at a stand near dawn. . . . I want to go home . . . and turn on the radio, eat some beans, and feel the fatigue in every cell. I want to feel the power of a .45 automatic tucked inside the belt of a paunchy Mexican federal cop as he sits in the hotel bar staring me down with contempt and malice. There is more but you get the idea: across the river and into the flesh.[20]

In Bowden's book, the pictures of bodies approach the representation of the abject. At first glance, the photographers documenting his story (Bailleres is among them) trudge the blurred and frail border that brings together Eros and Thanatos, primal desire and primal fear. The bodies represented in the pictures are at times the image of debris, the refuse that belongs in dumping grounds—young women workers treated as trash. There is a picture of a woman, found already in a state of decomposition, bloated, one leg bent backwards, her T-shirt covering only half of her breasts, her arms raised. This is such a composite and contradictory image that it constitutes an entryway into the psychology of a very troubled, wounded, and psychotic masculinity that permits us to peak into the fantasies of *lustmord,* the necrophiliac pleasure that lifts the shirt to show just half the woman's breasts, while he/they torture her, in the style of a model posing for a centerfold piece of a pornographic magazine. I know we don't want to entertain these thoughts, but the pictures of murdered women in Juárez, alongside the narratives about their ways of dying, lend credence to these readings more appropriate to the fantasies of horror film scenes. The pose makes us hear her killer advising her under threat to lift her arms before she is being hacked or raped by many, before dying. The bloated belly of death adds drama by suggesting an advanced state of pregnancy and contradicts the pose, placing the reader in quite an uncomfortable bind. Her sex, a dried-out piece of flesh clung to her wound, totally exposed, becomes a mere metonym of rape. What kind of mise-en-scène can we picture for this image? What kind of absolutely perverse affect enters into the capturing, torturing, raping, killing, and posing of this woman? What kind of intentionality and purpose, what kind of desire does it evoke in the photographer, the onlookers, in myself writing this piece? Undoubtedly, there is something erotic suggested in the positioning of the bodies as taken in the pictures, as there is in the representation of a truly maddening social development that speaks loudly about limits, such as the pleasure of inflicting pain, the killing at the moment of pleasure, the pleasure of torturing women—*lustmord.*

In snuff films, about which I will have more to say shortly, Sergio González suggests that women are beheaded so the body seizure produced by the occlusion of blood flow magnifies the pleasure of the orgasm of the rapist/serial killer and, vicariously, of the film audience. For us, scholars, this pleasure is permitted in theory, fiction, and art, but not in real life. In real life, we don't want to think or talk about it, right? However, the killing of women in Juárez and the illustrations of these murders in photographs all over the place situate us all, in a minor key, in exactly the same position as the executive voyeurs watching a movie where a woman is killed so that they get excited and fantasize about taking the place of the rapist in the film. So, the question is: why are representations of killed women pleasurable?

Psychoanalytical criticism of postmodern art and culture, along with theoretical works on horror films and pornography, provide readers with venues to answer some of these questions. In the psychoanalytical arena, Renata Salecl has explored the articulations of sex and death. In her article on Jenny Holzer, Salecl analyzes Holzer's project *Lustmord,* which relates sex and violence and illustrates the feeling of lust in a rapist. Holzer uses cropped photographs of texts, written on naked skin, whose messages underscore the juxtaposition of death and sex. Some of these messages are: "She fell on the floor in my room. She tried to be clean when she died but she was not. I see her trail." "With you inside me comes the knowledge of my death," "The color of her where she is inside out is enough to make me kill her." But what is most generative in Salecl's piece on Holzer for our reading of Juárez's pictures of murdered women is her suggestion that "Holzer presents in *Lustmord* three completely different viewpoints of a rape: that of the perpetrator, the victim, and the observer. It is crucial here that one cannot discern from which position the artist . . . herself speaks. One can guess that she speaks simultaneously from all three positions —and from none of them."[21] The question here is if the primal erotic is the position of the voyeur/observer—or reader, cameraman, artist—is it also the position of the torturer? To the degree that it is an eroticized gaze, the positions may be said to converge, but then the other question is, what is then the position of the victim? I think the representations of the murdered women in Juárez raise the same questions by situating the viewer/reader in the same positions, although scholars are reluctant to acknowledge it.

To answer this question Salecl invokes the category of the Big Other, which in our analysis can be juxtaposed to that of the state in that both invoke the presence, absence, erasure or betrayal of authority—that is, a situation of limits. In Lacanian theory, Salecl tells us, the Big Other/Authority does not actually exist, but it functions because people need that figure for their own self-perception, to create a self-binding mechanism to feel content in their choices. The Big Other is thus an invented, consistent structure which alleviates anxieties in the face of choices.[22] Thus, in Salecl, as in Juárez, the erasure/betrayal of the Big Other stands for the impotence or absence of authority—a place where artwork (*Lustmord*) and mass murder (*feminicidio*) dovetail, and where psychoanalytic categories of analysis come to explain what liberalism does not. In both cases, authority (moral, psychological, or statist) no longer holds sway over the subject. The absence or crisis of authority calls into question the place of the subject in contemporary society and forces a complete makeover of all the different relationships the subject holds with the symbolic and legal order. Consequently, one of the biggest effects of this erasure/betrayal is theoretically that the subject loses all his moorings and becomes psychotic. Here psychotic is understood "as people for whom social prohibitions have not been operative in the same way as they were, for example, for neurotics. . . . Psychotics are thus people who have their own very special view of reality. . . . Such individuals often function perfectly well for long periods of time until a small event in their life triggers a full-blown delusion."[23]

This is a powerful insight, because the erased point of view of the Big Other/Authority (in our case, the state) as related to social psychosis not only explains the pleasure of horror, *Lustmord,* but also constitutes a good hypothesis for explaining *feminicidio* in Juárez. In no other way can we understand the discussion of satanic practices performed during the killing of women discovered in Rancho Santa Fe or in more transnational cases such as snuff-film production. These practices evince the overbearing presence of social psychosis in that city at the same time that they underscore the conversion of eroticism into crime and crime into labor, trade, and profit. The role and place of the police is key here in two ways: first, they seem to easily destroy the evidence that connects eroticism, murder, labor, law, and justice; and second, they represent state authority, what the cultural refers to as impunity—or the absence or betrayal thereof. An extreme case of these social performances is represented by the industry of porno-violence of snuff films.

Snuff films are clandestine productions that yield considerable profits. They produce the actual performance of a crime with specific erotic purposes in mind. In regards to this production, Sergio González tells us, "When the images began to roll past, this is what you saw on the screen: 'two men were having sex with a young woman with black hair. . . . The woman's head hung over the edge of the bed while the man that was on top of her was penetrating her. The other man holding the blade knelt near the head of the woman. In a second everything was over. Spectators paid $1500 to watch the video.'"[24] Clearly, the climax of the film and of masculine orgasm converges in the act of slitting the woman's throat. Now, the question is, how to read this production? Are we located, as Salecl claims for Holzer, in the three positions of killer-rapist, observer, and victim and at once in none of them? Do we find ourselves before a work of art, as witnesses to a crime, as participants in a voyeuristic act, or all of the above? Is this a legal or an illegal form of labor?

Here is where scopic theories come to our assistance in the rearticulation of lust, labor, and murder.[25] In providing new models of vision, a newly corporealized immediacy of sensations and a rupture with previous codes, scopic theories blur the boundaries between body and machine and produce an amalgam of heterogeneous perceptions and different concepts of subjects. These new models enable, and even promote, the coalescence of an amalgam of heterogeneous perceptions, including the sadistic pleasure in horror: that is, viewing (and even paying to view) the murder of women as art or the performance of libidinal desires and fantasies with corpses. Seeing beauty in horror currently breaks down the idea of idealized selves that are separated from their object and the acceptance of the great variety of optical principles, and of all image-producing gadgets that practice constructing and deconstructing bodies. Judging by the availability of these films in marketplaces all over the world, this is good business, a profitable enterprise that provides excellent revenues. In films, lust is virtual, mediated by gadgets and special effects; in the case of Juárez, it is a live performance. Horror (and porno) films also imply a transition from high forms of art to a low type of realism—in representation, tastes, and consequently, markets—and more importantly, an observer with a high tolerance or desire for the macabre, one which is capable of disengaging sensations from a referent.

In scopic theories, the past is no longer tethered to the present or the future and spectators can now, with the mediation of visual technologies, move to a different time and place, to a different brand of sensibility without moving an inch from their own computers. Williams writes that Abigail Solomon-Godeau "maintains that the codes that characterize [the continuum between erotic show and hardcore event] are governed by a shift from a conception of the sexual as an activity to a new emphasis on specularity."[26] We like to see; we enjoy seeing, as in the case of scopophilia studied by Laura Mulvey.[27] Williams herself sustains that "while the psychoanalytically derived models of vision . . . have enabled the analysis of certain kinds of power—the voyeuristic, phallic power attributed to a 'male gaze'—they have sometimes crippled the understanding of diverse visual pleasures despite the importance and prevalence of the very term pleasure in them." This means subjects are very capable and willing to enjoy horror and the abject; they are ready to seek it and to find it; they are willing to pay for it. She then calls for the elaboration of "a model of vision that can explain pleasurable sensations that are primary to the experience of viewing images without . . . judging them as either perverse or excessive."[28] This is a theory of a subjectivity that is multiply positioned and of a subject whose gaze is disengaged and for whom authority and legitimacy have vanished—the Big Other is suddenly gone, any type of authority omitted. Distance from self and from others also accounts for the sadistic pleasure of real rapists, abductors, torturers, and killers in Juárez.

In tandem with this vision, Salecl tackles the question of choice. She believes that "postmodern subjects, no longer accepting the power of institutions or society to fashion their identity, often experiment with the power of self-creation, perhaps in the form of exploring different sexual identities or transforming their appearance, becoming 'works of art.' That is the range and nature of choice. However, in the process of the subject breaking free from the Big Other, one can also observe the subject's anger and disappointment in regard to the Big Other."[29] Thus, art, criminality, and a scopic and psychoanalytical performance commingle and become clear as mud in the case of *feminicidio*. Julia Estela Monárrez states, "'Sexual crime' could be defined and is present in the cases in which the murderer or murderers are motivated by sadistic sexual impulses, and the victim becomes a sexual object for the victimizers. In this relation, man would represent the 'subject, the real and essential,' while woman is reduced to the 'other, irreal, the nonessential.' Thus, to appropriate feminine sexuality, to torture and dispose of the body are parts of a strategy of gender that converts crime in a form of eroticism."[30]

Juárez is the meeting point of diverse types of subjectivities, the locus of a superimposition of historicities produced by the incessant flow of migrants coming from different stadiums of modern development, forming what Lyotard calls clouds of sociability. These migrants that come to the border are uprooted people who in Juárez are immediately immersed in a society governed by a *maquila* logic characterized by optimal performance. This logic erases all the traditional community signs of authority and disorients the subject, making it prone to psychosis. Living on the border also furthers this incessant sea change–producing disorientation regarding choice. Like borders, subjects are fluid, flexible, and disoriented, and *maquiladoras* are the accelerating devices that subtend the movement of subjectivities from communal to industrial to postmodern.

For young women who "choose" to migrate, *maquila* logic pushes them into spaces and times that were socially and traditionally assigned to men. Thus, women take over formerly masculine spaces and times at their own risk, with no supporting network or safety net to facilitate their transition. There is only a long, empty, and threatening corridor between the *maquila* and home. Leaving the house at dawn, returning in the middle of the night, walking through dark and empty streets, parks, or neighborhoods, riding an empty bus, not to mention the journey from southern to northern Mexico—all are inescapable conditions of the "forced choice" to work.

Men resent women's emancipation and oscillate between punishing them and enjoying their freedom. Punishment and enjoyment, primal pleasure and primal fear, are moods and actions corresponding to this double and contradictory articulation of fluid, sadomasochistic subjectivities. *Maquiladoras* benefit from this incessant flux of subjects and subject formation, and push hard towards maximum performance and cost reduction. Thus, in no way or manner does *maquila* logic enable the common good; it rather subtends the social evil, one of the side effects of which is the destruction of bodies, be it in the form of lowering costs of production or in the direct killing of women. The limit of *maquila* logic is the human body and its destruction. Thus, labor in the abstract, which in Hegel's philosophy is the condition for moving from civil to political society, is either aborted, or politics becomes the playing field of crime.

Maquila labor is legitimate, but it comes coupled with other forms of illegitimate labor that bloom in its shadow and that present themselves as partial forms of free and temporary contracts. They are the so-called black rubrics or traffics that are conjoined to large local, national, and transnational networks and are supported and covered over by the state. The killing of women in Juárez, their frequency and "normalcy" indicate that the traffic of human flesh is an ordinary postmodern scene; that it is a traffic of young women that grow younger and younger as the perversity of lust and profit grows and mutates, underscoring a set of emerging sensibilities and subjectivities. Robert K. Ressler, the expert on serial killers, believes that *feminicidio* could be the product of the traffic of organs, the traffic of images and porno-violence, sacrificial rites, or quarrels between gangs and *polleros* (smugglers of people across the border). What I add is simply the daring claim that "traffics" are postmodern forms of labor, and the stylistics of death a very lucrative business, one that accounts for *feminicidio*. Cultural workers agree that the culprits are the character of the state, the nature of labor, the complicity of the ruling and parallel forces, but also the twin evils of crime and impunity, crime and art, crime and sexuality. To me, danger coupled with impunity serves as aphrodisiac to murderers. Things being the way they are, I must conclude that the production, processing, and representation of death—criminal, artistic, or forensic—is an organic part of the new state of capitalism, yet another example of necropolitics. To understand this sea change in sensibility, sexuality, and production requires a visit not only to the common places of death and collective killings—the massive common burial grounds and graves—but also to the more legitimate, new, and vast universe of the culture and ideology of democracy and the theories of the state at the limits of liberalism.

epilogue

Essentially Contested Concepts
and Innocent Spaces

If women have a role to play . . . it is only in assuming a negative function:
reject everything finite, definite, structured, loaded with meaning, in the
existing state of society. . . . A feminist practice can only be . . . at odds
with what already exists so that we may say "that's not it," and "that's still
not it."

> Julia Kristeva, Nancy Hirschmann, and Christine Di Stefano,
> "Revision, Reconstruction, and the Challenge of the New"

In modern philosophical thought and European political practice and
imaginary, the colony represents the site where sovereignty consists
fundamentally in the exercise of a power outside the law.

> Achille Mbembe, "Necropolitics"

IT IS IMPORTANT to acknowledge the contributions of Enrique Dussel,
Iris Marion Young, and Achille Mbembe to the criticism of liberalism and
modern reason. These three thinkers excavate the occult sites of Western philosophy, radically questioning their social integrity and viability and obstinately

pointing to their flawed logic as ways of recognizing liberalism's ethical obligation to unassimilable Otherness—Dussel in his reconsideration of modernity from its underside, Young in her all-out offensive against liberalism's "innocent spaces" and "essentially contested concepts," and Mbembe in his redefinition of sovereignty as necropolitics, the power to decide who lives and who dies. They are eager to expose the aporias of modern thought so that the gates are opened to other constituencies—women, ethnic groups, and the poor. Dussel, Young, and Mbembe keep modernity under siege on the theoretical, political, and cultural fronts by asking Western philosophy to respond.

Feminist criticism's radical examination of what its theorists call "essentially contested concepts"—power, freedom, rights—has made it possible for me to understand the chasm between proper and improper conceptual environments. These thinkers, like us, take the realization of a lack of fit between concepts and the social real as their point of departure. Their claim is that political philosophy's foundational concepts don't fit women; consequently, the blueprint they offer for political analysis is flawed. Foundational concepts are grounded "on a vision of humanity that is historically specific and consistently exclusive in terms of class (propertied), race (white), sex (males), and gender (masculine subjects)."[1] Therefore, for each one of the exteriorities, to use Dussel's term, multiple adjustments are due. This is a tough recall of the political, very much in line with the gesture of this text. From feminists reflections we have taken their robust impulse for democratizing the foundational notions and scrutinizing the "innocent space" to encompass the excluded. Their analysis was particularly helpful in reading Rigoberta Menchú's discussion of civil society and in explaining the gap between publics and subaltern counterpublics in Menchú's uses of civil society. It was also insightful in explaining the tension between public and private in our exploration of the murder of women in Juárez.

One of the most important voices in this regard is Iris Marion Young's. She responds to some of the antinomies raised by multicultural philosophers such Will Kymlicka and Charles Taylor, and philosophers of justice such as John Rawls, examined in chapter 1 of this book. Her intervention can be read as a critique of liberalism's lack of ethical obligation to unassimilable Otherness. In particular I am interested in rehearsing her concept of justice, because she addresses questions relative to institutionalized domination and oppression not generally considered in standard and ordinary theories, which "tend to restrict the meaning of social justice to the morally proper distribution of benefits and burdens among society's members."[2] Hers is a position against the so-called distributive paradigm, for it limits itself to the allocation of material goods—things, resources, income, wealth—or the distribution of social positions. Public discussions on justice focus on inequalities of wealth and income, conceptualize issues of justice in terms of patterns, disregard processes, and, in taking the individual as the basis for all discussions, erase the importance of social groups and ignore their input. Concerning Young's intervention, I want to highlight her identification of nonmaterial, immeasurable quantities and intangible goods, such as self-respect, equal opportunities, and free speech, that are never discussed in debates on justice, and her critique of predominant approaches to justice that assume and accept current relations of production and distribution of wealth and justice, family structures, legal frameworks, and specific institutionalities that establish norms—as is the purpose of a text like *El silencio* examined in the previous chapter of this text, which identifies the criminals and reconstructs the lives of the murdered women to "save their dignity."[3] Young revisits the concept of justice to include agency and difference, "to displace talk of justice that regards persons as primarily possessors and consumers of goods to a wider context that also includes action, decisions about action, and provision of the means to develop and exercise capacities. The concept of social justice includes all aspects of institutional rules and relations insofar as they are subject to potential collective decision."[4]

Young's criticism of the distributive paradigm is that it does not take structural issues such as equality or inequality of wealth and income, division of labor, class relations, and power into account. In fact, theorists of justice rarely consider that the "decision-making structure operates to reproduce distributive inequality and the unjust constraints on people's lives," structures that Young labels "exploitation and marginalization."[5] The point, then, is to evaluate the social structure and not its distributive outcome. Justice concerns the distribution of rights and duties, both tangible and intangible; rights are institutionally defined rules that specify pertinent and permissible social relations. Rigoberta

Menchú's discussion of millenarian cultures and the right for them to be considered part of human knowledge would certainly be thought of as a call for justice. And Young and Menchú would certainly endorse Agnes Heller's shift from distribution to participation, deliberation, and decision making: "Justice is primarily the virtue of citizenship, of persons deliberating about problems and issues that confront the collectively in their institutions and actions, under conditions without domination or oppression, with reciprocity and mutual tolerance of difference. . . . For a norm to be just, everyone who follows it must in principle have an effective voice in its consideration and be able to agree to it without coercion. For a social condition to be just, it must enable all to meet their needs and exercise their freedom; thus justice requires that all be able to express their needs."[6]

Oppression is systematic and institutional; it is a process of disabling and inhibiting people's skills in socially recognized settings. Domination structurally prevents people from directly or indirectly determining the conditions of their actions. Discussions on justice undertaken by Alfredo Molano's and Alonso Salazar's interviewees square with the contents of this thought. Recall the case of Doña Azucena, a woman tough as nails, who demands to be heard. What would it mean for her to have control over the rules and practices governing her own actions and the way she is treated within social contexts and relations? Doña Azucena is deprived from policymaking, from furthering her autonomy. She is historically deprived, Othered, and exteriorized, as Dussel puts it; she is a real nonbeing who, notwithstanding oppression, is nevertheless also an autonomous agent and can interpellate justice. We bear witness to that!

In bringing to the cultural scene the plight of the oppressed, this book participates in the discussion on practical ethics and ethical theory. Practical ethics is principally related to moral choices, those that affect others and should be assessed on moral grounds; ethical theories are efforts to reintroduce morality into social practice, to pinpoint moral criteria and their moral weight, and move us away from individual into communal gestures and interests by indicating which judgments are best.[7] Feminist ethics take a position against the gender blindness of a great deal of traditional ethical theory and, in so doing, join multicultural thinkers' agenda.[8] Ill-fitting concepts inflict damage on people, primarily when describing situations that are, in practice, not true—such is the case of Liberals and Conservatives (*recalzados* or *volteados*—"refitted" or "turncoated") in Molano's testimonials. Moving the questions across time, space, and frame, or simply reframing them, spotlights the main theoretical inconsistencies of liberalism that hurt people, leave them ill prepared to contemplate issues, and lead to educational deficits in critical thinking. Some of the work of social scientists bears this out.

Ethical theory concurs in intention with liberation philosophy, also an attempt to expose the underside of Western philosophy. If feminist criticism highlights the adversarial position between community, family care, the state, and procedural politics, and calls attention to private and public as the fundamental duality of the modern, liberation philosophy takes ethics beyond the concept of community into intercontinental relations and beyond the modern into the transmodern. It is concerned with the most impoverished peoples of the peripheral nations of capitalism, whom it considers "the historical subjects of their own liberation."[9] Dussel's discussion of ethics from the perspective of liberation philosophy engages the works of Paul Ricoeur, Emmanuel Levinas, and Charles Taylor, philosophers of "ethical life" and "authenticity." He zeros in on the interpellation of the oppressed: his term is *exteriority,* that which irrupts within the horizon of the totality. The discourse of the oppressed is the true counterdiscourse to hegemonic or "cynical" reason, be it as communication (Habermas), as community (Apel), or as solidarity (Rorty).[10]

Liberation philosophy denounces eurocentrism, the pretension of modern reason to universality, and attempts to overcome "the philosophy of consciousness or its egological dialectic."[11] Liberation philosophy aims to transcend modern and postmodern from the perspective of its underside, its occluded Other, and, in so doing, merges its concerns with those of Norma Alarcón, Gayatri Spivak, and Wahneema Lubiano, discussed in the second chapter of this book. They all ask the fundamental question: how does a new transmodern discourse "disclose itself" or allow itself "to be disclosed within the already given horizon of meaning? . . . How are new moral-ethical claims allowed to shatter and re-constitute perspectives that do not allow for them?" The agenda of liberation philosophy is to politicize ontology. The Other is the other face of modernity which has paid with its misery and its "'non-Being,' for the 'Being,' the primitive accumulation and successive suppressions of the 'happy' capitalism of the center." Liberation philosophy argues against imposing the model of late and central capitalism without discontinuities on peripheral capitalism; it argues against the subjectivity of the cogito, like Spivak, and against "the developmentalist fallacy [that] thinks that the 'slave' is a 'free lord' in his youthful state, and like a child ('crude or barbarian')."[12] This is when slaves are, truly, the "other-part" or the counterpart of the exploitative relation, or, as Mbembe puts it, a shadow.

For Dussel the question is, from where is the critic of liberation philosophy announced? And the answer is, from the Other of the dominating of rationality, from Molano's and Salazar's witnesses, who are not the negation of the negation, or negativity itself but a positivity; from living labor and from feminism:

> . . . from the active subjectivity of feminine corporeality as constitutive of Eros and not an "object" . . . from popular culture as creator of a "new" ideology and symbols. From the "positivity" of this affirmation the "negation of the negation" can be performed. Liberation Philosophy . . . is a positive philosophy. This movement beyond mere negative dialectics we have called the "analectical moment" of the dialectical movement—essential and belonging to liberation as affirmation of a "new" order, and not merely as negation of the old. . . .
>
> The dialectical passage moves between an order and another, and all the problematic of the rupture within the old (1); order as system of domination, by the praxis of liberation itself (2); and of the constructive moment of the new order (3).[13]

We have thoroughly engaged this dialectics when analyzing the plight of children and their mothers in Colombia as an affirmation of the exteriority of the Other and a critique of capital.

Let us now move to Mbembe's concept of necropolitics. Mbembe's work subjects Enlightenment concepts—primordially sovereignty, freedom, and the full subject, that which feminist critics call "essentially contested concepts"— to a severe scrutiny in order to demonstrate that all of them are predicated on necropolitics. Necropolitics is a reformulation of Foucault's concept of biopolitics —its underside, for it does not sufficiently account for contemporary forms of subjugation of life to the power of death. Necropolitics maps out some of the repressed topographies of cruelty that profoundly reconfigure the nature of political resistance, sacrifice, freedom, martyrdom, and terror by blurring the lines between them, such as have been rendered evident in Salazar's work on Pablo Escobar. Necropolitics and necropower manifest the sundry ways "weapons are deployed in the interest of maximum destruction of persons and the creation of death-worlds, new and unique forms of social existence in which vast populations are subjected to conditions of life conferring upon them the status of living dead."[14] Viewed under the magnifying glass of necropolitics, sovereignty is not the production of norms elaborated by free and full subjects capable of self-understanding, consciousness, and preservation whose project is politics (i.e., attaining consensual agreement among a collectivity of equals through public discussion and recognition) but the right to decide who lives and who dies.

This is no conspiracy theory but rather the simple recognition of the system's dialectical underside. Sovereignty underlies the politics of indigenous extermination Rigoberta Menchú rejects, as so do the struggles between Liberals and Conservatives in Colombia exposed by Molano, and *feminicidio* in Juárez denounced by women activists. Women in Juárez are murdered, as argued above, by the coalescence of the politics of the state and the politics of *maquila* labor that account for massive migrations of women to areas where they are unprotected by law and therefore submitted to the necropolitics of globalization. *Feminicidio* is, too, "the generalized instrumentalization of human existence and the material destruction of human bodies and populations."[15] In *feminicidio,* as in plantation societies, it is self-evident that gender and race establish the biological caesura that split humans from infrahumans, men from women, and make possible the concatenation of necropolitics, the state of exception, and the state of siege. Part of sovereignty is to consider the Other as an absolute danger, a real threat to life, hence, the politics of biological annihilation. Sovereignty underwrites the idea that the Other's disappearance greatly enhance my potential to life and security; that each man is the enemy of every other; that the lowest form of survival is killing.

All the historical narratives plotted in this text support Mbembe's claim. Within their specific differences, they resemble fascism, apartheid, and fundamentalism. The struggles between Liberals and Conservatives in Colombia bear a resemblance to Germany's politics of the "final solution," which made the racist, murderous, and suicidal state one. They also echo the Palestinian politics of territorial fragmentation that render physical movement a matter of life and death—not to speak of the Drug Enforcement Agency politics of "overwhelming or decisive force," supported by the might of military technology that shuts down the enemy's life-support system and inflicts enduring damages to the population for generations. These are some of the modern and postmodern samples of necropolitics rehearsed in the chapters of this book. But what is generative, as an idea, and totally compatible with the aim of this text is Mbembe's proposal that all the examples are premised on the practices of colonial imperialism and plantation economies, sites "where sovereignty consists fundamentally in the exercise of a power outside the law . . . and where 'peace' is more likely to take on the face of a 'war without end.'"[16]

Colonies are treated as frontier territories inhabited by savages, and savages are "a horrifying experience, something alien beyond imagination or comprehension. . . . [They] are . . . 'natural' human beings who lack the specifically human character, the specifically human reality, so that when European men massacred them they somehow were not aware that they had committed murder.'" They are the "non-being" supporting "being." Is this not the case of *sicario* children like Antonio today? In savages there is no ethical responsibility, no human bond. In plantations, the premise is the perpetual state of exception: "The slave is . . . kept alive but in a state of injury, in a phantom-like world of horrors and intense cruelty and profanity. . . . Violence here becomes an element in manners." In the plantation "there is certainly no grammatical unity of speech to mediate communicative reason," there is no reciprocity "outside of the possibilities of rebellion and suicide, flight and silent mourning." Such is, for me, the plight of the poor today. We all know the poor do not speak this language, but they certainly speak of justice in the sense of Young, affirm positivities in Dussel's sense, and live necropolitics as Mbembe describes them.[17]

In dire contrast and contradiction, truth and reason are one and the same for the full subject (Gayatri Spivak's "S" subject) of liberal political economy, and politics is the public practice of both. Key to individual autonomy is the exercise of reason, which is the same as the exercise of freedom. The romance of sovereignty is that the subject is the author of his own meaning, which he masters and controls through self-institution and limitation. This is the credo of the Enlightenment, the normative theories that set democracy and reason as the main pillars of modernity, which have little or nothing to do with the necropolitics of transmodernities. But so too are the political economies of statehood, which in the last thirty years have changed dramatically. States no longer claim a monopoly over violence or the means of coercion within their territory. War machines have taken it over; their relation to the space is mobile and their functions plural. These war machines are constituted by segments of armed men that split up or merge with one another depending on the tasks at hand. They are polymorphous and diffuse organizations, characterized by their capacity for metamorphosis—the DEA is an emblematic example of it, but so too are the guerrillas, the army, and paramilitaries in Guatemala, Colombia, and Mexico. In the postmodern world, the serialization of technical mechanisms and the integration of instrumental, productive, and administrative rationality have refined the art of killing to the point that killing the enemy of the state has become an extension of play—remember how the first Gulf War was presented as a video game? Contemporary wars are hit-and-run affairs and require new techniques for managing multitudes, an unprecedented form of governmentality that spatially immobilizes whole categories of people or scatters them across the winds.

The conflation of modernity, terror, and reason has only been examined recently, but their roots go as far back as the French Revolution, utopian thinking, and narratives of mastery and emancipation, most of which are explored, expanded, and worked upon by Western philosophy. Western philosophy provides a workable understanding of truth and error, error and crime, without for one moment bearing in mind the workings of necropolitics. The only time philosophers began considering the underside of modernity was in World War II, when necropolitics was applied to the "civilized" peoples of Europe. Procedures previously reserved for the "savages," such as the "subjugation of the body, health regulations, social Darwinism, eugenics, medico-legal theories on heredity, degeneration, and race" were practiced at home.[18] For sure, all academic disciplines back up necropolitics, closely binding identity and topography. The efforts of this text, as are those of all the voices quoted here, are small attempts to push these ideas to their limits. This is the wager of humanities critical theory. If utopia is the affirmation of *ouk-tópos,* of that which has no place, of the "non-being" who nonetheless has a reality, utopia is the sense that future projects, alternatives to the ruling order coming from the non-ruling order, are possible. This is what many of us seem to believe.

notes

Introduction

1. Ileana Rodríguez, *Women, Guerrillas, and Love* (Minneapolis: University of Minnesota Press, 1996).

2. Ileana Rodríguez, *House, Garden, Nation: Space, Gender, Ethnicity in Post-Colonial Latin American Literatures by Women* (Durham: Duke University Press, 1996); Rodríguez, *Women, Guerrillas, and Love.*

3. See Renata Salecl, *The Spoils of Freedom: Psychoanalysis and Feminism after the Fall of Socialism* (London: Routledge, 1994).

Chapter 1: *Cultures, Nations, Differences*

1. See Linda Kints and Julia Lesage, eds., *Media, Culture, and the Religious Right* (Minneapolis: University of Minnesota Press, 1998).

2. We notice today that the term "liberal" has become a warning sign enjoying not quite yet the status of communism, but certainly moving into the area of a disclaimer. Remember that during the 2004 presidential campaign, President George W. Bush flung the word "liberal" at John Kerry to signify he was not a trustworthy candidate. Liberal became synonymous with "flip-flopper" during that campaign.

3. See Rob Wilson and Wimal Sissanayake, eds., *Global/Local: Cultural Production and the Transnational Imaginary* (Durham: Duke University Press, 1996); John C. Hawley and Revathi Krishnaswamy, eds., *The Postcolonial and the Global* (Minneapolis: Minnesota University Press, 2005).

4. As Bill Clinton noted in an interview during the presidential campaign of 2004, a war that cannot be won must not be waged. When the forces on the other side are so strong that one party cannot dominate the other, there is a need of politics. This is the obverse side of Clausewitz's dictum of war as the continuation of politics by other means.

5. See Naomi Klein, "The Rise of the Fortress Continent," *The Nation,* January 16, 2003.

6. For no matter where the discussion pertaining to social, political, economic, or cultural issues takes place, and regardless of the historical and local circumstances at hand, liberal frames of reference are truly hegemonic. Liberalism has come to be part of the world's common sense. This fact documents the effectiveness of a philosophy when it becomes organic—after Gramsci—and preserves the unity of the entire social bloc. Hence, for new ideas to gain currency, they must engage with liberalism not as a political ideology, or as a philosophy of rights, but as natural common sense—an engagement which politics always guarantees. The distinction Gramsci draws is that "in philosophy the features of individual elaboration of thought are the most salient," while "in common sense . . . it is the diffuse, uncoordinated features of a generic form of thought common to a particular period and a particular popular environment." Nevertheless, "every philosophy has a tendency to become the common sense of a fairly limited environment. It is a matter therefore of staging with a philosophy which

already enjoys, or could enjoy, a certain diffusion, because it is connected to and implicit in practical life, and elaborating it so that it becomes a renewed common sense possessing the coherence and the sinew of individual philosophy . . .the relation between common sense and the upper level of philosophy is assured by 'politics.'" *An Antonio Gramsci Reader: Selected Writings, 1916–1935,* ed. David Forgacs (New York: Schocken Books, 1988), 331–32.

7. Three books that speak about this conundrum are Giovanni Arrighi, *The Long Twentieth Century: Money, Power, and the Origins of Our Times* (London: Verso, 1994); Antonio Negri and Michael Hardt, *Empire* (Cambridge, MA: Harvard University Press, 2000); and Walter Mignolo, *Rethinking the Colonial Model* (Oxford: Oxford University Press, 2002).

8. See Michael Walzer, "Comment," in *Multiculturalism: Examining the Politics of Recognition,* ed. Amy Gutmann (Princeton: Princeton University Press, 1992), 99–103.

9. Stuart Hall, "Variants of Liberalism," in *Politics and Ideology,* ed. James Donald and Stuart Hall (Milton Keynes: Open University Press, 1986), 34.

10. Benjamin Arditi, *Politics on the Edges of Liberalism: Difference, Populism, Revolution, Agitation* (Edinburgh: Edinburgh University Press, 2007), 2.

11. Charles Taylor, "Politics and the Public Sphere," in *New Communitarian Thinking: Persons, Virtues, Institutions, and Communities,* ed. Amitai Etzioni (Charlottesville: University of Virginia Press, 1995), 183.

12. Hall, "Variants of Liberalism," 36.

13. See Étienne Balibar and Immanuel Wallerstein, *Race, Nation, Class: Ambiguous Identities* (London: Verso, 1991).

14. Walzer, "Comment," 99.

15. Achille Mbembe, "Necropolitics," *Public Culture* 15, no. 1 (2003): 11–40.

16. See Silvia Rivera Cusicanqui, *Oprimidos pero no vencidos: Luchas del campesinado aymara y quechua, 1900–1980* (La Paz: HISBOL, 1983); Clea Koff, *The Bone Woman: A Forensic Anthropologist's Search for Truth in the Mass Graves of Rwanda, Bosnia, Croatia, and Kosovo* (New York: Random House, 2004).

17. Hall, "Variants of Liberalism," 40.

18. Human rights are discussed in several manners: Michael Walzer discusses these rights within the distinction between societies and states, and Étienne Balibar within the relationship between nations and empires—these two distinctions, in turn, refer to Richard Rorty's philosophies of political pragmatism and to Charles Taylor's and Will Kymlicka's heterogeneity, multiculturalism, and multiethnicity that we will examine in more detail further on. Thus, whereas natural finds its context within states and empires, native is relative to groups, clans, hordes, tribes, or at the very best, societies and subaltern nations, rogue or failed states. See Michael Walzer, "Pluralism in Political Perspective," in *The Politics of Ethnicity* (Cambridge, MA: The Belknap Press of Harvard University, 1982), 1–28; Étienne Balibar and Emanuel Wallerstein, *Race, Nation, Class: Ambiguous Identities* (London: Verso, 1991); Richard Rorty, *Contingency, Irony, and Solidarity* (Cambridge: Cambridge University Press, 1989).

19. Ranajit Guha, *History at the Limit of World-History* (New York: Columbia University Press, 2002). In this piece, Guha eloquently argues for the history of people without history, in which he reviews Hegel's foundational philosophy of right, according to which history and state are coterminous.

20. See Michael Hardt, "The Withering of Civil Society," in *Deleuze and Guattari: New Mappings in Politics, Philosophy, and Culture,* ed. Eleanor Kaufman and Kevin Jon Heller (Minneapolis: University of Minnesota Press, 1998), 23–39.

21. Doris Sommer, *Foundational Fictions: The National Romances of Latin America* (Berkeley: University of California Press, 1991); Doris Sommer, *Proceed with Caution, When Engaged by Minority Writing in the Americas* (Cambridge, MA: Harvard University Press, 1999).

22. See Peter Hulme's discussion of Inkle and Yariko in *Colonial Encounters: Europe and the Native Caribbean, 1492–1797* (London: Methuen, 1986).

23. Part of the discrepancy between central and peripheral postcolonial writers can be read in an interesting exchange between Peter Hulme and Edward Kamau Brathwaite on the interpretation of Jean Rhys's *The Wide Sargasso Sea*. See Peter Hulme, "The Place of *Wide Sargasso Sea*," *Wasafiri* 20 (1994): 5–11; and Kamau Brathwaite, "A Post-Cautionary Tale of the Helen of Our Wars," *Wasafiri* 22 (1995): 69–78.

24. This is as an unfettered, primitive individual—a being that, in his natural needs of preservation and survival must compete with others to survive—which necessitates a concept of state to curb and regulate his primitive, natural dispositions, as in order to fend for himself and satisfy his natural needs, the individual must seek mutual protection in a social order that is established by its own will and on its own accord.

25. Hall, "Variants of Liberalism," 41.

26. Arditi, *Politics on the Edges*, 1.

27. Hall, "Variants of Liberalism," 49–50.

28. It is really not very clear if public and political spheres are two distinct spheres or just one. We know that the public sphere is part and parcel of civil society; however, it also partakes of political society, in that the public sphere is constituted as a corridor between civil and political societies. In this section I am taking them as separate. See Taylor, "Politics and the Public Sphere."

29. Taylor, "Politics and the Public Sphere," 185.

30. Ibid., 185–86.

31. Hall, "Variants of Liberalism," 43.

32. Feminism is to take these two questions to heart. See, for instance, Lauren Berlant, *The Queen of America Goes to Washington City: Essays on Sex and Citizenship* (Durham: Duke University Press, 1997).

33. Ibid., 184.

34. Taylor, "Politics and the Public Sphere," 190, 194, 193, 195, 186.

35. Ibid., 187. Liberalism presents itself as a total break with the historical and the meaning Taylor gives to "secular" captures it: "The eighteenth-century public sphere thus represents an instance of a new kind: a metatopical common space and common agency without an action-transcendent constitution, and agency grounded purely in its own common actions" (197). *Secular* means of the age, pertaining to profane time, a rejection of divine time: "Secularity is obviously related to this radically purged time consciousness" (198). Events exist in secular time. Simultaneity comes to be events utterly unrelated that are held together by their co-occurrence, vertical slices of time folding together the related and the unrelated.

36. Hall, "Variants of Liberalism," 42.

37. Will Kymlicka, *Liberalism, Community, and Culture* (Oxford: Clarendon Press, 1991).

38. Ibid., 169, 170.

39. See Antonio Cornejo Polar, *Escribir en el aire: Ensayo sobre la heterogeneidad socio-cultural en las literaturas andinas* (Lima: CELACP/Latinoamericana Editores, 2003); Edward Kamau Brathwaite, *The Development of Creole Society in Jamaica: 1770–1820* (Oxford: Claren-

don Press, 1971); Ralph Premdas, *Ethnicity and Elections in the Caribbean: A Radical Realignment of Power in Trinidad and the Threat of Communal Strife* (Notre Dame, IN: The Helen Kellogg Institute for International Studies, 1996); Ralph Premdas, "Race, Politics, and Succession in Trinidad and Guyana," *Modern Caribbean Politics,* ed. Anthony Payne and Paul Sutton (Baltimore: Johns Hopkins University Press, 1993), 98–124.

40. John Rawls, "Justice as Fairness" and "The Domain of Political Overlapping Consensus," in *Contemporary Political Philosophy: An Anthology,* ed. Robert E. Goodin and Philip Pettit (Cambridge: Blackwell, 1997), 187–202, 273–88.

41. Michael Walzer, "Critique of Liberalism," in Etzioni, *New Communitarian Thinking,* 66, 67.

42. Ibid., 67, 68.

43. Arditi, *Politics on the Edges,* 47.

44. Giles Deleuze and Felix Guattari, *A Thousand Plateaus* (London: Athlone Press, 1988); Jacques Rancière, *Disagreement: Politics and Philosophy* (Minneapolis: University of Minnesota Press, 1998).

45. Stuart Hall, "Pluralism, Race and Class in Caribbean Society," in *Race and Class in Post Colonial Society 1977,* ed. UNESCO (Paris: UNESCO, 1977), 153.

46. Ibid., 154, 158–59.

47. Ibid., 161.

48. Ibid., 164.

49. See, for instance, Marisol de la Cadena, *Indigenous Mestizos: The Politics of Race and Culture in Cuzco, Peru 1919–1991* (Durham: Duke University Press, 2000); Javier Sanjinés, *Mestizaje Upside Down: Aesthetic Politics in Modern Bolivia* (Pittsburgh: University of Pittsburgh Press, 2004).

50. Cornejo Polar, *Escribir en el aire.*

51. Ralph Premdas, "Public Policy in a Multi-Ethnic Caribbean State: The Case of National Service in Trinidad Tobago," *Journal of Ethno-Development* (1994): 76.

52. Arditi, *Politics on the Edges,* 3; Viktor Shklovsky, "Art as Technique," in *Literary Theory: An Anthology,* ed. Julie Rivkin and Michael Ryan (Malden: Blackwell Publishing Ltd., 1998), 15–21.

53. Charles Taylor, *Multiculturalism: Examining the Politics of Recognition,* ed. Amy Gutmann (Princeton: Princeton University Press, 1994), 39, 43–44.

54. Dinesh D'Souza, *The End of Racism: Principles for a Multiracial Society* (New York: Free Press, 1995); Joan Alway, *Critical Theory and Political Possibilities: Conceptions of Emancipatory Politics in the Works of Horkheimer, Adorno, Marcuse, and Habermas* (Westport, CT: Greenwood Press, 1995).

55. Enrique Dussel, *The Underside of Modernity: Apel, Ricoeur, Rorty, Taylor, and the Philosophy of Liberation,* trans. Eduardo Mendieta (New Jersey: Humanities Press, 1996); Walter Mignolo, *The Darker Side of the Renaissance: Literacy, Territoriality, and Colonization* (Ann Arbor: University of Michigan Press, 1995); Mignolo, *Local Histories/Global Designs.*

Chapter 2: *Western Texts, Indigenous Histories, Feminist Readings*

1. Rigoberta Menchú, *Rigoberta: La nieta de los Mayas* (Mexico City: El Pais/Santillana, 1998). Unless otherwise indicated, all translations are by Kathryn Auffinger.

2. Norma Alarcón, "Conjugating Subjects in the Age of Multiculturalism," in *Mapping Multiculturalism*, ed. Christopher Newfield and Avery Gordon (Minneapolis: University of Minnesota Press, 1996), 129;

3. Wahneema Lubiano, "Like Being Mugged by a Metaphor," in Newfield and Gordon, *Mapping Multiculturalism*, 66.

4. Hanna Arendt, *Between Past and Future: Eight Exercises in Political Thought* (New York: Viking Press, 1968).

5. Frantz Fanon, *Black Skin, White Masks*, trans. Charles Lam Markmann (New York: Grove Press, 1967); Jean-Paul Sartre, *Colonialism and Neocolonialism*, trans. Azzedine Haddour, Steve Brewer and Terry McWilliam (London: Routledge, 2001).

6. Jean-Luc Nancy, *Being Singular Plural*, trans. Robert D. Richardson and Anne E. O'Byrne (Stanford: Stanford University Press, 2000).

7. For a more complete and thorough discussion on the subject of particulars and universals, see Doris Sommer, *Proceed with Caution, When Engaged by Minority Writing in the Americas* (Cambridge, MA: Harvard University Press, 1999).

8. Alarcón, "Conjugating Subjects," 130, 132, 133.

9. Lubiano, "Like Being Mugged by a Metaphor," 64, 65.

10. Ibid., 69, 66.

11. Gayatri Chakravorty Spivak, *A Critique of Postcolonial Reason: Toward a History of the Vanishing Present* (Cambridge, MA: Harvard University Press, 1999), 272.

12. Rigoberta Menchú, *I, Rigoberta Menchú: An Indian Woman in Guatemala*, ed. Elisabeth Burgos-Debray, trans. Ann Wright (London: Verso, 1984). For a polemic on this text, see Arturo Arias, ed., *The Rigoberta Menchú Controversy* (Minneapolis: University of Minnesota Press, 2001).

13. *Ladino* is a term that invokes the presence of Spanish hegemony in the subject and the culture.

14. Menchú, *Rigoberta*, 30, 33, 34. In one passage of her book Rigoberta mentions the word *pul-ik,* and explains in detail that *pul-ik* "is a kind of food made out of pure seeds, condiments made from many kinds of seeds. It is a solemn food that one roasts for a long time and then grinds. It is a solemn food because it is made with a lot of patience. We call it *pul-ik* here. It is made from sesame seeds, winter squash seeds, *chilacayote* seeds, and gourd seeds. It has three kinds of seeds and that is why it is special . . . and chilies, three kinds of chilies, three kinds of tomatoes and a little bit of achiote." (33–34). Right after the word *pul-ik,* there is a footnote that, not withstanding Rigoberta's detailed explanation of the meal, simply reiterates what she has just explained. This footnote, however, presents itself as an addendum to Rigoberta's words, allegedly an authority to define meaning. It reads as follows: "also called *pulique.* It is a beef and vegetable stew with a lot of sauce. There are different ways to prepare this sauce, but essentially it is made from tomato, onion, garlic, pepper, cilantro or *apazote,* achiote and, naturally, chili. (Diccionario Quiche, Proyecto lingüístico Franciso Marroquín, Guatemala, 1996. From here on quoted as Marroquín)" (33).

15. See Friedem Schmidt-Welle, ed., *Antonio Cornejo Polar y los estudios Latinoamericanos* (Pittsburgh: Instituto Internacional de Literatura Iberoamericana, 2000); Ileana Rodríguez "Heterogeneidad y multiculturalismo: Discusión cultural o discusión legal?" *Revista Iberoamaericana* 66, no. 193 (Oct.–Dec. 2000).

16. For a thorough discussion on this subject, see Ileana Rodríguez, *Transatlantic Topographies: Island, Highlands, Jungle* (Minneapolis: University of Minnesota Press, 2005).

17. For a discussion on testimonial literature, see René Jara and Hernán Vidal, *Testimonio y literatura* (Minneapolis: Institute for the Study of Ideologies and Literature, 1986); Georg M. Gugelberger, ed., *The Real Thing: Testimonial Discourse and Latin America* (Durham: Duke University Press, 1996).

18. Menchú, *Rigoberta*, 334.

19. For a thorough discussion of the dangers of turning "difference" into another kind of essentialism, see Benjamin Arditi, *Politics on the Edges of Liberalism: Difference, Populism, Revolution, Agitation* (Edinburgh: Edinburgh University Press, 2007); Arditi, "El reverso de la diferencia," in *El reverso de la diferencia: Identidad y política,* ed. Benjamin Arditi (Caracas: Nueva Sociedad, 2000), 99–124.

20. See, for instance, the works of Daniel G. Brinton, *Library of Aboriginal American Literature,* vol. 1 (Philadelphia: Brinton's Library, 1882); Michael Coe, *The Maya Scribe and His World* (New York: The Grolier Club, 1973); Michael Coe, *The Maya* (London: Thames & Hudson, 1987); Munro S. Edmonson, *The Ancient Future of the Itza* (Austin: University of Texas Press, 1982). *The Book of Chilam Balam of Tizimin* (Austin: University of Texas Press, 1982); David Friedel, Linda Schele, and Joy Parker, *Maya Cosmos: Three Thousand Years on the Shaman's Path* (New York: William Morrow, 1993); Charles Gallenkamp, *Maya: The Riddle and Rediscovery of a Lost Civilization* (New York: Viking Rev. 1985); John S. Henderson, *The World of the Ancient Maya* (Ithaca: Cornell University Press, 1981); A. P. Maudslay, *Archeology-Biologia Centrali-Americana* (London: n.p., 1889–1902); Sylvanous G. Morley, George W. Brainerd, and Robert J. Sharer, *The Ancient Maya,* 4th ed. (Stanford: Stanford University Press, 1983); Linda Schele and David Freidel, *A Forest of Kings: The Untold Story of the Ancient Maya* (New York: Morrow, 1990); John L. Stephens, *Incidents of Travel in Central America, Chiapas and Yucatan,* 2 vols. (New York: Harper and Brothers, 1841); J. Eric S. Thompson. *The Rise and Fall of Maya Civilization* (Norman: University of Oklahoma Press, 1963); J. Eric S. Thompson, *Maya Archaeologist* (Norman: University of Oklahoma Press, 1963); J. Eric S. Thompson, *Maya History and Religion* (Norman: University of Oklahoma Press, 1970.

21. Menchú, *Rigoberta*, 336.

22. For a distinction between plural and multicultural or Creole societies, see my discussion on the works of Stuart Hall and Ralph Premdas in chapter 1 of this book; for a discussion of hybridity and the "underside of democracy" see Arditi, *Politics on the Edges.*

23. Alarcón, "Conjugating Subjects," 129.

24. Michael Warner, *Publics and Counterpublics* (New York: Zone Books, 2002); Lauren Berlant and Lauren Gail, *The Queen of America Goes to Washington City: Essays on Sex and Citizenship* (Durham: Duke University Press, 1997); Iris Marion Young, *Inclusion and Democracy* (Oxford: Oxford University Press, 2000); Iris Marion Young, *Justice and the Politics of Difference* (Princeton: Princeton University Press, 1990). I am particularly appreciative of Michael Warner's attempt to disengage the notion of "a" public from "the" public, as well as his countering of the claim that publics are contingent on state presences. However, in my view, Warner's notion of "the public" as discourse (text) existing only as "being addressed" responds to postmodern analyses based more on the modalities and logical figures of argumentation. I find his work very meticulous and his arguments very sophisticated and pertinent in the unraveling of hermeneutical tools that have become common sense and, in this regard, could be viewed under Benjamin Arditi's light of the underside of liberalism. However, my intention

in this essay is not in that vein. My aim is to juxtapose the common meanings of liberalism, liberalism as common sense, or liberalism as an imaginary political ideology, and the uses of these meanings that circulate in standard and modern Latin American social and cultural texts. In this sense, my engagement is not with the aporias of thinking. However much I appreciate efforts to relativize all hermeneutical tools of analysis, I am still swayed by Stuart Hall's dictum that the state can effectively bring semiosis if not to a halt, at least into clandestinity.

25. For an interesting contrast on the notions of hybridity in the Latin American field, see the works of Benajamin Arditi and Néstor García Canclini cited in this work. They provide two versions of the concept in the disciplines of political sciences and cultural studies. The use of the term in this book overlaps both.

26. Those interested in the civic organizations in Guatemala can consult http://www.peacebrigades.org/guate.html.

27. Menchú, *Rigoberta,* 284.

28. Craig Calhoun, ed., *Habermas and the Public Sphere* (Cambridge, MA: MIT Press, 1992), 2.

29. Nancy Fraser, "Rethinking the Public Sphere: A Contribution to the Critique of Actually Existing Democracy," in *Habermas and the Public Sphere,* ed. Craig Calhoun (Cambridge, MA: MIT Press, 1992), 116–17.

30. Ibid., 111.

31. Menchú, *Rigoberta,* 58–59, 159.

32. For a discussion on the difference between *oré* and *ñandé* in Guaraní, see Arditi, *Politics on the Edges,* 6; and Warner, *Publics and Counterpublics.*

33. Calhoun, *Habermas,* 7.

34. This disjunction opens up a vast gamut of discussions, from those related to the authority of disciplinary domains, which dictate the subjects a discipline is authorized to speak about, to the theories that address the performance of culture and identity, which dictate who litigates what for whom. I will speak to these questions later; here it is sufficient to acknowledge their presence in the discussion.

35. Renato Rosaldo, "Cultural Citizenship, Inequality, and Multiculturalism," in *Latino Cultural Citizenship: Claiming Identity, Space, and Rights,* ed. William V. Flores and Rina Benmayor (Boston: Beacon Press, 1997), 27–38.

36. Chela Sandoval, "Feminist Forms of Agency and Oppositional Consciousness: U.S. Third World Feminist Criticism," in *Provoking Agents: Gender and Agency in Theory and Practice,* ed. Judith Kegan Gardiner (Urbana: University of Illinois Press, 1995), 208–28.

37. Menchú, *Rigoberta,* 287.

38. Ibid., 197. See Jean Franco's argument on Deleuze's and Guattari's notions of the communal in primitive society, a notion than resembles Rigoberta's communal notion of the mother earth. Franco states that Deleuze and Guattari state that "in the primitive tribe, the socious is the mother earth." This notion is lost in the process of abstraction that takes place with the emergence of the despotic state. The interesting twist Franco gives to this notion is the power the family holds as a space of refuge and shelter in modern, bourgeois society. To me, this is an argument in favor of the counterpositions some old structures hold in modern society, the power of the traditional that for me can be applied to Rigoberta's defense of millenarian cultures' *creencias.* See Franco, "Killing Priests, Nuns, Women, Children," in *Critical Passions: Selected Essays,* ed. Mary Louise Pratt and Kathleen Newman (Durham: Duke University Press, 1999), 9–17.

39. See Arias, *Rigoberta Menchú Controversy.*

40. Rosaldo, "Cultural Citizenship."

41. Fraser, "Rethinking the Public Sphere," 121.

42. Guha, *History at the Limit of World History* (New York: Columbia University Press, 2002); Arditi, *Politics at the Edges;* Enrique Dussel, *The Underside of Modernity: Apel, Ricoeur, Rorty, Taylor, and the Philosophy of Liberation,* trans. Eduardo Mendieta (Atlantic Highlands, NJ: Humanities Press, 1996).

43. Menchú, *Rigoberta,* 338.

44. Ibid., 87–90.

45. As in all alternative models of civil society, the question for Gramsci involves how to handle the economic sphere, or to figure the place assigned to the economy in this model. So far the model is political and either presupposes a social democratic government that ensures that part of the social fund trickles down to the people, or an altogether different economic system.

46. Stanley Aronowitz, "Is a Democracy Possible? The Decline of the Public in the American Debate," in *The Phantom Public Sphere,* ed. Bruce Robbins (Minneapolis: University of Minnesota Press, 1993), 75–92.

47. For a discussion of the modern and postmodern in Latin America, see Beverley, Aronna, and Oviedo, *Postmodernism Debate in Latin America;* Hermann Herlinghous and Monika Walter, *Postmodernismo en la periferia: Enfoques latinoamericanos de la nueva teoría cultural* (Munich: Langer Verlag, 1994).

48. Carlos Franco, *Imágenes de la sociedad peruana: La "otra" modernidad* (Lima: Centro de Estudios para el Desarrollo y la Participación, 1991).

49. Fraser, "Rethinking the Public Sphere," 123.

50. Ibid., 125.

51. Arditi, *Politics on the Edges,* 8. For a very insightful discussion on multicultural rights, see Renata Salecl, *(Per)Versions of Love and Hate* (London: Verso, 1998).

52. See Rodríguez, "Heterogeneidad y multiculturalismo."

53. My point of departure is millenarian cultures and Menchú's secrets, and from there I will move on to cultural citizenship. But before I argue that point, let me make clear that a multicultural public sphere either presumes or requires multicultural literacy and respect. The point here is to look for what is common, what unifies. Menchú's proposal is that what unifies is respect for the *derecho de gentes.* Multicultural fora are among the best expressions of the public principle of having a plurality of perspectives on a given issue to discourage reified blocs. Publicity also enables people to participate in more than one public sphere.

54. Warner, *Publics and Counterpublics,* 119.

55. Ibid., 67–68, 73.

56. Ibid., 123–24.

Chapter 3: *Indigenous* Creencias, *Millenarian Cultures, and Counterpublic Persuasion*

1. Richard Rorty, *Truth and Progress: Philosophical Papers* (Cambridge: Cambridge University Press, 1998), 3:203; Jacques Rancière, *Disagreement: Politics and Philosophy* (Minneapolis: University of Minnesota Press, 1998).

2. Rorty, *Truth and Progress,* 205.

3. Ibid., 206–8.

4. Ibid. 214.

5. Scott Michaelson and David Johnson, *Border Theory: The Limits of Cultural Politics* (Minnesota: University of Minnesota Press, 1997), 26–27.

6. Menchú, *Rigoberta,* 123.

7. Doris Sommer, "No Secrets for *Rigoberta,*" *Proceed with Caution, When Engaged by Minority Writing in the Americas* (Cambridge, MA: Harvard University Press, 1999), 115–37.

8. Michel Maffesoli, "Identidades e identificación en las sociedades contemporaneas," in *El sujeto europeo* (Madrid: Editorial Pablo Iglesias, 1990); Gianni Vattimo, *The Transparent Society* (Cambridge: Polity Press, 1992).

9. See José Joaquín Brunner, "Notes on Modernity and Postmodernity in Latin American Culture," in *The Postmodernism Debate in Latin America,* ed. John Beverley, Michael Aronna, and Jose Miguel Oviedo (Durham: Duke University Press, 1995), 34–54.

10. Sommer, "No Secrets."

11. See Ileana Rodríguez, "Entre lo aurático clásico y lo grotesco moderno: La mayística moderna como campo de inversión y empresa postcolonial," in *Culturas imperiales: Experiencia y representación en América, Africa y Asia, 1850–1950,* ed. Ricardo Salvatore (Rosario, Argentina: Beatriz Viterbo Editores, 2005); Rodríguez, "Lugares minúsculos/grandes narrativas," in *Literatura de viajes: El viejo mundo y el nuevo,* ed. Salvador García (Madrid: Castalia, 1999), 287–97.

12. To have an idea of the range of the polemic around Rigoberta Menchú and her writings see Arias, *Rigoberta Menchú Controversy.*

13. For a discussion of ancient indigenous cultures as ruins see Quetzil Castañeda, *In the Museum of Maya Culture: Touring Chichén Itzá* (Minneapolis: University of Minnesota Press, 1996).

14. See my discussion on this subject in my book *Transatlantic Topographies: Islands, Highlands, Jungle* (Minneapolis: University of Minnesota Press, 2004).

15. See Astrid Ulloa, *The Ecological Native: Indigenous Movements and Ecogovermentality in Colombia* (London: Routledge, 2005).

16. Menchú, *Rigoberta,* 159.

17. Ibid., 185.

18. To better understand this argument against types and styles of multiculturalism, see Carlos Villa, *Worlds in Collision: Dialogues on Multicultural Art Issues* (San Francisco: International Scholars Publications, 1994); Coco Fusco, *English Is Broken Here: Notes on Cultural Fusion in the Americas* (New York: The New Press, 1995).

19. Cornel West, *Race Matters* (Boston: Beacon Press, 1993), 139; Renato Rosaldo, "Race and Other Inequalities: The Borderlands in Arturo Islas's Migrant Souls," in *Race,* ed. Steven Gregory and Roger Sanjek (New Brunswick: Rutgers University Press, 1994), 213–27; and Richard Rorty, *Contingency, Irony and Solidarity* (Cambridge: Cambridge University Press, 1989).

20. William V. Flores and Rina Benmayor, eds., *Latino Cultural Citizenship: Claiming Identity, Space, and Rights* (Boston: Beacon Press, 1997), 1.

21. Renato Rosaldo, "Cultural Citizenship, Inequality, and Multiculturalism," in Flores and Benmayor, *Latino Cultural Citizenship,* 37.

22. Warner, *Politics on the Edges,* 120–21.

23. Menchú, *Rigoberta,* 143–44.

24. Ibid., 143.

25. Ibid., 149.

26. Ibid., 149.

27. Ibid.

28. Ibid., 118, editorial interpolations in original.

29. Ibid., 121.

30. Ibid., 137.

31. Ibid., 338.

32. Ibid., 152, 153, 155.

33. An illustration of the imbalance between scientific knowledge and indigenous *creencias* when they come into conflict/dialogue can be seen in the 1998 film *Ya'ko'a'na* by Anh Crutcher. This film documents the marginalization of indigenous knowledge at the world ecological conference held in Rio de Janeiro in June 1992. Numerous indigenous groups, including the Xavante from Brazil, the Saami from Norway, the Ayta from the Philippines, the Monero from Australia, anticipate Menchú's belief system of communion with nature, but none of them sits at the conference table where the ecological problems of the planet are discussed. Although most of the indigenous *creencias* are validated by ecologists, indigenous communities do not even warrant a footnote. Now the ecologist speaks in the name of nature and of the different approaches to it. The ecologists' alternative points of view validate Menchú's mother's beliefs. In the film, the 109-point charter signed by the ecologists at the conference bears witness to how ecology takes over millenarian knowledges and, as Alarcón points out, translates them back to the modern epistemes of prestige. Whatever is produced in the past that serves for the future is snatched from the indigenous epistemologies and relocated in the Western text.

34. Walter Mignolo, Santiago Castro-Gómez, Catherine Walsh, and Freya Shiwy, eds., *Indisciplinar las ciencias sociales: Geopolítica del conocimiento y colonialidad del poder. Perspectivas desde lo andino* (Quito: Universidad Andina Simón Bolívar / Ediciones Abya-Yala, 2002).

35. Menchú, *Rigoberta,* 165; Hamid Dabashi, "No soy un subalternista," in *Convergencia de tiempos: Estudios subalternos/contextos latinoamericanos—Estado, cultura, subalternidad,* ed. Ileana Rodríguez (Amsterdam: Rodopi, 2001), 49–59.

36. Menchú, *Rigoberta,* 193, 196.

37. Ibid., 194.

38. Pat Seed, *Ceremonies of Possession in Europe's Conquest of the New World, 1492–1640* (Cambridge: Cambridge University Press, 1995).

39. Rawls, "Domain of the Political," 274.

40. Flores and Benmayor, *Latino Cultural Citizenship,* 69.

41. Menchú, *Rigoberta,* 195.

42. Arturo Escobar, *Encountering Development: The Making and Unmaking of the Third World* (Princeton: Princeton University Press, 1995), 4.

43. Charles Taylor, "Invoking Civil Society," in Goodin and Pettit, *Contemporary Political Philosophy,* 66.

44. Menchú, *Rigoberta,* 209–10.

45. Doris Sommer, "No Secrets."
46. Luisa Cabrera, "Efectos de la impunidad en el sentido de Justicia," *Psicología Política* 23 (2001): 37–58.
47. Escobar, *Encountering Development.*
48. Menchú, *Rigoberta,* 197.
49. Ibid., 197.

Chapter 4: *The Violent Text*

For the chapter epigraph, please see María Victoria Uribe Alarcón, *Limpiar la tierra: Guerra y poder entre esmeralderos* (Bogotá: CINEP, 1996), 25. Unless otherwise indicated, all translations from the Spanish by Kathryn Auffinger.

1. I was invited to participate in a panel on cultural studies at the Colombian National Anthropological Association Conference, which took place in Manizalez in September 2003. Interested as I was in violence, this was a magnificent opportunity to talk to Colombian intellectuals about this topic and to acquire further literature to help fill gaps in my research. I came back with a wealth of knowledge that made me realize the difference between writing one chapter on violence in one book and a national research dedicated to the topic. I am in debt to all the Colombian scholars who have dedicated their entire careers, and sometimes their lives, gathering the data and engaging in the discussion of the pressing theme of violence. But in particular I want to thank Mauricio Pardo and Fabio López de la Roche for providing me with valuable material that I could never have gotten otherwise and for introducing me to the richness of the Colombian debate on the matter.

2. Michel Foucault, *Discipline and Punish: The Birth of the Prison* (New York: Vintage Books, 1995).

3. A thorough review of the research literature on Colombian violence up to 1990 can be found in Ricardo Peñaranda, "Conclusions: Surveying the Literature on the Violence," in *Violence in Colombia: The Contemporary Crisis in Historical Perspective,* ed. Charles Bergquist, Ricardo Peñaranda, and Gonzalo Sánchez (Wilmington, DE: Scholarly Resources Inc., 1992), 293–314. For a summary of the different arguments on the theme, see Fernán E. González, Ingrid J. Bolívar, and Teófilo Vázquez, *Violencia política en Colombia: De la nación fragmentada a la construcción del Estado* (Bogotá: CINEP, 2003). Of equal value is Gonzalo Sánchez G., "Los estudios sobre La Violencia: Balance y perspectivas," in *Pasado y presente de la violencia en Colombia,* ed. Gonzalo Sánchez and Ricardo Peñaranda (Bogotá: CEREC, 1986), 183–94.

4. Arditi, *Politics at the Edges,* 2.

5. Étienne Balibar and Immanuel Wallerstein, *Race, Nation, Class: Ambiguous Identities* (London: Verso, 1991).

6. Ibid., 93.

7. See Norbert Lechner's notion of disenchantment in "La democratización en el contexto de una cultura posmoderna"; and José Joaquín Brunner's idea of a segmented and differentiated participation in "Tradicionalismo y modernidad en la cultura latinoamericana," both in *Postmodernismo en la periferia: Enfoques latinoamericanos de la nueva teoría cultural,* ed. Hermann Herlinghous and Monika Walter (Munich: Langer Verlag, 1994), 197–209, 48–82.

8. Daniel Pecaut, "Guerrillas and Violence," in Bergquist, Peñaranda, and Sánchez,

Violence in Colombia, 217–40; Daniel Pecaut, *Orden y violencia: Colombia, 1930–1953* (Mexico City: Siglo XXI/CEREC, 1987).

9. This is another great point of debate. See Paul Oquist, *Violence, Conflict, and Politics in Colombia* (New York: Academic Press, 1980); Gonzalo Sánchez and Donny Meertens, "La Violencia, el Estado y las clases sociales," *Anuario Colombiano de Historia Social y de la Cultura* 10 (1982): 254–61. In this article the authors debate the relationship between Oquist's theories of the collapse of the state with Pecaut's thesis of the dissolution of the state.

10. For a discussion on the Hegelian nature of the state as it comes to bear on the nature of non-European historiographies, see the work of Ranajit Guha, *History at the Limit of World-History* (New York: Columbia University Press, 2002); Craig Calhoun, *Habermas and the Public Sphere* (Cambridge, MA: MIT Press, 1992); Hardt, "Withering of Civil Society." Hardt argues that Hegelian education in civil society is a process of formal subsumption: that is, a process whereby particular differences, foreign to the universal, are negated and preserved in unity. For Hegel, the institutions of civil society are the networks that orient the particular to the universal and the individual to the social. In this model, civil society is intimately related to labor, and labor is the device that enables the transition from natural to civil, and from civil to political society. This movement implies a transcendence of individual needs and conflicts for which concrete labor must be transformed into abstract labor. Labor brings together the individual needs of the society and creates a sphere of relatedness whereby subjective self-seeking turns into the satisfaction of everybody's needs. Civil society is then defined as "the society of organized labor." Ergo, a postlabor society must, by necessity, be a post-civil society, and the process of subsumption and absorption of the concrete into the abstract, the individual into the social, the particular into the universal, and the different into the unitary is therefore curtailed and stunted.

11. Testimonials and fiction have also greatly contributed to the discussion of these issues, and their renditions of Colombian struggles can in no way be held in contempt. In fact, one of the most well-known Colombian internal migrations due to violence is that of the Buendía family in Gabriel García Márquez's acclaimed text *One Hundred Years of Solitude* (New York: Harper and Row, 1970). Although we cannot construe the Buendía's migration to the Colombian hinterland as a simile for the migration of people throughout at least half of the last century or take this original wandering as an allegory of nation formation and read Macondo as a metaphor for the frontier settlement of dirt-road hamlets (the so-called *veredas*), a sample of the "independent republics" spoken about by the social text, there is a great temptation to do so. The distance between fact and fiction here is perplexing. In *One Hundred Years,* fiction falls short in its rendering of the dramatic drifting of people without names, people who, due to violence, have to migrate away and beyond Aracataca, Santa Marta, and Macondo, the Neverland of the Buendías, to the frontier, opening it up to agriculture. This is, however, not the case in Fernando Vallejo's *La virgen de los sicarios.* The second wave of violence had already marked the cultural text and permeated aesthetics. In this text, the leading questions are: How can we explain the fact that extreme violence in Colombia is carried out by children? What is the relationship between standard Spanish and murder? And finally, why does the older man insists on teaching a young *sicario* the correct use of grammar, while the young *sicario* insists on teaching him the adversary nature of Colombian postmodern history? The answer is that in Vallejo's text, grammar is instrumental in drawing the distance between a seigniorial, oligarchic age of presumed respect and safety and

the new postmodern era signed by murder. By interrogating normative grammar and insisting in the correct phonetics of words and verb tenses, the old man distinguishes, through language, who classifies as citizens and who does not, whereas by the indiscriminate use of bullets the young man renders that difference inconsequential.

Testimonial literature is the genre that comes closer to the social text in documenting the logic of violence. Testimonials are closer to the popular in that they gather the voices of the people who were directly involved in the massacres and violence throughout most of the last century in Colombia. Alfredo Molano's and Alonso Salazar's testimonials are the main focus of the present chapter. Very useful in this regard is the discussion of the state and disciplinary formations in Ranajit Guha's three lectures on Hegel, whose subject is the history of people without history. Both Vallejo's novel and Guha's historical analysis directly engage questions pertaining to the state and citizenship. Vallejo's novel does so through the use of good grammar, while Guha argues the importance of the presence of the state in determining the competence of history and of nonhistory, and, consequently, argues the same distinctions between people as those that Vallejo makes regarding citizenship.

12. Fernán E. González, Ingrid J. Bolívar, and Teófilo Vázquez have done a superb job at summarizing the discussion in their text *Violencia política en Colombia.*

13. Fabio López de la Roche underscores this point. See his "Culturas políticas de las clases dirigentes en Colombia: Permanencias y rupturas," in *Ensayos sobre cultura política colombiana,* ed. Fabio López de la Roche, Controversia no. 162–63 (Bogotá: n.p., 1990), 99–201; and his *Izquierdas y cultura política: Oposición alternativa?* (Bogotá: CINEP, 1994).

14. Uribe Alarcón, *Limpiar la tierra.*

15. Catherine LeGrand's study constitutes a solid basis for understanding the struggle of colonists and big landowner struggles over land-tenure systems. See her *Frontier Expansion and Peasant Protest in Colombia, 1850–1936* (Albuquerque: University of New Mexico Press, 1986).

16. In his article "De las violencias a La Violencia," Daniel Pecaut undertakes analysis of Gaitanismo and makes reference to these positionings and repositionings as "barbarism." The interesting thing is that this sign remits us to the representation of the people as barbarians. It seems that every time there is a popular response to state or oligarchic aggression, the term used to refer to the people is that of barbarian. Barbarian then stands as a metaphor for real threats to the established oligarchic social order. In this respect, when La Violencia comes up, Pecaut argues, we can say that barbarism has materialized itself, taken form. Pecaut, in Sánchez and Peñaranda, *Pasado y presente de La Violencia,* 183–94. Pecaut also calls the absence of a civil spirit of debating issues barbaric in "Politics, the Political and the Theory of Social Movements," in *Alain Touraine,* ed. Jon Clark and Marco Diani (Washington, DC: Falmer Press, 1996), 159–72.

17. Alfredo Molano, *Trochas y fusiles* (Bogotá: Instituto de Estudios Políticos y Relaciones Internacionales, 1994), 26–27.

18. Germán Palacio and Fernando Rojas, *La irrupción del paraestado: Ensayos sobre la crisis colombiana* (Bogotá: ILSA / CEREC, 1990). González, Bolívar, and Vázquez, *Violencia política en Colombia,* 26; see also Carlos Vilas, "(In)justicia por mano propia: Linchamientos en el México contemporaneo," in Rodríguez, *Convergencia de Tiempos,* 185–228.

19. Samir Amin, *Empire of Chaos* (New York: Monthly Review Press, 1992).

20. See Luis Alberto Restrepo, "The Crisis of the Current Political Regime and Its Possible Outcomes," in Bergquist, Peñaranda, and Sánchez, *Violence in Colombia*, 273–92.

21. For the full argument (which I rehearse in the epilogue of this book), see Enrique Dussel, *The Underside of Modernity: Apel, Ricoeur, Rorty, Taylor, and the Philosophy of Liberation*, tr. Eduardo Mendieta (New Jersey: Humanities Press, 1996).

22. Fernando Coronil, *The Magical State: Nature, Money and Modernity in Venezuela* (Chicago: University of Chicago Press, 1997); Michael Taussig, *The Magic of the State* (London: Routledge, 1996).

23. Louis-Ferdinand Celine, quoted in Julia Kristeva, "The Speaking Subject Is Not Innocent," in *Freedom and Interpretation: The Oxford Amnesty Lectures 1992*, ed. Barbara Johnson (New York: Basic Books, 1993), 171; Kristeva, *Powers of Horror: An Essay on Abjection* (New York: Columbia University Press, 1982).

24. Molano. *Los años de tropel.*

25. Readers interested in pursuing this topic further may wish to consult David Bushnell, Catherine LeGrand, and Charles Bergquist, "Waging War and Negotiating Peace: The Contemporary Crisis in Historical Perspective," in Bergquist, Peñaranda, and Sánchez, *Violence in Colombia*, 1–74; Fernán E. González, *Violencia en la región andina: El caso Colombia* (Bogotá: CINEP, APEP, 1994); López de la Roche, *Izquierdas y cultura política.*

26. Maria Victoria Uribe, "El bipartidismo como encubridor de la venganza de la Sangre," in López de la Roche, *Ensayos sobre cultura política colombiana*, 15–28. One of my editors, John Crider, tells me that *bipartisanship*, in English (or at least in the United States), connotes a high level of effective cooperation between two political parties. *Bipartisan* has some of this connotation of cooperation, but it can also be used as neutral descriptive term for a two-party system. Still more neutral is the term *bipartite.* His clarification further underscores the difficulties of using classical liberal and democratic terms to speak about societies where these categories do not apply. In commenting on material later in this chapter, Crider also notes that *bipartisan* and *bipartisanship* are used to refer to a situation of two ideologies/parties in extreme conflict, which is true for the case of Colombia. In these cases, he continues, because there is a reference to struggle or conflict, he does not think that *bipartisanship* or even *bipartisan* is the right word. However, those are the words used to describe sociopolitical struggles in Colombia by Colombian and non-Colombian scholars.

27. Alfredo Molano, *Los años del tropel: Relatos de la violencia* (Bogotá: CEREC, 1985), 19.

28. Peñaranda, "Conclusions."

29. Restrepo, "Crisis of the Current Political Regime," 292.

30. Pecaut, "Guerrillas and Violence," 222.

31. Though rarely explicitly invoked in the Colombian research literature, a master trope of Western social scientific research casts its shadow, for the repeated emphasis on the split between *the social* and *the political* reveals that in the dominant academic model, there is a presumed coalescence between the two terms. In Colombian political development, this coalescence is wanting; this variation on the Hegelian model has possibly served to read the country's political history. In Hegel's epistemology, the coalescence of the social and the political is presented as the outcome of a seamless lineal transition from natural to civil to political society.

32. Pecaut, "Guerrillas and Violence," 223.

33. There is a rich discussion about Andean Colombia vis-à-vis the "other country"—perhaps Caribbean or Amazonian Colombia, a literature that makes strong references to racist conceptions of the Colombian nation. See López, "Culturas políticas de las clases dirigentes en Colombia," and *Izquierdas y cultura política.*

34. Uribe, *Limpiar la tierra*. 25. Fabio López de la Roche's study of the culture of the political classes, *Ensayos sobre cultura política colombiana,* which sufficiently documents the hegemonic role of the church in the formation of the ideological climate of the nation during the first half of the twentieth century, offers an example of how traditional the ideas motivating early forms of violence (which constitute the genealogies of present forms of violence) were.

35. López de la Roche, *Ensayos sobre cultura política colombiana,* 117.

36. For an outstanding analysis of this deadlocked situation, see Restrepo, "Crisis of the Current Political Regime."

37. Molano. *Trochas y fusiles;* Molano, *Los años de tropel;* Alfredo Molano, *Los bombardeos de El Pato* (Bogotá: Editorial CINEP, 1978).

38. Alfredo Molano, "Violence and Land Colonization," in Bergquist, Peñaranda, and Sánchez, eds. *Violence in Colombia,* 195.

39. Molano, *Los años del tropel,* 109.

40. Molano, *Trochas y fusiles,* 31–34.

41. Molano, *Los años del tropel,* 44–45.

42. For a different point of view, see Patricia Lara, *Las mujeres en la guerra* (Bogotá: Planeta, 2000).

43. Molano, *Los años del tropel,* 76.

44. María Clemencia Ramírez presents a series of testimonials regarding the right to work and argues that civic-defense organizations formed to struggle for that right. "We can assert that in Western Amazonia the armed conflict is forcing civil society to organize itself and to make itself visible as such through civic movements that tend to turn themselves into political movements, and its assigned identity as delinquents (drug dealers or guerrilla fighters) not only has been rejected but has motivated the emergence of a social movement that seeks to define its own collective identity as 'social actors' independent from drug traffic and guerrillas." Her unpublished piece, "Las paradojas de la economía de la coca: Re-configurando historias de violencia y desarraigo a través de la promoción de organizaciones comunitarias y espacios públicos de participación ciudadana," is a chapter of her dissertation in progress to be presented to the Department of Anthropology at Harvard University.

45. This production has been labeled the illicit economy. María Clemencia Ramírez's paper, cited in the previous note, cogently argues against defining both labor and capital forms of accumulation represented by this production as "illegal." Her discussion on this topic from the point of view of the *cocaleros* is quite compelling.

46. Participation of peasant from Mandar *vereda,* Puerto Guzmán, at the Foro sobre Paz y Convivencia, held in Puerto Asís, 1997, as recorded by Ramírez, "Las paradojas de la economía de la coca."

47. See Maria Victoria Uribe, "Dismembering and Expelling: Semantics of Political Terror in Colombia," *Public Culture* 16, no. 1 (2004).

Chapter 5: *Constituting Subaltern Subjectivities, Disclosing Acts of Violence*

1. Molano, *Los años del tropel,* 29–31.
2. See Colin Harding's introduction to Alonso Salazar, *Born to Die in Medellín* (London: Latin America Bureau, 1992).
3. Molano. *Los años del tropel.*
4. A good article on the representation of violence is María Cristina Rojas de Ferro, "Civilización y violencia: La lucha por la representación," in *Cultura, política y modernidad,* ed. Luz Gabriella Arango, Gabriel Restrepo, and Jaime Eduardo Jaramillo (Bogotá: Universidad Nacional de Colombia, 1998), 217–46.
5. Kristeva, "The Speaking Subject," 161.
6. Arditi, *Politics on the Edges,* 3.
7. Molano, *Los años del tropel,* 96.
8. Ranajit Guha, *Elementary Aspects of Peasant Insurgency* (Durham: Duke University Press, 1999).
9. Molano, *Los años de tropel,* 135.
10. Ibid., 61.
11. Gabriel García Márquez, *La mala hora* (Buenos Aires: Sudamericana, 1970).
12. Molano, *Los años del tropel,* 97–98.
13. Ibid., 98.
14. For a discussion on justice in the metaphorical sense rather than the distributive sense, see Iris Marion Young, "Reflections on Families in the Age of Murphy Brown: On Gender, Justice, and Sexuality," in *Revisioning the Political: Feminist Reconstructions of Traditional Concepts in Western Political Theory,* ed. Nancy J. Hirshmann and Christine Di Stefano (Boulder: Westview Press, 1996), 251–70.
15. Molano, *Los años del tropel,* 54–55.
16. Arditi, *Politics on the Edges,* 37.
17. Molano, *Los años del tropel,* 47.
18. See Arturo Alape, *El Bogotazo: Memorias del olvido* (Havana: Casa de las Américas, 1983); see also Restrepo, "Crisis of the Current Political Regime."
19. Molano, *Los años del tropel,* 39.
20. Ibid., 63.
21. Achille Mbembe, "Necropolitics," *Public Culture* 15, no. 1 (2003): 11–40.
22. Molano, *Los años del tropel,* 62–63.
23. Ibid., 42.
24. Sigmund Freud, *Three Essays on the Theory of Sexuality* (New York: Basic Books, 2000).
25. Molano, *Los años del tropel,* 37.
26. There is a radically different conception of the body that is revealed in the form it is treated and killed. Uribe tells us that it is not the same to kill a body conceived in the modern sense of the term with anatomic and physiological modern concepts as it is to liquidate a body that is conceived as an aggregate of parts proceeding from an animal. During La Violencia, the classificatory system in use was that of the peasants. Several words in use come from an economic context, like those of hunting and meat processing, or forms of killing animals; others emerge from the practices and beliefs associated with illness and health. In these rituals of death, the role played by different organs is significant: for instance, the heart or the head.

There is not one single cut that directly affects the heart, but the cuts give us the impression that it is the head which is the part of the body that the *cuadrilleros* (gangs) are most concerned with and toward which they direct their efforts. The same occurs with the zone around the neck, considered by the peasant the most vulnerable part of the body.

27. Ibid., 132, 65, 62.

28. For a comparative analysis of modern and postmodern torture, see Clea Koff, *The Bone Woman: A Forensic Anthropologist's Search for Truth in the Mass Graves of Rwanda, Bosnia, Croatia, Kosovo* (NewYork: Random House, 2004).

29. Molano, *Los años del tropel*, 44.

30. In writing this section, I was fully aware that the use of terms such as primitive, archaic, and premodern troubles postmodern analysis, but, when at a loss for words, testimonials use this terminology. In Alejandro Angulo's reading of Alfredo Molano's work, for instance, Angulo reiteratively turned to the idea of the prepolitical and the archaic that could well be read either as unwittingly referring to the Hegelian idea of natural societies as expressions of the traditional, and premodern where needs prevail, or to Freudian ideas regarding a return to primitive, instinctual psychical formations during trauma. I am miles away from absurdly suggesting here that Angulo and the testimonialists read Hegel and Freud in order to use the word archaic or prepolitical. What I want to convey in my repositioning of these terms back to their theoretical genealogies is that the convergence of the two interpretive models to discern Colombian violence underscores the purchasing power of these theoretical frames of reference. Angulo's (and Molano's and subsequently Alonso Salazar's in the next section) sense of the prepolitical and the archaic are also in tune with Kristeva's idea, apropos of Louis-Ferdinand Céline and fascism, that "the conflictual [read primitive and archaic psychic forms] subject can be roused in each of us once the grip of judging rationality is loosened" ("The Speaking Subject," 166). Bourgeois rationality interferes in the reading and writing of what, in the absence of the bourgeois state, comes to be interpreted as expressions of the instinctual and archaic. *Archaic* here enjoys a referentiality that is more psychoanalytic than sociological or developmentalist. It means what is subjectively primary and visceral, not what is backward and underdeveloped. If loss of meaning produces psychosis in the subject, in the political arena it produces social anarchy—or the separation of the social and the political. In Alonso Salazar's testimonials examined in the following section, I interpret the use of like terminology in terms of a postmodern sensibility prone to relativizing the whole universe of meaning. My argument is, simply, that these postmodern forms of violence are ordinary sequels to those officially practiced during La Violencia. Scores unsettled in the latter come to be borne out in the former and distressed subjectivities produced in the former come to inflect the latter.

31. Mbembe, "Necropolitics."

32. Alonso Salazar, *La parábola de Pablo: Auge y caída de un gran capo del narcotráfico* (Bogotá: Planeta, 2001), 39.

33. Amin, *Empire of Chaos;* Masao Miyoshi, "A Borderless World? From Colonialism to Transnationalism and the Decline of the Nation-State," in *GLOBAL/LOCAL: Cultural Production and the Transnational Imaginary,* ed. Rob Wilson and Wimal Dissanayake (Durham: Duke University Press, 1996), 97.

34. Alonso Salazar, *Born to Die in Medellín* (London: Latin America Bureau, 1992). The book has also been translated into French, German, Japanese, and Italian.

35. Salazar, *Born to Die*, 8.

36. Alonso Salazar, *Mujeres de fuego* (Medellín: Corporación Región, 1993); Salazar, *Profeta en el desierto: Vida y Muerte de Luis Carlos Galán* (Bogotá: Planeta, 2003); and Salazar, with Ana María Jaramillo, *Medellín: Las subculturas del narcotráfico* (Bogotá: CINEP, 1992).

37. Salazar, *Born to Die,* 109.

38. Ibid., 126, 110. For a discussion of politics as biopolitics and the use of the body as a weapon, see Mbembe, "Necropolitics."

39. *Maras y pandillas en Centroamérica* (Managua: Universidad Centroamericana, 2001).

40. Jorge Franco Ramos, *Rosario Tijeras* (Colombia: Plaza & Janés, 2000).

41. Salazar, *Born to Die,* 15.

42. Ibid., 34.

43. For a discussion on cyborgs, see Donna Haraway, "A Cyborg Manifesto: Science, Technology, and Socialist-Feminism in the Late Twentieth Century," in *Theorizing Feminism: Parallel Trends in the Humanities and Social Sciences,* ed. Anne C. Herrmann and Abigail J. Stewart (Boulder: Westview Press, 1994), 424–57.

44. Salazar, *Born to Die,* 11.

45. See Maria Victoria Uribe, "Dismembering and Expelling: Semantics of Political Terror in Colombia," *Public Culture* 16, no. 1 (2004): 79–95.

46. Salazar, *Born to Die,* 12, 32, 31, 15.

47. Ibid., 16.

48. Ibid., 12.

49. Ibid., 20, 24. A very good article to read on this subject is Alejo Vargas Velásquez, "Violencia en la vida cotidiana," in González, *Violencia en la región andina,* 141–96.

50. Salazar, *Born to Die,* 21.

51. Arditi, *Politics on the Edges,* 2.

52. Salazar, *Born to Die,* 22.

53. For a discussion of the effects of violence on the physical, social, and political body, see Hernán Vidal, "La sesión de tortura, espacio de las metamorfosis corporals," *Chile: Poética de la tortura política* (Santiago, Chile: Mosquito Comunicaciones, 1998), 143–202.

54. See Restrepo, "Crisis of the Current Political Regime."

55. See Vilas, "(In)justia por mano propia."

56. In Salazar's text, the continuity between La Violencia in the countryside and the later urban violence of the *sicariato* is written through the blood relation of Doña Azucena and her son Antonio. Antonio is the youth assassin, *sicario,* whose deathbed testimonial at the San Vicente de Paul hospital opens up *Born to Die in Medellín.* Antonio is beholden to his mother and admires her fortitude, endurance, and toughness—her being and status as a *tesa.* The blood relation between mother and son paradigmatically synthesizes a number of other social and affective relations in the text, including the fact that the shantytown *comuna* is made up of rural drifters who came to the city as a result of La Violencia.

57. In this regard, Hobsbawm's explanation of social banditry is useful. After establishing a divide between types of law and types of criminality, he then claims that social banditry is, above all, a rural phenomenon proper to precapitalist societies and that it manifests itself during severe moments of instability or the social and political collapse of rural societies. Social banditry is thus a symptom of destructuration, as is gang formation. Like social banditry, gang formation is favored by certain environmental conditions, such as the profusion of young people without property or permanent employment, and by certain political and ad-

ministrative circumstances, such as the weakness or fragmentation of public power. Gang members, like bandits, are defined by their functions. These positions are political because they imply a rejection of the authority of the law and the mediation of the state. Conversely, banditry and gangs prove the inability of state power and law; Eric Hobsbawm, "Historiografía del bandolerismo," in Sánchez and Peñaranda, *Pasado y presente de la violencia en Colombia,* 367–77.

58. Uribe Alarcón, *Limpiar la tierra.*

59. Fabio López de la Roche has demonstrated how the imaginaries of "nation" and "people" work in tandem to construct an idea of the elite as civilized, reasonable, and calm, and an idea of the people as passionate, anarchistic, and disorderly. Of particular interest in this respect is Laureano Gómez's provocative comparison of the popular to the basilisk—the mythic beast whose horror and abjection derive from its hybridity, thus representing a genetic composite of the incompatible. A basilisk conjures up several animal species in one, and it is this kind of multispecies embodiment that gives it the power to kill with his look. Later in the chapter I will have a few more words to say about the basilisk as a figure for the elite terror of the popular.

One intriguing observation López and others have made about the imaginary of political violence in Colombia is that ideology is not conveyed through conversation, teaching, or open debate, which leads an individual to acquire a personal sense of political conviction. We heard one of Molano's protagonists say that people choose their political affiliation through imitation. If the parents are Conservatives, so are the children. When political persuasion is not derived by free choice, when it is not considered part of a decision-making process, the liberal frame of reference is wanting. Political affiliation is then erroneously conceived as something people are born with, as part of the genetic code transmitted from parent to child. Uribe, like many other Colombian scholars, explains this way of conceiving and living politics in terms of precapitalist agrarian formations and argues that political ideologies, expressed as party allegiances in Colombia, are subcultures that generate oppositional views of the social order. That is, Liberal and Conservative political ideologies in Colombia are misnomers. They are not what are commonly understood by these terms in political science texts or in highly developed capitalist democratic societies. The problem, then, lies in using categories of analysis that in no way or manner correspond to the social environment one is analyzing. Hence the adjustment: although political ideologies in Colombia are called Liberal and Conservative, they in no way or manner correspond to the modern ideas indicated by these names. They are used to refer to what in another context would be considered archaic manners of expressing the social self. Conservative and Liberal political ideologies in Colombia are not political ideologies, but a pretext to kill. Liberal and Conservative ideologies are not modern forms of political organization but premodern forms of social relations operating within the context of modernity. They are not constituted ideologies of state power that organize and regulate the common good, but anarchy that produces ideologies. That is, Colombian scholarship is caught up in opposite and contradictory ways of political predication.

This problem haunts me. To solve it I think of the residual, that which is premodern but inhabits the modern. I also think of the time line established for the modern and how it does not coincide with the political development of this nation. In most regions there is perhaps a kind of uneven or arrested development that accounts for a mixture of overlapping temporalities. And this all takes me back to the hypothesis of a failed state: that is, a state that never constituted itself into a modern form of governance. However, and here we come back to the problem full circle, understanding political ideologies in terms of affect and acting upon other members of the community violently because they do not share the same party affiliation is a way of conceptualizing the Colombian state's failure to be fully modern. These interpretive dilemmas would explain to me why the political praxis of modern political ideologies, such as Liberal and Conservative, are interpreted as primary loyalties, structures of parentage, collective memories, and shared feelings, and why affect and proximity constitute the substratum of the modern that is being inaugurated in such a bloody fashion in the Colombian countryside. My take on the use of this vocabulary by social scientists betrays not only their main frame of analysis but also the political unconscious that inflects their vision of subaltern politics. It is the type of peasant sociality and sensibility, its tensions with the modern, its responses to bipartisan politics that are read as archaic. Consequently, killing a neighbor brings together the solidarity of the rest of the community that claims revenge. To err in a contrary direction, we can also understand revenge as an act of self-defense—which is Doña Azucena's interpretive choice. Following Hobsbawm's thesis that subaltern politics in rural areas are premodern expressions of peasant societies (that is, natural, not civil) and even less so political forms of behavior, the treatment of the body at the massacres conforms to a code of dismemberment that is more pertinent to animals than to people, in Uribe's view.

60. María Victoria Uribe, "El bipartidismo como encubridor de la venganza de la sangre," in López de la Roche, *Ensayos sobre cultura política colombiana,* 15–28.

61. In the second chapter of *Elementary Aspects of Peasant Insurgency,* Ranajit Guha speaks about the difference between criminality and rebellion as operating within a logic of ambiguity. He first demonstrates how the definition of criminality uses the instrumentalities of punishment to interpret and defend a preordained meaning of the term upon which the material bases of power and prestige rest; second, he shows how this type of hermeneutics creates a blind spot for interpreting the two different codes of violence: namely, crime vs. insurgency. He states, "The conceptual inertia that refuses to acknowledge, at first sight, the altered figure of violence, feeds on the sharp increase in criminal activity which often inaugurates a peasant revolt" (81). For Guha, criminality in no way can be related to the satisfaction of one's basic needs for survival, particularly in the case of hunger or oppression. Minimum subsistence is an overriding right, and when people steal food to eat, no matter what the criminal code is, morality is on the side of the thief. How to distinguish criminality from hunger must then be made very plain, as must be the distinction between self-defense and criminality. Social oppression makes crime the only way of life for the poor and dispossessed, and crime is the precursor of rebellion. Ranajit Guha, *Elementary Aspects of Peasant Insurgency* (Durham: Duke University Press, 1999).

62 Although Camilo Torres, Orlando Fals Borda, and Eric Hobsbawm present excellent positions on the subject, the impetus now is for going after the imaginaries that make the political possible. See Peñaranda, "Conclusions."

63. Shoshana Feldman, *The Juridical Unconscious: Trials and Traumas in the Twentieth Century* (Cambridge, MA: Harvard University Press, 2002); Nora Strejilevich, *A Single, Numberless Death,* trans. Cristina de la Torre (Charlottesville: University Press of Virginia, 2002).

64. Salazar, *Born to Die,* 10.
65. Kristeva, "Speaking Subject," 171.
66. Molano, *Los años del tropel,* 62; Kristeva, "Speaking Subject," 165.
67. Molano, *Los años del tropel,* 44.
68. Guha, *History at the Limit.*
69. Kristeva, "Speaking Subject," 168.
70. Salazar, *La parábola de Pablo,* 103–4.
71. Dipesh Chakrabarty, "The Time of History and the Times of Gods," in *The Politics of Culture in the Shadow of Capital,* ed. Lisa Lowe and David Lloyd (Durham: Duke University Press, 1997), 35–60.
72. Salazar, *La parábola de Pablo,* 83–88.
73. For a more complete rendition of this situation, see Ramírez, "Las paradojas de la economía de la coca."
74. Salazar, *La parábola de Pablo,* 23. For a discussion on the role of development and underdevelopment to explain the historiographies and identities of people in Colombia, see Escobar, *Encountering Development.*
75. For a theoretical development of this idea, see Chakrabarty, "Time of History," 35–60.
76. Laura Restrepo, *Delirio* (Madrid: Alfaguara, 2004).
77. Laureano Gomez, *El Siglo* (Bogotá), June 27, 1949, 4, quoted in Uribe, "Dismembering and Expelling," 82–83.
78. Salazar, *La parábola de Pablo,* 37.
79. Ibid., 37
80. Ibid., 56.
81. Ibid., 75, 76.
82. Ibid., 19–20.
83. Ibid., 36.

Chapter 6: Feminicidio, *or the Serial Killings of Women*

1. Héctor Domíguez, "Desierto lleno de gente: Avatars de la multitud en la frontera"; and "La educación de los hombres o cómo producir victimarios," both in "Las muertas de Juárez," ed. Sergio González Rodríguez, special issue of *Metapolítica* (2003): 27–32.
2. Hardt, "Withering of Civil Society."
3. "Through needs, work, exchange, and the pursuit of particular self-interests, the 'unorganized atoms of civil society' are to be ordered toward the universal" (Hardt, "Withering of Civil Society," 24). Concrete labor cements the articulations of civil society and allows for the transcendence of the particular for the sake of the universal.
4. Ibid., 25.
5. Ibid.
6. Ibid., 24, 26.
7. Ibid., 27–28.
8. Ibid., 25.
9. For an interesting proposal for global forms of political governance, see Amin, *Empire of Chaos;* Miyoshi, "Borderless World?"

10. Hardt, "Withering of Civil Society," 25.

11. For a discussion on the ungovernable nature of the world, see my article "Globalization as Neo-, Post-Colonialism: Politics of Resentment and Governance of the World's *Res Publica,"* in *The Postcolonial and the Global: Connections, Conflicts, Complicities,* ed. John Hawley and Revathi Krishnaswamy (Minneapolis: University of Minnesota Press, 2007).

12. Hardt, "Withering of Civil Society," 27.

13. Margo Glantz, "También la muerte se maquila," in "Las muertas de Juárez," special issue of *Metapolítica* (2003): 61–62.

14. Ximena Andión, Adriana Carmona, Sofía Lascurain, and Laura Salas, "Violencia de género e irresponsabilidad política," in "Las muertas de Juárez," special issue of *Metapolítica* (2003): 20.

15. "Manifiesto," In "Las muertas de Juárez," special issue of *Metapolítica* (2003): 33.

16. Sergio González Rodríguez, "Una década de violencia y feminicidio," in "Las muertas de Juárez," special issue of *Metapolítica* (2003): 39.

17. Candia et al., *El silencio.* Unless otherwise indicated, all the translations are by Kathryn Auffinger.

18. Ibid., 103. Emphasis added.

19. Thus, when reading the documents on *feminicidio* in Juárez, when seeing films or pictures about the same subject, the first thing to notice is a series of criminal events concerning which nothing is certain. They come up as the daily events of a city and call for our attention due to their frequency, as much as for their way of making themselves present in the public sphere. As social events, their massive character and the way they make their appearance are cause for much restlessness among the citizenry, to the degree of involving several social institutions and mobilizing civic action and women's groups. But as more institutions, persons, and juridical persons are involved in the matter, the more obscure the panorama becomes. This paradox is the cause of further perplexity and produces more documentation, until the expansive wave reaches the U.S. academy and cinematography. The criminal acts, the bodies of women, and the informative body over the events have created a sensation of mystery that lends itself to multiple interpretations. Hector Domínguez and Patricia Ravelo have discerned about twenty interpretative moods. See Hector Domínguez and Patricia Ravelo, "La batalla de las cruces: Los crímenes contra mujeres en la frontera y sus intérpretes," *Desacatos: Revista de Antropología Social* 13 (Winter 2003): 122–33. See also the film *La batalla de las cruces: Protesta social y acciones colectivas en torno de la violencia sexual en Ciudad Juárez* (2006), directed by Rafael Bonilla.

20. Candia et al., *El silencio.*

21. Sergio González, *Huesos en el desierto* (Barcelona: Anagrama, 2002), 14.

22. Diana Washington, "Ricos y poderosos en los crímenes de Ciudad Juárez," in "Las muertas de Juárez," special issue of *Metapolítica* (2003): 102.

23. González, *Huesos en el desierto,* 66–67.

24. This situation resembles what Renata Salecl argues for Chickatilo, the serial murderer in the former Soviet Union whose psychosis was manifested in the blinding of his victims. Salecl reads this blinding action as a text which signifies a gesture against the overbearing presence of the state and its police apparatuses. See Salecl, "Crime as a Mode of Subjectification," in *The Spoils of Freedom, Psychoanalysis and Feminism after the Fall of Socialism* (London: Routledge, 2002).

25. González, *Huesos en el desierto*, 45–46.

26. Directed by Steven Soderbergh, 2000. Several other films have come out since I finished writing this text, among them, *The Virgin of Juarez* (2006), starring Minnie Driver, and *Bordertown* (2006), starring Jennifer Lopez. One of the most interesting works of fiction regarding this subject is Roberto Bolaños's outstanding novel *2666* (Barcelona: Anagrama, 2004), which I don't examine here because I am devoting this book to testimonial literature.

Chapter 7: *The Perverse Heterosexual*

1. A very good representative summary of these works is outlined in the special number of *Metapolítica,* amply quoted in this section. See also *Quimera: Revista de Literatura* 258 (June 2005), a special issue dedicated to literature. See also Rita Laura Segato, "Territorio, soberanía y crímenes de segundo estado: La escritura en el cuerpo de las mujeres asesinadas en Ciudad Juárez," *Serie Antropológica* (Brasilia) 362 (2004): 2–16; Nuria Vilanova, "Violencia y anonimato en la frontera norte de México: Los cuerpos desaparcedios," *Quimera: Revista de Literatura* 258 (June 2005); and María Socorro Tabuenca, "Ciudad Juárez como espacio testimonial," *Entorno* 60–61 (2004): 118–23; Jorge Balderas Domínguez, *Mujeres, antros y estigmas en la noche juarense* (Chihuahua: Instituto Chihuahuense de la Cultura. 2002); Balderas, "Luis Arturo Ramos y el arte de narrar en *La mujer que quiso ser dios*" *Revista de Literatura Mexicana Contemporánea* 8 (2004): 71–75; Balderas, *"Baile de fantasmas* en Ciudad Juárez al final/principio del milenio," in *Más allá de la ciudad letrada: Crónicas y espacios urbanos,* ed. Brois Muñoz and Silvia Spitta (Pittsburgh: Instituto Internacional de Literatura Iberoamericana, 2003), 411–37; Ricardo Aguilar and Socorro Tambuenca, eds., *Lo que el viento a Juárez: Testimonio de una ciudad que se obstina* (Torreón, Coahuila / Las Cruces, NM: UIA / Laguna / Editorial Nimbus, 2002); Julia Monárrez Fragoso, *Elementos de análisis del feminicidio/sexual sistémico en Ciudad Juárez para su viabilidad juridica,* (Chihuahua: La Gota, 2005); Víctor Ronquillo, *Las muertas de Juárez: Crónica de una larga pesadilla* (Mexico City: Planeta: 1999).

2. Candia et. al., *El silencio*; González, *Huesos en el desierto.* Unless otherwise indicated, all translations are by Kathryn Auffinger.

3. Marianne Hirsch, "Projected Memory: Holocaust Photographs in Personal and Public Fansaty," in *Acts of Memory. Cultural Recall in the Present,* ed. Mieke Bal, Jonathan Crewe, and Leo Spitzer (Hanover, NH: University Press of New England, 1999), 3–23.

4. See *8mm,* a film by Joel Schumache (1999); and *Irreversible,* a film by Gaspar Noé, (2002).

5. Carlos Monsiváis, "El femicidio y la conversión de Ciudad Juárez en territorio de la impunidad," "Las muertas de Juárez," special issue of *Metapolítica* (2003):14.

6. González, *Huesos en el desierto,* 283

7. Iris Marion Young, "Displacing the Distributive Paradigm," in *Ethics in Practice: An Anthology,* ed. Hugh LaFollette (Cambridge: Blackwell, 1997), 547–58; Young, "Reflections on Families in the Age of Murphy Brown."

8. Héctor Domínguez, "Desierto lleno de gente."

9. Mbembe, "Necropolitics."

10. Domínguez, "Desierto lleno de gente."

11. González, *Huesos en el desierto,* 284–85.

12. You can see a picture of this face in Charles Bowden, *Juárez: The Laboratory of Our Future* (New York: Aperture, 1998), 66.

13. Julie Rivkin and Michael Ryan, eds., *Literary Theory: An Anthology* (Balden, MA: Blackwell, 2000), enact this theme in the front cover of their book. The image, an idealized portrayal of a dead woman lying on top of a flat surface and observed by the gaze of a respectable older man, is Barbara Kruger's piece "Untitled." Onlookers cannot help but gaze at the beauty of the woman, at her body barely covered by a white sheet stained with blood that suggests the deciphering of an enigma. The scene brings together the scientific, artistic, and theoretical discourses poured over the dead body of a woman. See also Jean Franco, "Killing Priests, Nuns, Women, Children," in Pratt and Newman, *Critical Passions*, 9–17. As in Kruger's picture, Bowden's book, and Bailleres's photographs, the images unwittingly feed on the artistic representation of death, however much, in the case of Juárez, the representation has fatally slipped away from a respectable aesthetic to the low areas of criminality and labor. We know that the photographer's aim is to baste together the storyline of aggression and violence to women.

14. Bowden, *Juárez,* 67.

15. Here I take the sublime to mean not so much the power of killing, that horror that feels like a heart attack, as Stephen Greenblatt reads Kant's concept, but rather how horror, libido, and death commingle at the intersection of gender relations and labor in Juárez. Julia Kristeva tells us that for Freud, Eros is masculine, that the libido is made up of fragments and appropriations and reaches its capacity of idealization by displacing the drive's logic towards another object, different from the sexualized body, which in its ultimate instance is, on the one hand, the attraction towards the phallus, and on the other, the object of knowledge which in infancy comes from the energy or wisdom of motherhood. Julia Kristeva, *Tales of Love* (New York: Columbia University Press, 1987). See also Domínguez, "La educación de los hombres o cómo producir victimarios."

16. André Bazin, *What Is Cinema?* vol. 2, trans. Hugh Gray (Berkeley: University of California Press, 1971).

17. Sigmund Freud, "The Uncanny," in *The Standard Edition of the Complete Psychological Works of Sigmund Freud,* trans. James Strachey (London: Hogart, 1963), 27:25.

18. Julia Kristeva, *Powers of Horror: An Essay on Abjection* (New York: Columbia University Press, 1982).

19. Stephen Greenblatt, *Marvelous Possessions: The Wonder of the New World* (Chicago: University of Chicago Press, 1991); Homi Bhabha, *The Location of Culture* (London: Routledge, 1994).

20. Bowden, *Juárez,* 30.

21. Renata Salecl, "Focus: Cut-and-Dried Bodies or How to Avoid the Pervert Trap," in *Jenny Holzer,* ed. David Joselit, Joan Simon, and Renata Salecl (London: Phaidon Press, 1998), 78–89; 92; 78.

22. Renata Salecl, "Worries in Limitless World," *Cardozo Law Review* 26, no. 3 (2005): 101–19.

23. Ibid., 112–13.

24. González, *Huesos en el desierto,* 77

25. Linda Williams, "Corporealized Observers: Visual Pornographies and the 'Carnal Density of Vision,'" in *Fugitive Images: From Photography to Video,* ed. Patrice Petro (Bloomington: Indiana University Press, 1995), 3–41.

26. Williams, *Techniques,* 27.

27. Laura Mulvey, *Visual and Other Pleasures* (Bloomington: Indiana University Press, 1983).

28. Williams, *Techniques,* 6.

29. Salecl, "Focus," 85.

30. González, *Huesos en el desierto,* 36–37.

Epilogue

1. Hirschman and Di Stefano, *Revisioning the Political.* In Seyla Benhabib's words, "As a vision of feminist politics we are able to articulate a better model for a future than a radical democratic polity which also furthers the values of ecology, nonmilitarism, and solidarity of peoples." The purpose of feminist conceptual analysis is "(1) interrogating and contesting the apolitical postures of concepts that claim to be nonpolitical; (2) scrutinizing what may be termed . . . the 'innocent space' of political theorizing; (3) rethinking concepts that are already understood as political" (Hirschman and Di Stefano, "Revision, Reconstruction, and the Challenge of the New," 4, 6).

2. Iris Marion Young, "Displacing the Distributive Paradigm," in LaFollette, *Ethics in Practice,* 547.

3. Candia et al., *El silencio;* González, *Huesos en el desierto.*

4. Young, "Displacing," 548.

5. Ibid., 551.

6. Young, "Displacing the Distributive Paradigm," 556–57.

7. Young, "Reflections on Families in the Age of Murphy Brown."

8. Patrice DiQuinzio and Iris Marion Young, eds., *Feminist Ethics and Social Policy* (Bloomington: Indiana University Press, 1998).

9. Dussel, *Underside of Modernity,* 6.

10. Craig Calhoun, ed., *Habermas and the Public Sphere* (Cambridge, MA: MIT Press, 1992); Karl-Otto Apel, *The Response of Discourse Ethics to the Moral Challenge of the Human Situation as Such and Especially Today,* Mercier lectures, Louvain-la-Neuve, March 1999 (Leuven: Peeters, 2001); Richard Rorty, *Contingency, Irony and Solidarity* (Cambridge: Cambridge University Press, 1989).

11. Dussel, *Underside of Modernity,* xxii.

12. Ibid., xxiii, 3, 5.

13. Ibid., 6–7, 5.

14. Mbembe, "Necropolitics," 40.

15. Ibid., 14.

16. Ibid., 23.

17. Ibid., 24, 21.

18. Ibid., 23.

index of names

233